Thomas Campion

Twayne's English Authors Series

Arthur F. Kinney, Editor

University of Massachusetts, Amherst

TEAS 450

Inigo Jones's design for "Torchbearer: A Fiery Spirit" in Campion's
The Lords' Masque (1613), from the Devonshire Collection, Chatsworth.
Reproduced by permission of the Chatsworth Settlement Trustees.

Thomas Campion

By Walter R. Davis

Brown University

Twayne Publishers
A Division of G.K. Hall & Co. • *Boston*

Thomas Campion

Walter R. Davis

Copyright © 1987 by G.K. Hall & Co.
All Rights Reserved
Published by Twayne Publishers
A Division of G.K. Hall & Co.
70 Lincoln Street
Boston, Massachusetts 02111

Copyediting supervised by Lewis DeSimone
Book production by Janet Zietowski
Book design by Barbara Anderson

Typeset in 11 pt. Garamond
by P&M Typesetting, Inc., Waterbury, Connecticut

Printed on permanent/durable acid-free paper
and bound in the United States of America

Library of Congress Cataloging-in-Publication Data

Davis, Walter R.
  Thomas Campion.

  (Twayne's English authors series ; TEAS 450)
  Bibliography: p.
  Includes index.
  1. Campion, Thomas, 1567–1620—Criticism and
interpretation.   I. Title.   II. Series.
PR2229.D38   1987   821'.3   87-11
ISBN 0-8057-6949-8 (alk. paper)

For my mother, Helen K. Davis,
and in memory of my father, Walter Y. Davis

Contents

Editor's Note

"Except for Shakespeare," T. S. Eliot wrote, "Thomas Campion is the most accomplished master of rhymed lyric of his time." Walter R. Davis, the distinguished editor of the *Works of Thomas Campion*, examines here why this is so. He shows how instrumental Campion was in every field he touched: Latin poetry (where he wrote some of the best that remains in his period), theory (where he championed classical verse), poetry (where he changed the direction of Renaissance lyric), and music (where he joined the great John Dowland in replacing the madrigal with the ayre). From the beginning, Campion stressed brevity, lack of ornamentation, invention, compression, and complexity, seeking in them the exacting marriage of word and music so that they were mutually reinforcing and inseparable. Such work led to the apex of his career in court masques performed before the monarch James I, for Campion's talents, "the perfect form." Campion's reputation built slowly at first, according to Davis—"He was not worth the silent reading until he had been sung"—but he became in time, in his age as in our own, "the preeminent poet of the auditory imagination." Davis's study brings a wide knowledge of poetic theory, poetic practice, and the history and practice of music into clear and illuminating discussion; this Twayne study is learned, comprehensive, and eminently useful. "The image of Thomas Campion stands at a boundary or limit, for the point at which poetry and music meet," Davis concludes. This is a book about both, by a scholar whose gifts are precisely in identifying and revealing that boundary.

—Arthur F. Kinney

About the Author

Walter R. Davis is professor of English at Brown University. He received his degrees from Trinity College and Yale University, and taught at the University of Rochester, Dickinson College, Williams College, M.I.T., and Notre Dame. He has published *A Map of Arcadia* (1965), *Idea and Act in Elizabethan Fiction* (1969), and edited both *The Works of Thomas Campion* (1967) and *Twentieth-Century Interpretations of "Much Ado About Nothing"* (1969). He has written articles on Giovanni Boccaccio, St. Thomas More, Henry Howard Earl of Surrey, Sir Philip Sidney, Edmund Spenser, Michael Drayton, Thomas Campion, Thomas Lodge, Ben Jonson, Sir Francis Bacon, John Donne, Henry Smith, Richard Crashaw, Sir Thomas Browne, and John Milton, and is preparing a book on Edmund Spenser and the allegorical tradition. A few of his poems have been published, and he has recently finished a volume entitled *Illustrations: Captions for Partially Unearthed Chinese Artifacts*.

Preface

Thomas Campion is known to us in our time as "except for Shakespeare . . . the most accomplished master of rhymed lyric of his time" (T. S. Eliot) and as "the only man in English cultural history who was both a poet and a composer" (W. H. Auden). In this study I try to do justice to both his lyric poetry and his music, by showing how the two interact. In short, I take him seriously as both poet and musician, as an accomplished artist in combining media. The interaction I wish to explore is what Stephen Ratcliffe expresses metaphorically by "rhyme": that is, the poetry and the music resemble each other with differences, while the balance between them varies, as the music sometimes points up elements of the poetic text, sometimes seems analogous to the text in its melodic development or structure, or sometimes develops its own loosely related interests.

This study is an exploration of combined media. It is framed by chapters on Campion's life and his reputation. In the chapter on "Song" I outline the aesthetics of Campion's art, starting with the poetic text and ending with the music. In the next two chapters (which "rhyme," being analogous in their structures) I separate the two, treating his poetry in the context of his time and tracing its development, then doing the same for his music. In the chapter on "Theory" I return to his comments on musico-poetic form, and treat his individual works on metrics and composition (with an appendix on the Latin poems). Finally, I treat his most ambitious work in that great multimedia show the court masque, where he joined music and poetry with stage spectacle, dance, and drama, and where he used these various media to pursue questions of significance and final meaning.

In the twenty years since I edited Campion, I have profited by conversations and aid from many people, and I set down as many as I can remember here. I am grateful to Elise Bickford Jorgens, Edward Doughtie, and John Hollander for a word or an insight now and then, to Stephen Orgel for a bit of help at the last minute, to Kimberly Blaeser and the students in my graduate workshop in scholarly method at Brown in 1985 for joining me in my explorations, especially to Deborah Weiner for pointing out to me several specific facts.

I wish to thank Dennis Flynn for sharing his knowledge of English Roman Catholicism with me. To my colleague Andrew J. Sabol I owe thanks for sharing his enormous store of musical knowledge and for looking over my manuscript. When I proudly showed Nancy Donegan my first few pages of text, she turned and asked, "Can't you get a little more life into your prose?" She then proceeded to help me do that very thing; if it fails to live the fault is hers. I am grateful to my daughter Alison Greenberg for helping me with Campion's music: when her father absentmindedly erased a tape she had sent him, she cheerfully did it over again, even though she had a sore throat. Finally, I wish to thank David McSweeney for additional help with the music, Edward Holgate for his painstaking work on the manuscript, and Brown University for a grant covering costs of manuscript preparation.

Walter R. Davis

Brown University

Acknowledgments

I wish to thank the following for their kind permission: Excerpts from *The Works of Thomas Campion* edited by Walter Davis. Copyright © 1967 by Doubleday & Company, Inc. Reprinted by permission of the publisher.

Robert Creeley, "Air: Cat Bird Singing," "The Love of a Woman," and "A Token" from *For Love: Poems 1950–1960*. Copyright © 1962 by Robert Creeley. Reprinted with the permission of Charles Scribner's Sons and Marian Boyars, Ltd.

Selections from *W. H. Auden: Collected Poems,* edited by Edward Mendelson, copyright © 1966 by W. H. Auden. Reprinted by permission of Random House, Inc., and Faber and Faber Ltd.

The frontispiece from the Devonshire Collection, Chatsworth, is reproduced by permission of the Chatsworth Settlement Trustees.

Chronology

1607   *The Lord Hay's Masque* performed at court, 6 January.

1613?   *Two Books of Ayres.*

1613   *Songs of Mourning* on the death of Prince Henry (died 6 November 1612), "worded" by Campion, the music by Giovanni Coperario. *The Lords' Masque* for the wedding of the Princess Elizabeth performed, 14 February; *The Caversham Entertainment* for Queen Anne performed, 27–28 April; *The Squires' Masque* performed at court, 26 December.

1613–1614   *A New Way of Making Fowre Parts in Counter-point* (?).

1615   Examined and cleared of complicity in the murder of Sir Thomas Overbury, 26 October.

1616   Allowed to administer physic to his friend Sir Thomas Monson, imprisoned in the Tower for the murder of Overbury, 14 January.

1617?   *The Third and Fourth Booke of Ayres.*

1617   *The Ayres That Were Sung and Played at Brougham Castle,* by George Mason and John Earsden, perhaps with words by Campion, performed for James I's return from Scotland in August (published in 1618).

1619   *Tho. Campiani Epigrammatum Libri II* (entered 21 August).

1620   Campion dies 1 March and is buried at St. Dunstan's in the West, Fleet Street.

Chapter One
Life

Many writers have imaged Thomas Campion as a ghost or hovering spirit. Edmund Gosse imagined him lying in London by the Strand in a "music-haunted dream," and Ezra Pound prayed "To Thomas Campion his ghost" for the revival of music. Even his contemporary George Peele, in the first written tribute to him, asked why he did not go join Philip Sidney in the Elysian fields, when the poor fellow was only twenty-six years old![1] Perhaps he appeared ethereal to people. We know that he considered himself small and skinny, and suffered insomnia.[2] Perhaps because we can still hear his poetry as music in performance he seems to be here and not here, a spirit that hovers in the air of our climate. But he did live and breathe, and he had a life in the flesh though we do not know as much about it as we would like to. He was a poet, he was a musician, he studied law, he wrote masques or pageants for the political stage, and he was a physician who knew at firsthand the pains and frailties of the body. It is the business of this chapter to set down what we know about that life.

We are questioning a ghost. First let us list some things we do not know. He may have been of Irish descent. His grandfather was described in 1565 as "John Campion, late of Dublin, Ireland, deceased." But his editor and biographer Percival Vivian can find no trace of his grandfather in Ireland and concludes that he must have held a petty office for the English government in Dublin (V, ix). Instead, he traces the family to villages like Anstey in Hertfordshire, not very far from London, Oxford, and Cambridge. He was probably of solid English stock.

Campion seems never to have married or had children, since he left all his worldly goods at his death to a friend. He may have been Roman Catholic. The question is an important one, for if he had been of the Roman faith it would have affected the quality of his life in England under Elizabeth and James. Roman Catholics could not take university degrees, for a person had to subscribe to the Oath of Supremacy on graduation, and so they were effectively blocked from some professions; they were regarded with suspicion, too, especially after the Gunpowder Plot of 5 November 1605 when the Jesuits had tried to blow up the Houses of Parliament. We may remember that John Donne explained his lifelong bouts of depression by the fact that he had been raised in a haunted and fugitive religion. The man who called himself "Peter Warlock" wrote that Campion left Cambridge without a degree, "a fact which suggests that he may have been a Roman Catholic."[3] The rest of us are not so sure. It was common to leave a university without a degree. In a Latin poem of 1595 he praised Chaucer for his supposed attack on the Papacy—but then omitted the poem from a later collection. In 1602 he called Elizabeth "Faiths pure shield" and in 1613 he congratulated James I on the discovery of the Gunpowder Plot.[4] Nobody has been able to establish a connection with the Jesuit martyr St. Edmund Campion. Some of his friends—the three Michelbourne brothers and John Dowland the lutenist—were Roman Catholics and suffered for it, and his great patron Sir Thomas Monson *may* have been. Many of his other friends were not. We simply do not know: Vivian thinks not (V, xxvii).

Early Years

We do know Campion was born 12 February 1567, three years after Shakespeare and four after Dowland: "borne upon Ash Weddensday being the twelfth day of February, An. Rg. Eliz. nono, and cristened at St. Andrewes Church, in Houlborne" (V, xiii). He had an older sister, Rose, born 21 January 1565. His father, John Campion, was a minor law clerk, having been admitted to the Middle Temple in 1565 and having been appointed as "Cursitor" or clerk of the Chancery Court. John Campion seems to have been rather prosperous, perhaps because of his marriage, owned property and even rented farms; he called himself a gentleman, aspired to a coat of arms with the campion flower on it, and was vestryman of St. Andrew's Church (V, xvi–xvii). His mother Lucy was the comfortable widow of Roger Trigg, and remarried to John Campion in 1564, bringing her daughter Mary into the household with her. John Campion was apparently a litigious man, and his wife's previous marriage raised several law suits for him to pursue. He died in October of 1576, when his son was only nine years old. His mother left a brick and timber house on Chancery Lane for Wiltshire, and was soon married again, to Augustine Steward on 21 August 1577, having first made a contract guaranteeing legacies for her children. Lucy had no children by

Steward, and did not survive the marriage long, dying in March 1580 and leaving Rose and Thomas orphans in the guardianship of Steward. Steward, saddled with two orphan stepchildren, did not long remain a widower but married Anne, widow of Clement Sisley, on 26 January 1581.

Young Thomas certainly knew much of death: his mother a widow, his stepfather married to a widow, his father dead when he was nine and his mother when he was thirteen. What is more, a few months after Steward's remarriage, in May, Thomas was packed off to Cambridge along with Thomas Sisley, Anne's son and Steward's new stepson. At fourteen, he was enrolled at Peterhouse, Cambridge. We do not know what happened to Rose; we lose sight of her after 1592, when she was still living, unmarried at twenty-seven, with the Stewards (*V*, xxv). It is likely that Thomas and his half-brother Thomas Sisley were sent to Cambridge because of family tensions, since it is clear they did not go home for vacations (*V*, xxvii). The two boys must have been close: they shared a bedroom but each had his own study. Their stepfather kept close accounts of their expenses, thirteen pounds yearly for food, four pounds for tuition, four pence quarterly for paper, "At Cristmas, a cap, a band, a shirt, a doblet, a payer of hose, a gowne, a payer of netherstockes"; he even recorded ten shillings for laundry and seven shillings 6 pence for mending their clothes and shoes (*V*, xxvi). From a modern perspective it seems to have been a rather cheerless life; the boys rose at 4:00 or 5:00 A.M. with prayer and were to study till 10:00 P.M.; they were required to eschew finery and wear "sad colours."[5]

Peterhouse was a popular college at Cambridge, mostly because of the prestige of the master, Dr. Andrew Perne: he was a broad-minded churchman who has had the misfortune of being remembered as a turncoat, reverting to Catholicism under Mary Tudor, attacking the pope when Elizabeth came to the throne. We meet his name in W. B. Yeats's "perne in a gyre." Yet he encouraged not turning but latitude in religion, and contemporary with Campion were both Henry Walpole the Jesuit, afterwards hanged, and "Elder Brewster" of the *Mayflower*. As for Cambridge University at large, it was famous for its music degrees and literary study. It had been Spenser's university, Spenser having received his M.A. in 1576; Spenser's friend Gabriel Harvey was a don at Pembroke College in Campion's day. Who else might Campion have known there? He might have met Sidney's protégé Abraham Fraunce, who received the M.A. in 1583 and then went to Gray's Inn, which Campion entered three years later; George Peele coupled their names in a poem of praise, and Fraunce was the chief practitioner of the attempt to write English verse in classical meters that Campion was to defend in his *Observations in the Art of English Poesie* of 1602. It is probable that he knew William Percy, author of the sonnet sequence *Coelia* (1594) at Peterhouse, and later celebrated him in an epigram of 1595 (see *V,* xxvii).[6] It is probable, too, that he first met his friend Thomas Nashe there, Nashe having matriculated at St. John's in 1582.

We do not know how fully he participated in the intellectual life of the university.[7] If he had any time left after preparing his intense readings in classics, he might have read Spenser's exciting volume *The Shepheardes Calender* (1579) or John Lyly's extravagantly stylish prose romance *Euphues* (1578): Nashe did, and indicated its vogue when he wrote of it, *"Euphues* I readd when I was a little ape in Cambridge, and then I thought it was *ipse ille* [the real thing]."[8] For some reason hard to fathom, Vivian calls Campion "one of the last of the Euphuists" (*V,* lvii); one looks in vain for Lyly's influence on him, but certainly the imprint of Spenser was deep and lasting, as we shall see. We know that Campion immersed himself in the Greek and Latin classics. He left without a degree in 1584.

In April 1586 the nineteen-year-old Campion was admitted to Gray's Inn, possibly intending, at the start, anyway, to follow his father's career in law. Gray's Inn, like the other so-called "Inns of Court"—the Middle Temple, the Inner Temple, and Lincoln's Inn—was nominally a law school. But really, the academic organization was so loose that they operated as much like residential clubs as they did graduate schools. Probably only one fourth of the men in attendance or residence were actually studying law, the rest being noblemen or gentry who had "come up" to London in order to refine manners and gain access to the royal court to which the Inns of Court were loosely attached. Sir John Fortescue described an Inn as "a sort of academy or gymnasium fit for persons of their station, where they learn all kinds of music, dancing and other such accomplishments and diversions which are suitable for their quality and such as are usually practised at Court . . . knights, barons and the greatest nobility of the kingdom often place their children in the Inns of Court not so much to make the laws their study, much less to live by the profession, having large patrimonies of their own; but to form their manners and to preserve them from contagion and vice."[9]

According to John Carey, writing of Donne's residence at Lincoln's Inn, the gentry in residence there "despised the poorer students who were in search of a professional qualification, and adopted aggressively cultivated and aristocratic manners to distinguish themselves from these career lawyers. They were great dabblers in poetry, and they enjoyed organizing revels and masques, which gave them the feeling that they were in touch with court life."[10]

The evidence suggests that the atmosphere of Gray's Inn was much more congenial to Campion than Cambridge had been. He may have been in residence for the most part of eight years, from 1586 to 1594. He acquired many friends: Edmund Bracy; Francis Manby, who drowned at sea in his youth; John Stanford and William Hatcliffe, who acted in plays with him; George Gervis, James Thurbane, and Robert Castell; Thomas Michelborne, brother of the Latin poet; and James Huishe, the son of a wealthy grocer. Abraham Fraunce was there, one of the poor students actually studying for the law (but he had known Sidney). So was Francis Davison the poet and anthologist who was to print two songs attributed to Campion in his Sidneian *Poetical Rhapsody* in 1602 (*D*, 474–75, 507–8). Vivian suggests that the sort of passion with which Campion embraced friendships was a reaction to the early loneliness of an orphan boy whose stepfather and stepmother seem to have offered little in the way of affection (*V*, xxviii).

He also took part in social occasions, most notably the dramatic performances that brought the members of Gray's Inn to the attention of the royal court. Shortly after he was admitted the elder members of the Inn wrote and produced the important play *The Misfortunes of Arthur* before the queen at Greenwich. We do not know if Campion took part in it, but we do find his name listed among "The Names of ye Gētillmē of Gray's In yt played ther a Comedy" as part of the Christmas celebration of 17 January 1587 (*V*, xxix–xxx). What the comedy was we do not know; it looks like a mélange—perhaps even two different plays—of Roman comedy like Terence, with old man, parasite, and courtesan, and Roman history with Catiline, Cato, Cinna, and other actual Romans. Campion played two parts, "Hidaspes ye sonn" and "Melancholy": if it was Roman comedy, the part of the son or dissolute young man would have been the lead. And it would have brought him to the attention of the honored guests Lord Burghley, the earl of Leicester, Ormond, and Lord Grey of Wilton.

Seven years later he probably collaborated with Francis Davison in an entertainment before the queen in the Christmas festivities of 1594 that apparently included a performance of *The Comedy of Errors*.[11] The piece was called *The Masque of Proteus and the Adamantine Rock*, and historians of the masque find in it a turning point in the development of that genre.[12] It seems likely that Davison wrote the speeches and Campion the songs. It is an elaborate compliment to Elizabeth in a myth: the "Prince of Purpoole" (i.e., the resident of Gray's Inn chosen to be master of the revels) having caught the sea-god Proteus (after he has run a gamut of emotions by turning into a lady, a serpent, a casket of gold, and so forth), refused to release him until he turned over to him the "Adamantine Rock" which draws with its magnetism the empires of the sea. Proteus agrees only if the Prince can offer an attractive virtue greater than the rock, and takes the Prince and seven knights hostage. Of course, the great power that can move men's hearts and arms as well as rocks is Eliza, for upon her "appearance" Proteus strikes the rock, the Prince and the knights emerge, and all join in a dance. Two beautiful songs attributed to Campion have been preserved: "Of Neptunes Empyre let us sing," sung by the ensemble at the beginning, and the song for Eliza, "Shadowes before the shining sunne do vanish," at the end (*D*, 474–75).

While Campion was at Gray's Inn momentous things happened. The Armada was routed and he wrote a rather disjointed Latin poem about it attributing the invasion to Satanic manipulation, the vices of envy, pride, avarice, and such, and attributing the defeat to the power of the Thames River to disturb the oceanic currents. In 1589 Nicholas Yong's *Musica Transalpina* appeared, presenting in print for the first time the Italian madrigals of Luca Marenzio, Palestrina, and others; it must have been popular with the gentlemen of the Inns of Court, noted as they were as great singers and copiers of music, and it certainly sparked a new wave of musical development in England as *The Shepheardes Calender* had in poetry ten years before.

Then in 1591 his first verse was published. Sidney's *Astrophil and Stella* was an important part of the new wave of poetry that had been sweeping the country since 1579, and manuscript copies had been avidly sought for several years. In 1591 Thomas Newman obtained a copy and issued it in a pirated edition; he hired Thomas Nashe to write a preface, and he filled up the eighteen pages at the end of his quarto with "Poems and Sonets of Sundrie other Noblemen and Gentlemen," which included one poem by Sidney's boyhood friend Fulke Greville, Lord Brooke, twenty-eight sonnets by Samuel Daniel, and a set of five songs by a poet who signed himself "Content" but was really Thomas Campion. Nashe, whom he may have known back at Cambridge, appears to have been a close friend until his premature death in 1601; the son of a clergyman, educated at Cambridge, he made his living by his writings, collaborating on plays with Marlowe and Ben Jonson, along with his own *Summers Last Will and Testament,* issuing a stream of brilliant, entertaining, and frequently outlandish prose pieces like *Piers Pennilesse his Supplication to the Divill, The Unfortunate Traveller,* and *Nashes Lenten Stuffe* (containing a parody of *Hero and Leander*). Campion's relation with Daniel was less calm. Daniel, the son of a musician and the brother of another, was educated at Oxford and became a member of the Pembroke circle under the patronage of Sidney's sister Mary. He composed a sonnet sequence *Delia,* several closet dramas, a wonderful defense of poetry and the tradition entitled *Musophilus,* and a historical poem, *The Civil Wars.* Campion and Daniel appeared together peaceably enough between the boards of the 1591 *Astrophil and Stella* volume, but a dozen years later, when Campion issued his *Observations in the Art of English Poesie* attacking rhyme as a relic of mediaeval barbarism and advocating using Latin meters for English poetry, the conservative and tradition-loving Daniel was outraged and attacked it (perhaps egged on by Fulke Greville)[13] in *A Defence of Ryme* (1603). Also, during the first decade of the seventeenth century, Daniel, along with Ben Jonson, was Campion's rival as a composer of court masques.

When Campion's verse was first published, he was probably not there to see it because he was out of the country. This is what probably happened. The English and the Spanish had been skirmishing with each other on and off since 1586, when Sidney received his death wound from a Spanish bullet at Zutphen in Holland. The defeat of the Armada was one episode, as was the privateering raid the English, among whose volunteers was Donne, made on Cadiz in 1596. In 1591 the Queen levied 4,000 men to assist Henri IV of France against the Spanish invaders of Brittany; an expedition headed by the earl of Essex arrived on 2 August and was promptly dispatched to lay siege to Rouen. The siege failed and Essex returned in the spring of 1592. A company of 100 Londoners and fifty men of Surrey commanded by Sir Robert Carey went over with Essex, and Campion may have joined them as a volunteer or gentleman adventurer. One event he witnessed there was the heroic death of Essex's brother Walter Devereux. On 8 September 1591 Essex sent out a reconnaissance force to Rouen that occupied a hill close to the town. In the course of several skirmishes, a soldier in ambush behind a hedge shot Walter Devereux in the head, and several of the English captains—John Wotton, Sir Conyers Clifford, and others—struggled with the Spanish over the body and brought it back to camp where it was mourned by all. He witnessed the bravery of Captain Thomas Grimston who commanded 150 Suffolk men and Captain John Goring with his 180 York and Rutland men. And he saw the cowardice of Barnabe Barnes at firsthand (V, xxxii–xxxiii).

The way his friend Nashe was to tell it, Barnes, "Having followed the Campe for a week or two . . . to the Generall he went and told him he did not like of this quarrelling kind of life . . . wherefore hee desir'd license to depart, for hee stood everie houre in feare and dread of his person." But when Barnes returned to London he boasted of great feats of soldiership.[14] As Nashe tells it, it was "that universall applauded Latine Poem of Master *Campions*," *In Barnum*, that stopped this braggart: "You vow that ten men were slain among the Gallic foe when you 'played Mars.' There is shame in the number: if you were to say 'no men,' Barnes, you would have kept the meter of the verse and also the truth" (D, 432–33). Nashe said, "he shewes how hee bragd, when he was in *France* he slue ten men, when (fearfull cowbaby) he never heard piece shot off but hee fell flat on his face."[15] Barnes was a classic butt of ridicule: raised in Holborn in Campion's neighborhood, he achieved notoriety if not fame with the fustian sonnet cycle after Sidney he called *Parthenophil and Parthenope* (1593). In the infamous sonnet 63 he wishes to be transformed into wine, "which down her throat doth trickle, / To kiss her lips, and lie next at her heart, / Run through her veins, and pass by Pleasures part" (see D, 409). This produced howls of laughter from Nashe, John Marston the satirist, John Harington the epigrammatist, and Campion, who wrote in another epigram: "Perhaps you will touch her heart; but Barnes, after they fish you out of the chamber-pot, what a fine lover you will be!" (D, 409). The relation goes on for years, in the usual epigrams mocking Barnes for a cuckold, in the rather unusual complimentary poem to a prose work in 1606 (D, 196).

The Norman expedition had been important for Campion, and perhaps turned him against warfare—"a lover of peace, I had to endure military service," he later wrote (V, 345). What he did was to return to England before the end of the campaign in 1592, when he proceeded to turn this rich fund of adventure into literature. He wrote

Latin epigrams lamenting the death of Devereux, praising Grimston and Goring, revealing Barnes's cowardice. These were published in 1595, his first solo volume of Latin verse, *Thomae Campiani Poemata*, consisting of the partly epic poem to the Thames on the Armada, called "Ad Thamesin," an interestingly incomplete mythological poem "Umbra" ("Shadow"), sixteen elegies after Ovid, and 129 epigrams. What is interesting about the Latin epigrams is what they reveal about his friends and acquaintances. There are epigrams addressed to his old friends at Gray's Inn, Manby, Thurbarne, Castell, Bracy, Gervis, and Stanford. There are poems addressed to Edward Michelborne, the most noted Latin poet of his day, as well as to his brothers Thomas and Laurence, an elegy on Sir Philip Sidney, a long intimate and rather obscure poem to Nashe urging him to attack somebody in print, another one to George Chapman, the famous translator of Homer, on a mutual acquaintance, one to Sir John Davies the author of *Orchestra* with whom he hopes to exchange poems, and one to Edmund Spenser telling him how much he loves his poetry whether it be pastoral or epic (i.e., both *The Shepheardes Calender* and *The Faerie Queene*, which had started to come out in print in 1590).

From Poet to Musician

One epigram is addressed to a new sort of acquaintance. "Dowland," Campion writes, "you steal away my mind in my misery, and the chords you strike overwhelm my foolish heart" (*D*, 440–43). Dowland's music puts him in mind of sweet-voiced Lygia emerging from the resounding waves to sing her own song against them (like Wallace Stevens's singer in "Idea of Order at Key West"), of lapsing muscles and other falling things like rose petals shed abroad on the ground. Two years later he repeated this striking compliment in a poem prefaced to the first book of new solo lute songs to be printed in England (type founts for lute tablature having recently been acquired by Richard Field),[16] John Dowland's *The First Booke of Songs or Ayres* (1597): he praises him for his "innovation" in issuing songs, "pressing the fleeing sounds into print" (see *D*, 195).

Campion had probably left Gray's Inn for ordinary dwelling in the city of London by this time. He loved the city and complained about it, writing, "why did you thrust a helpless young man into this town with its dark roads and filthy ways? Here it is easier to go astray than in the labyrinth at Cnossus" (*V*, 219). How was he supporting himself? When his mother, a woman of considerable means on account of her first marriage, had married Augustine Steward in 1577, she had stipulated that certain sums of money should be held in trust for her children, fifty pounds to her daughter by her first marriage, Mary Trigg, two hundred pounds to Rose Campion at her marriage, and either an annuity of forty pounds a year or a single payment of 260 pounds to Thomas at his attaining majority. Accordingly, on 2 March 1587 he released Steward of all claims except for the 260 pounds, and on 20 October 1588 he executed a further deed (*V*, xxxi). He was twenty one, in possession of a goodly sum. And that seems to have lasted ten or twelve years until some time after 1600, when he was forced to learn a profession. For the time being, he read Spenser and exchanged poems with Davies, he wrote poetry, and he consorted with musicians whose work clearly excited him tremendously.

In the "Eumaeus" episode of Joyce's *Ulysses,* Leopold Bloom and Stephen Dedalus roam the dark streets of Dublin talking of many things. Stephen

launched out into praises of Shakespeare's songs, at least of in or about that period, the lutenist Dowland who lived in Fetter Lane near Gerard the herbalist, who *anno ludendo hausi, Doulandus,* an instrument he was contemplating purchasing from Mr Arnold Dolmetsch, whom Bloom did not recall, though the name certainly sounded familiar, for sixty-five guineas and Farnaby and son with their *dux* and *comes* conceits and Byrd (William), who played the virginals, he said, in the Queen's Chapel or anywhere else he found them and one Tomkins who made toys or airs and John Bull.[17]

Of course, Stephen is showing off, part of the comedy being the contrast of his pretentious parade of musical knowledge out of books to Bloom's totally inaccurate but feeling love of "light opera of the *Don Giovanni* description" or "the severe classical school such as Mendelssohn." But it does present a telling picture of a community of musicians that it is tempting to explore. In the parish of St. Dunstan's-in-the-West lived John Dowland, Philip Rosseter, and Thomas Campion.[18] It was contact with his neighbors that made Campion a musician as well as a poet.

John Dowland was four years older than Campion, and the finest musician of his age. A virtuoso performer on the lute as well as a composer, he traveled widely—performing often and to great acclaim—in France, Germany, and Italy (where he may have met Luca

Marenzio). He was in and out of London, and from 1598 to 1606 was lutenist to Queen Anne's alcoholic brother, King Christian IV of Denmark, after which he returned to England until his death twenty years later. We know nothing of Dowland's friend and neighbor Philip Rosseter before 1601, when he and Campion published *A Booke of Ayres* together. Besides that, he arranged and published a collection of instrumental chamber music or "consort" pieces for "Treble lute, Treble Violl, Base Violl, Bandora, Cittern and Flute," in 1609, containing instrumental arrangements of several Dowland songs and of the song "Move now" from Campion's wedding masque for the Lord Hay in 1607. From 1604 to 1609 he was employed as one of the king's lutenists, and beginning in 1610 managed the court revels, being in charge of the sort of company of child actors Hamlet despised, and they performed plays by Jonson, Chapman, and others at court. He and Campion were lifelong friends: when Campion made out his will in 1619 "he did giue all that he had vnto Mr. Philip Rosseter and wished that his estate had bin farr more" than the twenty-two pounds it was (*V*, xlvii).

Up through 1595 Campion was a poet whose chief relationships were with literary men, chiefly with the Latin poets among whom his *Poemata* of 1595 placed him, like Edward Michelborne and Charles Fitzgeffrey, and he was praised for his Latin verse by William Covell, Nashe, Fitzgeffrey, and Francis Meres. But then in 1601 he appears as a composer of songs in a celebrated volume that did not even bear his name: *A Booke of Ayres, Set foorth to be song to the Lute, Orpherian, and Base Violl, by Philip Rosseter Lutenist: And are to be solde at his house in Fleetstreete neere to the Grayhound.* That he did not set his name to the title page for any fool to gaze at seems to be a result of both diffidence and aristocratic disdain: he called the songs "after the fascion of the time, eare-pleasing rimes without Arte" (*D*, 15),[19] and Rosseter is careful to explain in the dedication to Sir Thomas Monson that the first twenty-one songs are actually by Master Campion, "of his owne compostion, made at his vacant houres, and privately emparted to his friends . . . though his selfe neglects these light fruits as superfluous blossomes of his deeper Studies, yet hath it pleased him, upon my entreaty, to grant me the impression of part of them, to which I have added an equall number of mine owne" (*D*, 14). In 1595 and again in 1597 Campion appeared as a Latin poet in his complimentary poems to Dowland. By 1601 he is Rosseter's collaborator, and soon Dowland and other composers would pay him the compliment of setting his texts to their own music.

We know nothing whatever of Campion's musical education. It is a tempting speculation to suppose that Dowland and Rosseter as his friends and neighbors might have advised or overseen or at least provided models for his musical compositions. As we shall see later, his method of structuring a song by setting rhyming lines to analogous melodies was first employed by Dowland and was used throughout Rosseter's songs—and by the singer Robert Jones, too, who may have known Campion.[20] In Rosseter's case, the relationship seems to have gone two ways. As Campion's music resembles Rosseter's at the start, so Rosseter's texts resemble Campion's to such an extent that they have been printed as Campion's in some editions, and in others are included as doubtful poems. But they are more awkward in articulation and in meter than Campion's, as if they were, for example, first drafts of finished lyrics. That gives rise to the speculation that Campion might have supplied the lyrics for Rosseter's twenty-one songs in the 1601 volume, possibly in rough form; that might indicate a way of working with music, starting with a rough form of the poem to be polished along with the musical setting (like having a vague idea of a lyric text and letting it evolve along with the music). Rosseter in his dedication says that he encouraged Campion to publish his ayres, and for the two of them to come out together in print may have been an instance of mutual support.

It is hard to overestimate the importance of these musicians in Campion's life, for they made him a poet. It was music that changed him from a coterie poet in Latin, who would never be remembered today, to a lyric English poet whose songs would later attract poets as diverse as A. C. Swinburne, Ezra Pound, W. H. Auden, and Robert Creeley. It is *A Booke of Ayres* and the four song books that followed it that established him as one of the finest lyric poets in English. Paradoxically, though we usually read him today as a poet only, his texts detached from their music in modern print, it was not till he issued his poems in the form of sheet music in English songs that he found his own voice. He was not worth the silent reading until he had been sung.

It was all tentative, though, and he still shrank from the public notice. He prefaced his volume of the next year with a little dialogue poem, "The Writer to his Booke":

> Whether thus hasts my little book so fast?
> To Paules Churchyard. What? in those cels to stand,

With one leafe like a riders cloke put up
To catch a termer? or lye mustie there
With rimes a terme set out, or two before?
(*D*, 292)

This is very colloquial verse echoing common speech, concerning
Paul's Churchyard, the bookstall district of London where books and
other wares were set out to attract "termers" or men who came up
from the country for the legal term; it is very much about the business of bookselling rather than ideals. He was right to be diffident,
though. The book was *Observations in the Art of English Poesie* (1602),
and in it he proposed composing English verse by the Latin system
of long and short, instead of accented and unaccented syllables. It
was, he said, a project he had thought up several years before (perhaps
as early as 1591) (see *D*, 288), strongly influenced by the theory and
practice of his hero Sir Philip Sidney, and perhaps by Abraham
Fraunce who had been at Cambridge and Gray's Inn in his time. It
was doomed to failure and even ridicule, and Samuel Daniel attacked
it vigorously and successfully in *A Defence of Ryme* (1603). Campion
dropped the idea: henceforth he was to be a purely English song-
writer.

Court and Public Life

We hear nothing of any literary projects from him until 1607. It
was not that he was sulking after Daniel's attack. Rather, the 260
pounds he had received in 1588 had most certainly run out, and he
was seeking a profession by which to support himself. Reality was
coming in on him from all directions. It was not law but medicine
he chose. Some time in 1602 he enrolled as a medical student at the
University of Caen, in Normandy, and on 10 February 1605—two
days before his thirty-eighth birthday—he received the M.D. from
Caen. It was customary for Englishmen to take medical degrees
abroad. Of the university, Lowbury, Salter, and Young write, "The
University of Caen, founded by Henry VI of England in 1431 . . .
was easy of access and popular with students from England; something, in fact, of an English university abroad. With its spires and
its mediaeval legacy the city of Caen had much in common with Oxford and Cambridge, and its population in the later part of the sixteenth century included a majority of Protestants."[21] It was notable

for pageants, like the one celebrating the new heir to Henri IV in 1602, and for poetry contests. As a medical school it was less distinguished, Paris, Montpellier, Padua, and Leiden being the really important medical centers on the Continent. It offered the usual reading in anatomy, pathology, materia medica, pharmacy, and the rest, and its faculty was never accused of incompetence as some were in other universities. Yet it took only three years to earn a degree, and some universities did not honor such degrees. It was what we would call today a "degree factory." Campion, verging on forty and in need of money, had not troubled to enter on a long and painstaking education.

Some time in 1605 he returned to set up practice in London, probably in his familiar area of Fleet Street. Though he was not admitted to the Royal College of Physicians—few who did not hold their medical degrees from Oxford or Cambridge or a prestigious continental university were—there is evidence that he was respected in the profession. On at least one occasion, Thomas Moundeford, M.D., at several times president of the college, accompanied him on his rounds (see V, xlv).[22] Otherwise we know no more than that he occupied himself as the usual general practitioner of his time did.

When Campion returned to London in 1605, he came home to a new profession in a new country: Elizabeth had died while he was away and James I was now on the throne. James himself was a poet who had produced a treatise on poetry in 1584, and as king he knew how to harness literature and the other arts to his service. James was learned—Lancelot Andrewes quoted the Greek Septuagint when he preached before him—and he had aspirations as a theologian. The Bible most of the English-speaking world uses bears his imprint. He was venial, and sold knighthoods and offices to the highest bidder. He was bisexual. He believed in the divine right of kings and witchcraft. Most important for our purposes he had been James VI of Scotland before becoming James I of England. When he came to the throne, he intended to make England part of Great Britain. One way among many he used to bring that about was marriages: marriages of his Scots lords to English ladies. James wanted his messages to his new English subjects to be read clearly: how could this be done better than by public entertainments, or court masques?

The masque was an old form, and we can find it in England before the time of Henry VIII. It began as the interruption of a dance by costumed or masked strangers—as at Capulet's ball in *Romeo and Juliet*—but gradually explanations and significances expanded it so far that it resembled a play with music and dance like Milton's *Comus*. The masque of *Proteus and the Adamantine Rock* that Campion had a hand in at Gray's Inn in 1594 was actually one of the pieces that brought the masque form to its maturity in the seventeenth century: an introductory song and dialogue laying out the mythic story that forms the basis of the "plot," the entry of the masquers or featured dancers, a debate ending in a spectacular transformation (the rock breaks open and the knights emerge dancing), a triumphal dance followed by "revels" or social dancing, ending with a song dedicated to the monarch. It was similar to modern musical comedy. It was an old form; what was new was James's constant employment of it as an official court occasion—at tremendous expense—in order to convey his messages to his subjects and solidify his reign. The major composers of masques were Daniel, Campion, and of course Ben Jonson. The first one in James's reign of which we have record is Daniel's *Vision of the Twelve Goddesses* (1604), the second and third Jonson's *Masque of Blackness* (1605) and *Hymenei* (1606).

Campion's *Lord Hay's Masque* (1607) is the fourth in a long list. He was commissioned to write it by the court. We do not know how that came about, but we may assume that he had some powerful friends at court—perhaps Sir Thomas Monson. The occasion was one of the first big weddings, that of James's favorite James Hay, first earl of Carlisle and Baron Hay, to Honora Denny, daughter of the high sheriff of Hertfordshire who had welcomed James to England and was now a baron himself. For his libretto Campion created a story of a wedding under the auspices of Flora being interrupted by Night who represents virginity, her pacification by Apollo, and her transformation. He had long admired the Spenser of *The Faerie Queene,* and was to admire Francis Bacon's elucidation of natural allegory in *The Wisdom of the Ancients* when it came out in 1609 (see *D,* 418–19), and so it was natural for him to turn to allegory (which we find little trace of in his previous work) as a method for drawing out meaning. In one sense his story was about the bride and groom, her cool regressive fears and his hot desires. As we shall see, it means much more besides that. But one thing Campion made sure people realized was that it was about the joining of two kingdoms, the reluctant and cool one that had been a female domain with a hot and energetic male kingdom. The politics was obvious: fertility was to result. It moved Campion himself from cultivating music to exploring significance, and it also moved him from private practice into the public eye.

To compose court masques was to enter the political arena; it meant he had to risk offending, to subject himself to the possible censure of king or chamberlain, and to experience rivalry with other composers like Daniel who had attacked him in print or Jonson who was to parody one of his masques (see *D*, 264). Writing the libretto was only half the job. He had to work with the set designer, and as we know from the conflict of Ben Jonson and Inigo Jones that could be very trying indeed. He had to work with the dancing-master, and fit his words to dance movement. He may have had to direct, and at least attended rehearsals; since most of the cast—the dancers surely— were both amateurs who needed direction and noblemen who may have found it hard to take direction, it may have been frustrating.[23] He was busy, and had to farm out much of the music to other composers—Thomas Giles, the organist; Thomas Lupo, the violinist (see *D*, 205); and Giovanni Coperario and Nicholas Lanier.

Campion's life was busy and his circle of acquaintances—friends and fellow workers—was large. Inigo Jones the famous architect, artist, and designer did the sets and costumes for two of his masques, an Italian, Constantine de Servi, did them for the third. Of the musicians, three are especially important for his career. John Cooper (ca. 1575–1626), after an extended visit to Italy, Italianized his name to Giovanni Coperario and returned to England to bring the art of playing the viola da gamba to new heights and to produce a "monodic" style of song writing that would be perfected by his students William and Henry Lawes. He composed songs, instrumental pieces, a treatise on composition, and he collaborated with Campion on two masques and other works. Nicholas Lanier (1588–1666) created a sensation with his monodic setting of Campion's "Bring away this sacred tree" in *The Squires' Masque* (1613), which embarked him on a long career of masque music, including what may have been an entire setting of Jonson's *Lovers Made Men* (1617) in "recitative style," including speeches, that may have propelled masque toward opera.[24] Alfonso Ferrabosco the younger (ca. 1580–1628), son of the man who first brought madrigal style to England, later composer-in-ordinary to Charles I and Jonson's collaborator, drew Campion and Jonson together in a single volume: in his *Ayres* of 1609 he set texts by both Campion and Jonson to music (also Donne's "The Expiration"), and both contributed commendatory verses to his volume. These three musicians had a profound influence on changes we shall find in Campion's musical style, and they quickened his interest in music in general by their experiments with new styles, especially "monody" or "recitative" whereby vocal music abandoned melody to approach impassioned speech. When Campion published a book of theory drawn from their practice, *A New Way of Making Fowre Parts in Counter-point* (ca. 1614), he carved a place for himself in the history of music theory.

Campion's big year was 1613. It saw the publication of his second volume of songs, *Two Bookes of Ayres* (his books, unlike others, always came out in pairs), to which he put his own name as author-composer for the first time. The year probably began with the publication of *Songs of Mourning,* a linked set of seven songs bewailing the premature death of James's eldest son, Henry Prince of Wales (who died 6 November 1612), the words by Campion, the music by the newly popular Coperario. While we do not know that this was a royally commissioned work, it does have the look of an official public expression of grief, its songs variously addressed to King James, Queen Anne, Prince Charles, Lady Elizabeth (Henry's sister), and Frederick Count Palatine, his brother-in-law. Then on 14 February Campion had the honor to compose the libretto for an important royal wedding, that of Princess Elizabeth (who was to be known as "the winter queen" of Bohemia) to Frederick Count Palatine, the Bohemian monarch. It was an event of great importance both for international politics and for the Protestant cause, uniting the British and German states; Campion brought that fact out at the end of the masque when he had the Sibyl deliver a prophecy in Latin of the fertility and political order resting on the Roman roots of European civilization. This he published as *The Lords' Masque* together with an outdoor entertainment given for Queen Anne on her way to take the waters of Bath, by Lord Knollys at Caversham near Reading on 27–28 April. Campion was now not simply seeing his work performed before royalty, he was composing for royalty, and he had gathered around him a whole group of designers, musicians, and dancers.

Then on 26 December was performed Campion's masque for another wedding, that of Robert Car, earl of Somerset and King James's new favorite, to the powerful family of the Howards in the person of Frances Howard, who had been countess of Essex before her marriage was annulled. It was celebrated on a grand scale by four masques:

Campion's *Squires' Masque* on the wedding night; Jonson's *Irish Masque* on 29 December; Thomas Middleton's *Masque of Cupid* on 4 January; and *The Masque of Flowers* put on by Gray's Inn on 6 January. It was Christmas and a wedding; Donne wrote an epithalamion for the occasion. Campion wrote that he founded his text on enchantments, because to him the age of myth and fiction was over (see *D*, 268).

It was true: the myths exploded; it all blew up. A little over a year later it came out that the marriage of Robert Car and Frances Howard was founded on murder. When Frances Howard fell hopelessly in love with Car she employed all sorts of legal trickery to have her marriage to the earl of Essex annulled, and finally succeeded on 25 September 1613. While the annulment was in process, Car's friends exerted their influence to prevent the marriage, and one of them, Sir Thomas Overbury, the famous writer of "characters," told him, "Well, my lord, if you do marry that filthy base woman, you will utterly ruin your self" (*V*, xlii). Car and Frances, still countess of Essex, resented that so much that they decided to do away with Overbury. They had him imprisoned in the Tower on 6 April 1613 on a bald pretext, and then sought to poison him. In order to do that, they managed to pave the way by replacing the lieutenant of the Tower, Sir William Wade, with their agent Sir Jervis Elwes, and getting Overbury's keeper, one Cary, replaced by one Weston. This was all accomplished by 6 May, at which point Weston and Anne Turner the infamous serving-woman of the countess administered blue vitriol, which made Overbury sick but did not kill him. Car sent him a powder to cure his illness: it turned out to be white arsenic. Gullible as Overbury was, his constitution was strong enough to prevent him from suffering from his gullibility overmuch, so that the arsenic made him sicker but still did not kill him. But he was growing suspicious! When he wrote a note to Car accusing him of treachery, Car replied with convincing assurances and offered to send him any food he might fancy. He asked for tarts and jellies, and Car dutifully sent them—laced with corrosive sublimate. Apparently Overbury did not eat the tarts, and the royal favorite and his mistress finally resorted to a poisoned glyster, which took Overbury off on 14 September. The annulment took place eleven days later, and, after Car had been made earl of Somerset to equal his wife's rank as he was her equal in morals, the wedding took place on 26 December, celebrated by Campion's lovely masque.[25]

By the autumn of 1615 the rumors of foul play had burst forth. As the result of a series of prosecutions, the whole affair was brought to light. Elwes, Anne Turner, and Weston were hanged. Car and Frances Howard were condemned to death, then reprieved and confined to the Tower until 1622, when they were released and allowed to live out their lives in retirement. What was worse, Campion's friend and patron Sir Thomas Monson (1569–1641) was involved. Monson was a dependent of the Howards and a favorite of King James, who first made him master falconer and later in 1611 master of the armory at the Tower. He was well known for his musical entertainments and his patronage of young musicians, and he took charge of Dowland's son Robert while his father was away.[26] Monson had set his coat of arms on the reverse of the title page of *A Booke of Ayres* in 1601 to signify his protection of it, and from then on his relationship with Campion was close—really a friendship more than patronage. It was customary under James I to sell offices, and when Elwes took over the lieutenancy from Wade he was to pay 2,000 pounds for the privilege. Car's agent in the sale was Monson, already an officer of the Tower, who told Elwes in prophetically dark language "that Wade was to be removed, and that if he succeeded Sir William Wade, he was to bleed, that is, give 2,000 li." What was even worse, it was Campion who had acted as receiver in the sale; Elwes "came into the place, and payd 1400 li of the money at his unkle alderman Helvash his house to Doctor Campian" (*V*, xliii).

On October 1615 Campion was examined and Monson arrested. Here is Campion's deposition:

The exāīation of Thoms Campion docter of phisicke taken this 26 of Oct. 1615.

He confesseth that he receiued of alderman Helwys for the vse of Sr Thoms Mounson fourten hundred pounds wch Sr gervis Elwis left or provided for him there, and this event was about the midsommer after Sr gervis became lievetenant of the tower, and that pt of that 1400 li was in gold, and pt in white money and the gold Sr Thoms Mounson took wth him and the white money being in Bagge, Darwyn Sr Thoms Mounson's man caused to be caried to Sr Thoms Mouns. as he taketh it, And for what consideration it was payd this exāīate saith he knoweth not.

J. Ellesmere, Canc.   Tho: Campion

E. Zouch.   Lenox (*V*, xliv–xlv)

Campion was cleared immediately since the justices believed that he knew nothing of the purpose of the money. But Monson was kept prisoner in the Tower for lack of evidence. It was not until 13 February 1617 (the day after Campion's fiftieth birthday) that Monson was cleared and released, it being established that while he sold the office he knew nothing of the plot with poison. But while he was in the Tower his health failed, and on 24 January 1616 a warrant was issued "to allow Dr. Montford and Dr. Campian, physicians, to have access to Sir Thomas Monson, Knt., a prisoner in the Tower, to confer with the said Sir Thomas on matters relating to his health in the presence of the said Lieutenant," Sir George More (V, xlv).

Shortly after Monson's release in 1617, Campion issued his final set of songs, *The Third and Fourth Bookes of Ayres*. Dedicated to Monson (as the 1601 volume had been) and to his son, Campion made it into a kind of celebration for his friend's release:

> Since now those clouds, that lately over-cast
> Your Fame and Fortune, are disperst at last:
> And now since all to you fayre greetings make,
> Some out of love, and some for pitties sake:
> Shall I but with a common stile salute
> Your new enlargement? or stand onely mute?
> I, to whose trust and care you durst commit
> Your pined health, when Arte despayr'd of it?
> (D, 133)

After that horrendous series of events, Campion retired from court notoriety and pursued his profession. It is possible that he wrote the texts of a set of songs sung for the entertainment of King James by the earl of Cumberland at Brougham Castle in Westmoreland in 1617, but when the songs were published the next year they bore only the names of the musicians George Mason and John Earsden on the title page.[27]

Campion had only a few years to live. He must have felt death approaching, perhaps knew he had a terminal illness, even though he was only fifty-two years old. In 1619 he revised and augmented the Latin poems of his youth, published as *Tho. Campiani Epigrammatum Libri II* (1619). And then he made his will: "MEMORANDUM that THOMAS CAMPION, late of the parishe of St. Dunstons in the West, Doctor of Phisicke, being in p̄fect mynde and memory, did with an intent to make and declare his last will and testament vpon the first of March, 1619, and not longe before his death saie that he did giue all that he had vnto Mr. Phillip Rosseter and wished that his estate had bin farr more, or he vsed words to that effecte, being then and there present divers credible witnesses" (V, xlvii). A year later Campion died, on 1 March 1620, and was buried the same day at St. Dunstan's-in-the-West, Fleet Street. Philip Rosseter, who inherited the estate he wished had been far more than a mere twenty-two pounds, died three years later, on 5 May 1623, and was buried near his old friend.

Chapter Two
Song

This is the way Thomas Campion characterized his work in the genre that he perfected:

What Epigrams are in Poetrie, the same are Ayres in musicke, then in their chiefe perfection when they are short and well seasoned. But to clogg a light song with a long Praeludium, is to corrupt the nature of it. Manie rests in Musicke were invented either for necessitie of the fuge, or granted as a harmonicall licence in songs of many parts: but in Ayres I find no use they have, unlesse it be to make a vulgar and triviall modulation seeme to the ignorant strange, and to the judiciall tedious. A naked Ayre without guide, or prop, or colour but his owne, is easily censured of everie eare, and requires so much the more invention to make it please. And as *Martiall* speakes in defence of his short Epigrams, so may I say in th'apologie of Ayres, that where there is a full volume, there can be no imputation of shortnes. The Lyricke Poets among the Greekes and Latines were first inventers of Ayres, tying themselves strictly to the number and value of their sillables, of which sort, you shall find here onely one song in Saphicke verse; the rest are after the fascion of the time, eare-pleasing rimes without Arte. The subject of them is for the most part amorous, and why not amorous songs, as well as amorous attires? Or why not new Ayres, as well as new fascions? (D, 15)

An ayre like an epigram is short, it is "naked" or without ornament, it is relatively simple, and it stresses "invention" or the imaginative discovery of ideas. He reiterated the comparison from *A Booke of Ayres* (1601) some years later in the preface to *Two Bookes of Ayres* (ca. 1613), adding the implications of compression and complexity: "Short Ayres, if they be skilfully framed, and naturally exprest, are like quicke and good Epigrammes in Poesie, many of them shewing as much artifice, and breeding as great difficultie, as a larger Poeme" (D, 55).

Campion's words will govern our own exploration of his songs. We will begin with the epigrammatic traits of his texts. But of course they are not epigrams but love lyrics in the form of epigrams, and we will therefore proceed to discuss their lyric traits. Finally, Campion's comparison is between epigram in poetry and ayre in music, and so we must end with music.

Epigram

An epigram is short: so are Campion's ayres, especially those in his favorite two-strophe contrastive form (their shortness appears even more dramatically by contrast to his peers like John Dowland and Philip Rosseter). It is economical: he uses few words, few lines, even few notes in his music, as David Greer has shown. It is compressed, showing the fruit of much craft and labor in small compass (as Campion insists in his prefaces, which in themselves exemplify a curt, disconnected style). His ayres frequently incorporate compressed aphorisms, like "Once false proves faithfull never" (*Third Booke,* 2) or "Action alone makes the soule blest" (*Third Booke,* 5) or "For what is courtship, but disguise?" (*Third Booke,* 27). Or they reach toward a couplet-rhetoric of tight interrelation of terms (like "The first step to madnesse / Is the excesse of sadnesse," *Fourth Booke,* 14). Their structures use devices of logical argument conveyed by syntax as means to compress complex relationships of terms and subjects.

An epigram is simple and relatively unornamented. Campion's ayres use direct statement and eschew visual imagery that expands statement. A strophe like the following is unusual in the amount of visual appeal it contains, but it is noteworthy that the detail is compressed into metaphor and that it is, even at that, indicated only by a few words ("sunne," "shaddowe," "blacke," "night," "light") that make the argument expand into something seen, while other words move in other directions and the action conveyed by syntax is uppermost:

> Followe thy faire sunne, unhappy shaddowe:
> Though thou be blacke as night,
> And she made all of light,
> Yet follow thy faire sunne, unhappie shaddowe.
> (*A Booke of Ayres,* 1.4)

More often, the visual comes to us in the form of "submerged metaphor" wherein compressed diction suggests imagery briefly by indicating action. Such is the case with this strongly argumentative strophe wherein the human term "dive" applies to suns, the solar term "set" to lovers, thus both extending the imagery of the heavens and intensifying the interaction between suns and lovers that comes to dominate the song:

> My sweetest Lesbia, let us live and love,
> And, though the sager sort our deedes reprove,
> Let us not way them: heav'ns great lampes doe dive
> Into their west, and strait againe revive,
> But, soone as once set is our little light,
> Then must we sleepe one ever-during night.
>
> (*A Booke*, 1.1)

An even more delicate implication of metaphor is envinced by the following:

> No more can I old joyes recall:
> They now to me become unknowne,
> Not seeming to have beene at all.
> Alas, how soone is this love growne
> To such a spreading height in me
> As with it all must shadowed be!
>
> (*Fourth Booke*, 6)

The most characteristic trait of epigram is its emphasis on structure. Closure is held back and then delivered quickly, with a sense of surprise, so that the structure highlights the "invention" that is so central to its appeal: that is, the listener "comes upon" the close ("invenire"—"to find") suddenly, then realizes its inevitability. A classic example is "When to her lute":

> When to her lute Corrina sings,
> Her voice revives the leaden stringes,
> And doth in highest noates appeare
> As any challeng'd eccho cleere;
> But when she doth of mourning speake,
> Ev'n with her sighes the strings do breake.
>
> And, as her lute doth live or die,
> Led by her passion, so must I:
> For when of pleasure she doth sing,
> My thoughts enjoy a sodaine spring;
> But if she doth of sorrow speake,
> Ev'n from my hart the strings doe breake.
>
> (*A Booke*, 1.6)

Syntax governs the movement and gives it a logical as well as narrative progression: the first line of the first strophe sets up a condition that the next three lines fulfill and then expand; the final two lines set up a countercondition—the mournful one—and then rapidly follow through with the pathetic conclusion full of new feeling. The second strophe works similarly, though condition and countercondition are compressed more tightly into the last four lines. Each strophe has the structure of an epigram. And they go together to form another epigram; part of the surprise effect of the last line of the song, which in repeating line 6 ties the two strophes together, is the realization that the first strophe has been reset as a metaphor for the second, the lute an image of his heart, its strings of his veins and arteries. It is no exaggeration to say that Campion took the loose and repetitive lyric form of his time and disciplined it by epigrammatic form with its argumentative and even logical means. Ralph W. Berringer writes, "In his favorite two-stanza form, the second stanza answers the first by application or conclusion, the whole giving much the same effect as a well-constructed sonnet. The point is frequently driven home by an epigrammatic turn, sometimes lightly accenting each stanza, more often clinching the whole with an unexpected ending."[1] The logicality of such structure is frequently indicated by the syntax, as in "When to her lute," "Thou art not faire" (*A Booke,* 1.12) or "Breake now my heart" (*Third Booke,* 10).

The emotional effect of epigram consists in sudden and surprising changes in tone. A good example is "Thou art not faire" (*A Book,* 1.12), which begins in the first strophe to condemn the woman, positing that she can be neither fair nor sweet unless she loves him. In the second strophe he heightens insult to exaggerated refusal of her, only to lift the veil at the end wherein the very act of condemnation he has been engaged in becomes a reason for her to grant his desires, and the whole song becomes reset as a seduction piece. "When thou must home" has a more weighty turn. The suspense created by the subordinate clause moves across the strophes, "Then" moving toward completion of the first strophe's "When," and the movement is recapitulated in the last two lines of the song. Until those last lines, the song presents itself as high courtly compliment, and suspends the mistress in a heady atmosphere of a romantic, classical Hades with the shades of famous beauties; the names are evocative, the sounds suave (note how each line tends to be a unit of sound, a word near the beginning of each in assonance with its rhyme-word):

When thou must home to shades of under ground,
And there ariv'd, a newe admired guest,
The beauteous spirits do ingirt thee round,
White Iope, blith Hellen, and the rest,
To heare the stories of thy finisht love,
From that smoothe toong whose musicke hell can move:

Then wilt thou speake of banqueting delights,
Of masks and revels which sweete youth did make,
Of Turnies and great challenges of knights,
And all these triumphes for thy beauties sake:
When thou hast told these honours done to thee,
Then tell, O tell, how thou didst murther me.

(*A Booke*, 1.20)

She is as great a celebrity in the afterworld as she had been on earth:
even her position as narrator is an image of dominance there, surrounded by the famous beauties who hang upon her lips. But the last
line changes all: not only does it reveal the true sarcasm lurking beneath the praise, but it also cuts beneath the heady romance to assim-
ilate the classical Hades to the Christian Hell reserved for sinners, and
to show in that context the real brutality of the celebrated mistress by
means of that final unexpected verb that breaks the spell, "murther."

Lyric

Epigram provided Campion with an aesthetic, and the epigrammatic structures we have been examining provided the muscle beneath Campion's lyric grace and polish. In moving from structure to
emotional effect, we have also been moving from considering his
songs as epigrams toward realizing their nature as lyrics.

Campion is the preeminent poet of the auditory imagination. More
fully than any other lyric poet or song writer of his age or any, he
offers us experiences that strike the ear: structures of sound, the implications of words, tones of voice. In his usual manner he is so little
likely to be concerned with specificity of image, color, or shape, that
when we encounter an occasional "yellow Frog" or some "Gray
Snakes" we react with surpise—until we realize that the primary effect of such images is subtly and comically to overplay a fearful state
of mind ("So quicke, so hot," *Third Booke*, 28). It is far more typical
of him to reach out and convert visual experience into auditory terms,

as when he calls Lawra's face "thy beawties / Silent musicke" ("Rose-cheekt *Lawra*"). As Catherine Ing writes, "His Corinnas and Lesbias and Bessies may be related to the Delias and Chloes and sweet Kates, but they have their individuality, and it arises partly from the fact that Campion draws attention to qualities in them hardly noticed by other poets. They may have golden wires for hair and pearls for teeth, but he is not particularly interested if they have. Yet if they move or speak or sing, his awareness quickens at once."[2]

The visual is usually expressed as static. It is the auditory that moves, and there is analogy between flying feet, falling or rising sound, and the movement of the vocal chords in singing (see "Follow your Saint"). Campion's pursuit of the movements of sound is recorded in that strange but subtle treatise on metrics, *Observations in the Art of English Poesie*. Its fruits are preserved in his song books. His theoretical speculations on the emotional effect of a final unaccented syllable, the marchlike effect of iambs in short lines, or the quickening of the pulse by an inserted trochee gave rise to his mastery of metrical effects in the songs. Consider, for example, the totally different metrical shapes given to the following pentameter lines by variations in stress and pause: "Constant to none, but ever false to me," "My sweetest Lesbia, let us live and love," "Followe thy faire sunne, unhappy shaddowe," "Follow your Saint, follow with accents sweet." His efforts to contain movement in "stands" produced in his songs a variety of interesting stanzaic or strophic forms; some of them give an effect of articulating movement without stoppage, others use rhyme (which he had denied himself in the *Observations*) to dilate movement before contracting it into a couplet or to balance contrasting movements, others employ an occasional quantitative line to quiet the action of an accentual strophe.

His theoretical care to measure the exact length of vowel sounds and insure their independence by regularly intervening consonants, as well as his use of echo-effects to fix metrical equivalences, led him in his songs to use sound as a means of organization. Sometimes he centered individual lines on variations of one vowel sound, as in "O then I'le shine forth as an Angell of light," "Though you are yoong and I am olde," "There is ever one fresh spring abiding," "Follow her whose light they light depriveth." And often he conceived of an entire strophe as a unit of massed sounds, as in the first strophe of "Shall I come, sweet Love" (*Third Booke*, 17) where the *l* sounds beginning every line but one frame a movement from the first four lines dominated by "sweet," "thee," "beames," "be" and related sounds to the last two dominated by the *o* sounds of "for," "more," "your dore," and other words—the movement of sounds delineating a change in tone.

Campion was concerned in these technical matters with the effects of meter and massed sounds on tone; they represent, therefore, the means by which the accents of a voice full of significance move and fall upon the ear.

His management of diction is both precise and significant. Sometimes he will juxtapose two nearly cognate words for an effect of precise definition gained with ease, as in "All their pleasure is content" ("Jacke and Jone," *First Booke,* 20). At other times he uses diction to suggest imagery briefly, as we have seen. Most frequently, he will place a telling word where it will reverse the tone and show a final movement of mind; one example is the placement of "murther" in "When thou must home," another the placement of that "Comfit maker's" oath (as Hotspur calls it in *Henry IV,* Part 1), "forsooth" in "I care not for these Ladies":

> Her when we court and kisse,
> She cries, forsooth, let go:
> But when we come where comfort is,
> She never will say no.
> (*A Booke,* 1.3)

"Blame not my cheeks" moves us through several tonal modulations by switching levels of diction:

> Blame not my cheeks, though pale with love they be;
> The kindly heate unto my heart is flowne,
> To cherish it that is dismaid by thee,
> Who art so cruell and unsteedfast growne:
> For nature, cald for by distressed harts,
> Neglects and quite forsakes the outward partes.
>
> But they whose cheekes with careles blood are stain'd
> Nurse not one sparke of love within their harts,
> And, when they woe, they speake with passion fain'd,
> For their fat love lyes in their outward parts:
> But in their brests, where love his court should hold,
> Poor Cupid sits and blowes his nailes for cold.
> (*A Booke,* 1.14)

The lover's solemn and rather cool physiological argument linking pale cheeks to flaming heart leads, in the second strophe, to satire of other lovers; and at that juncture the defensive posture and under-played condemnation of the mistress in the first strophe come to the fore (perhaps even suggesting a link between her and the false lovers). The satire peaks in the dip in diction of "their fat love lyes in their outward parts" (indicating sloth as well as a grotesque obesity), and that leads in the end to plain low diction ("Poore Cupid sits," "blowes his nailes") and the comic spatial image, which stops move-ment, of Cupid as a poor, cold little boy rather than a god holding court.

Tonal complexity—produced both by diction and by other means—is one of Campion's most pervasive lyric qualities. It is of course supported by an epigrammatic structure with its surprising turns, as we saw in "When to her lute," "Thou art not faire," or "When thou must home." But such complexity is not always reserved for the ending, as we saw in "Blame not my cheeks." In "Though your strangenesse frets my hart" complexity is achieved thoughout by multiple voices, by the singer's incorporating the lady's voice into his own: the juxtaposition of her excuses, which, couched in easy senti-mental cliché, illustrate her brutal off-handed indifference to the lover's plain hard comments, is devastating; and the two voices exist-ing side-by-side create a strongly bitter effect:

> When another holds your hand,
> You sweare I hold your hart:
> When my Rivals close doe stand
> And I sit farre apart,
> I am neerer yet then they,
> Hid in your bosome, as you say.
> Is this faire excusing? O no, all is abusing.
> *(Second Booke,* 16)

Tonal complexity sometimes reveals a dark side of Campion, as in "the humanity and wise disillusionment" Yvor Winters finds in "Now winter nights,"[3] or in the gradual revelation in "I must com-plain" that the lover who criticizes the deceit of a fair woman is him-self tired and cynical. More often, though, it reveals an impressive fullness of response. A good example is "Where are all thy beauties now" (*First Booke,* 3), which may be glancing at Queen Elizabeth.[4] One of the finest examples of the complex and responsible attitude achieved with lyric grace in these songs is 'Were my hart as some mens are" (*Third Booke*, 3). In the first strophe the lover establishes himself as an honest man both by his conversational style and by his balanced view of himself: he is less patient than some lovers but his very impatience is a token of his concern for the beloved. Her faults, moreover, are forgiven but not at all mitigated by his confession of his own faults (though the mild "curious" pulls against hot condemnation):

> Were my hart as some mens are, thy errours would not move me:
> But thy faults I curious finde, and speake because I love thee;
> Patience is a thing divine and farre, I grant, above mee.

This man explains his stance in the second strophe by reference to friendship's duty to reveal faults to the friend, and gives his explanation substance by opposing "th' obsequious bosome guest" who flatters to destroy. Finally, by a sentence that starts as an oath of allegiance but turns to a hard-headed promise (thus utilizing syntax to control tone), he reaches a final balance of critic, servant ("observer"), and detached though tender well-wisher:

> While I use of eyes enjoy, and inward light of reason,
> Thy observer will I be, and censor, but in season:
> Hidden mischiefe to conceale in State and Love is treason.

By relating his finely balanced attitude to those proper to serious affairs in life such as State and Friendship, the lover impresses on the listener the fact that his kind of love is just such a serious affair, and demands fully as much care. He has located his feelings in a rich context of what is above ("divine"), below (the obsequious), and round about him and them (some men, state).

Song

In his provocative study of "Now winter nights" (*Third Booke,* 12)—a tour de force of 200 pages devoted to a single lyric—Stephen Ratcliffe locates the relations between words and music in a song within the associative aesthetic that lyric so frequently exhibits:

"Rhyme," then, describes the relationship of identities unified by a strong but strongly imperfect likeness; while maintaining and even emphasizing the separation between the parts, it forces them together, binds them, makes them cohere. In the chapters that follow I argue that what we like about a Campion song is its multiplicity of relationships among parts and patterns whose simultaneous likeness and unlikeness pull them simultaneously together and apart. My topic throughout this book is the *principle* of such relationships—the principle of *rhyme*—and my conclusions are (a) that that principle recurs in every artistic relationship in all media, (b) that that principle is the common denominator of aesthetic pleasure, (c) that the simplest fact about any song—that it is the unification of two detachable identities, one in words and one in music—demonstrates the rhyme principle and explains the fact that the pleasure of a Campion song is potentially much greater than the pleasure of either Campion's words or his music separately, and (d) that Campion gets and deserves the special admiration he receives because his words and music together multiply the manifestations of simultaneous likeness and difference to an astonishingly high degree.[5]

Ratcliffe provides a good framework for discussing Campion's songs as songs because his concept of "rhyme," by the very fact of its metaphorical quality, is broad enough to include a variety of relations between text and music of varying similarity and difference, beyond the predictably rigid one-for-one relation of syllable and note. Campion's own favorite metaphor was copulation or marriage: he wrote, "In these *English* Ayres, I have chiefly aymed to couple my Words and Notes lovingly together" (*D, 55*).

There are at least four different kinds of rhyme or coupling to be found in Campion's practice of setting words to music: music can imitate individual words, it can underline verbal structure, it can become analogous to verbal structure, and it can generate an independent but related structure. The most obvious and open is a form inherited from the older practice of the madrigalists, termed "word-painting," the attempt to make the movement of the notes imitative of ideas expressed in the words. In this representative passage, Thomas Morley gave a few basic hints to amateur musicians:

Moreover you must have a care that when your matter signifieth "ascending," "high," "heaven," and such like you must make your music ascend; and by the contrary where your ditty speaketh of "descending," "lowness," "depth," "hell," and others such you must make your music descend; for as it will be thought a great absurdity to talk of heaven and point downwards to the earth, so will it be counted great incongruity if a musician upon the words "he ascended into heaven" should cause his music descend, or by the contrary upon the descension should cause his music to ascend.[6]

Campion used such devices of "word-painting" frequently: for example, in repeating "but a little higher" each time a note above the preceding musical phrase ("Beauty since you so much desire"), or in stressing the weariness of "long houres" by a repeated long descending phrase ("Shall I come, sweet love, to thee"), or in expressing "my dying spright" by a falling phrase, "wander as a stray" by an uncertain cross-rhythm, and "mists and darkness" by a tonally unstable chromatic phrase ("Author of light").[7] In Campions's hands such effects often took on fuller meaning than those implied in Morley's rules. In "Follow thy faire sunne," for instance, the steady beat and up-down movement of the first line obviously represents the concept of relentless walking, and that is resumed in the similar but slightly more jagged music to the fourth line.[8] But that movement is broken momentarily by the two central lines where the music first descends on "black as night" and then ascends in an unusual chromatic passage on "And she made all of light." The words are about darkness and light, but the music is about lowly and high: here the music presents Campion's favorite light-dark imagery with a new, a spatial dimension. She becomes even more firmly established with the sun in its element of air while her shadow is bound to the dark and heavy element of earth he falls upon. Subsequent strophes build on this dual symbolism—the second underlining high and low again, the third relating high to pure and low to defiled—until the two join in the death predicted by the final two strophes.

But Campion saw fit to mock techniques like Morley's in the preface to *A Booke of Ayres,* and asserted that music ought chiefly to give stress to important portions of the text:

But there are some, who to appeare the more deepe and singular in their judgement, will admit no Musicke but that which is long, intricate, bated with fuge, chaind with sincopation, and where the nature of everie word is precisely exprest in the Note, like the old exploded action in Comedies, when if they did pronounce *Memini,* they would point to the hinder part of their heads, if *Video,* put their finger in their eye. But such childish observing of words is altogether ridiculous, and we ought to maintaine as well in Notes, as in action, a manly cariage, gracing no word, but that which is eminent, and emphaticall. (D, 15).

There are at least two varieties of this skill of gracing eminent and emphatical words: one is using repeated or "rhyming" melodic motifs that point up the structure of total effect of a text; the other is using motifs and other elements to create a musical structure that runs parallel to the verbal structure—pointing a text or creating its analogue.

An example of the first sort is the way in which "My sweetest Lesbia" indicates the structure of the text by melody. There is word-painting in this song, with an octave leap to high D on "heav'ns" that then yields to a descending phrase on "lampes doe dive" that is repeated lower by "Into their west," to rise again on "againe revive." There is a remarkable unity of tone produced by the fact that a few figures and their inversions compose most of the melody, as Lowbury, Salter, and Young observe.[9] But the most striking element in the music is the identical descending phrase repeated (it is, by the way, the only repeated phrase in the entire song, so much composed of variants and inversions) beneath the words "live and love" at the end of the first line and "ever-during night" at the end of the last. This remarkable echo draws together the two concepts of love and the hostile universe whose conflict, strophe by strophe, determines or generates the development of the entire lyric. "Though you are yoong" (*A Booke*, 1.2) intensifies its generating conflict of youth and age in each half line by using a different rhythmical motif for each, three half notes and a whole for youth, two half notes and two whole notes for age (in addition, "yoong" and "old" are both set to A, "hot" to C and "colde" to C-sharp, "youth" and "age" to D). But then in the fourth line of the strophe age's reversal over youth is indicated in the music by setting age to the motif hitherto associated with youth, and youth to that of age. Here the music does more than merely point up the basic terms of the text; it also makes the whole a pervasive structural statement.[10]

"Follow your Saint" goes one step further in underlining tone and imitating the feelings of the singer in its music. The four-note descent on D for "Follow your Saint" is resumed on C for "follow with" but then amplified to the end of the line—all this giving an effort of hesitation, perhaps fatigue in beginning again. The music is repeated for line 2, where "fall" underscores the descending motif. Line 3 starts by repeating the motif still one note lower on B-flat as if beginning a third time, but it suddenly switches direction with a leap of a sixth from F to D and stays near the top of the octave with "sorrow pity move" in expressing sudden then sustained anguished appeal. This underlining of mood is familiar to us from several other songs: the slow hovering melody of "The Sypres curten of the night" (*A Booke*, 1.9) emphasizes its fear and grief, and the irregular rhythm of

"See where she flies" (*A Booke,* 1.13) interprets her various moods, flight, and fury. But there is a difference, the point being that "Follow your Saint" is addressed to the song itself—the singer sings not to the mistress about her traits, but to his song about his song—and it is particularly plangent that the song should therefore incorporate the feelings of its singer into its music. The fourth line, which starts to incorporate the song's intended message to the mistress, begins with the familiar four-note motif on F, its highest point, and the actual words that the song is to deliver, "I perish for her love," begins its descent on D as the song had at the start—the song within the song repeating the song, as it were.

The creation of a musical structure analogous to the verbal structure is like very deliberate and exact "rhyme"; its best examples occur where the music pursues an epigrammatic structure in which suspense, cadence, and other elements of the musical vocabulary clarify the verbal structure. For the concept of the lyric as epigram we explored extensively before was not merely a poetic concept but a radically new theory involving music and poetry as an undifferentiated unit of sound, a theory of the short, simple unrepetitive ayre (music) as terse and pointed epigram (poetry).

Part of the epigrammatic effect of "When to her lute" (which we explored as text above) depends on its music. The suspense proper to the logical condition set up in the first four lines is intensified in the melody by phrases ending in the dominant D, but constantly frustrated in their movement toward closure and rest in the tonic G. The new condition arising in the fifth line ("But when she doth of mourning speake") supersedes the first condition and therefore is represented by repeating the melodic pattern of the first line and then reversing direction. From this point, the music leads us toward the climax by building suspense in a sequence on "her sighes" (and "my hart" in the second strophe), then displacing the rhythm and subsiding to the tonic G on the nodal phase "the strings doe break" (which is punctuated by a dissonant chord in the lute part imitating the breaking of the strings). The rich effect of a song like this one comes neither from strikingly complex music nor from conceited or strong-lined texts, but rather from the meaningful sounds produced by words and notes bound inextricably together.

"Blame not my cheeks" is another example of the total ayre as epigram. Each line begins with an analogous motif of four half-notes rising, usually over the interval of a fourth: "Blame not my cheeks,"

"The kindly heate," "For nature, cald," and "Neglects and quite." But as the text approaches the explanation in the fifth line that will intensify the epigrammatic surprise, it pursues symmetry, so that there seems to be closure in setting "(dis)-tressed harts" to an exact retrograde of "For nature." The closure is false, the motif begins once more in the sixth line in its lowest setting, starting on F, but then suddenly leaps a fourth from A to D with "and quite," that surprise becoming the basis of resolution in the final descending phrase.

A fourth variety of "rhyme" or copulation between text and music is suggested by two songs from *The First Booke of Ayres* where the music achieves imitative form, not pointing up important words or total structure, but operating independently in its own unique way to create a form that "rhymes" with the form of the text, at a distance, as it were. In "Come, chearfull day," each strophe contains a little *peripeteia* in which the couplet totally revalues the opening statement. Reversal becomes the governing principle of the music, related to, but in large part independent of, the text: it is accomplished by means of an extensive network of echoes and inversions. For example, the second occurrence in line 3 of "Part of my life," which resets its first occurrence in line 1 with considerable new irony, is set to an exact repetition of its music (bars 3–4 and 10–11). The music expresses the nature of reversal in the last line by a complex symmetry of the line and then the song: "So ev'ry day" is set to a near retrograde of "Come, chearfull day," as if beginning again with contrast, but then "we live we live" is set to a retrograde of "So ev'ry day" and this becomes, of course, an exact repetition of "Come, chearfull day." Here the music shows the structure of the text, but it does so by exhibiting the same kind of structure in itself, separately.

"Tune thy Musicke to thy hart" presents a more complex case of such "mirroring" of the text in the music. The lyric's construction is quite simple: in each strophe two stylistic directions are followed by a longer affirmation that gives substance to the imperatives. And so, as the text attempts to unite religion and art, a religious statement justifies the directions for style. The music expresses perfectly the relation of the second half of the strophe to the first, both transcending it and explaining it as it does. The basic musical idea of the song is a tetrachord from C to G, with each of the notes repeated, as established in the descending motion of the first line. The second line works this in retrograde in an obvious movement toward symmetry, but the symmetry is broken after the B-flat and never reaches the necessary repeated C. The second half of the strophe reworks the second line, starting again on the repeated G; but it augments the motif by repetitions, by adding half steps (thus giving a plaintive chromatic tone to the upward movement), and by rising above the tetrachord once only, on "the rich." It also pushes the song finally to the symmetry we have been seeking, and makes it end where it began. In this song Campion created a musical form, independent of the verbal structure but inspired by it, which perfects the lyrical statement. By forcing on the listener a desire for completion of a pattern that cannot be satisfied until he reaches the religious level of thought at the end, it implies that devotion is necessary to art not only for its inspiration, but for fulfillment of its being, its form as well.

These last two songs show a human striving toward the heavenly, and Campion's concept of the goal of poetry and music wedded or united owes much to the heavenly. In his prose comments on art, he links art to the nature of the created universe with its order, symmetry, proportion: "The world is made by Simmetry and proportion, and is in that respect compared to Musick, and Musick to Poetry" (D, 293). His characteristic image for this concept is light, the light of the world as first ordered in Genesis by the "Author of light" (First Booke, 1). As this image echoes and reechoes throughout the songbooks, it acquires a rich combination of meanings that span the heavenly—"Celestiall things . . . fullest are they in themselves of light" (First Booke, 7), "walke the wayes of light" (First Booke, 16), "O then I'le shine forth as an Angell of light" (A Booke, 1.21)—beauty—"dim all her light" (A Booke, 1.4)—the soul—"our little light" (A Booke, 1.1)—reason—"inward light of reason" (Third Booke, 3)—clarity, and even, by a pun, the weightless and happy—"Lighten, heavy hart" (First Booke, 1.9), "Light Conceits of Lovers" (D, 51).[11] Light for him thus gathers up the qualities of integrity, consonance, and clarity that had dominated Christian aesthetics since the time of St. Thomas Aquinas at least.[12] By stressing the elements of reason and proportion it moves toward the interpretation of claritas as perspicacity or having structure (rather than being simply dazzling and intuitively suggestive) that Abraham Cowley gave it by the mid-seventeenth century.[13] Campion's penchant for brevity was even related to it, since he opposes giving a brief glimpse of light to what is contained "in large and obscure volumes" (D, 343). And music founded on the brief, clear, orderly, and "light," will "yeeld a sweetnesse and content both the eare and minde, which is the ayme and perfection of Musicke"

(*D*, 55), music in his vision having in it something of the satisfaction and rest of a momentary glimpse of heavenly order.[14]

It is interesting that Campion encloses an image of music in the visual. It is also interesting to see how the image changes, for in his later work light is often presented as the literal light of the sun or human artifice—"Why should I languish, hating light?" (*Fourth Booke*, 16), "O why invented Nature light?" (*Fourth Booke*, 6), "Now yellow waxen lights" (*Third Booke*, 12). The key to a change of orientation and perspective is contained in the lines of a lover, "Others may the light admire, / I onely truely feele the fire" (*Third Booke*, 19). There the experiential becomes the center and the dominant imagery becomes that of the extremes of heat and cold—a contrast and a feeling one. This imagery is inaugurated in *The Third Booke* by "Now winter nights" (12), and proceeds through "Fire that must flame" (15), "While these cold nights freeze me dead" (17), "yon blew fire" (18), "Fire, fire" (20), "mayden flame" of love or "Summers frost" (26), and "roofes too hot . . . for men all fire" (28) into *The Fourth Booke* (9 and 19, for example).

Order and proportion in his later songbooks become located less in the metaphor of a visual light and more in sound itself, in a woman's beautiful voice (*Third Booke*, 21), in speech that shows forth the soul in articulation (*Third Booke*, 13), or in Apollo singing "the motions of the Spheares" (*Fourth Booke*, 8). As Campion proceeded in his career the ideal of perfection and formal grace yielded to the experiential and expressive, and we can see that both in the poetry and in the music. Throughout his career, his favorite technical critical term was "invention," meaning to discover or find out.[15] An epigrammatic lyric laid out the objective correlative of a feeling, as the plot of a masque entertainment found the right myth to encompass its occasion. We may apply the term to his career, also. Sight led him to find out what is felt, as light leads to fire.

Chapter Three
Poetry

Campion's songs are unique. Campion is the only poet in English whose work has a place in music history, and he is the only musician who has a place in literary history. He brought music into contact with the latest poetry. He developed his own style out of contemporary poetic movements at a time when his fellow song-writers were either borrowing texts from him or still working with texts of the old "copie" or copious style of the 1560s and 1570s, with their penchant for phrasing and rephrasing a statement. The most popular of madrigal texts, "Tichborne's Lament," which goes on for twelve lines in this fashion, is a good example:

> My prime of youth is but a frost of cares;
>> My feast of joy is but a dish of pain;
> My crop of corn is but a field of tares;
>> And all my good is but vain hope of gain.[1]

English poetry began to turn away from this style in 1579, two years before Campion was to enter Cambridge. That was the year Spenser's *The Shepheardes Calender,* dedicated to Philip Sidney, was published. With its apparatus of introduction, notes, woodcuts, and arguments before each poem, it was as much a manifesto like the *Lyrical Ballads* of 1798 as a first book of poetry; since its author was referred to as the "new Poete," we may call his movement "the new poetry."

The New Poetry and After

Basically, the new poetry was the manifestation of an aesthetic impulse succeeding the moral earnestness that had dominated the 1560s and 1570s in the *Mirrour for Magistrates* and the work of Googe, Turberville, and Gascoigne. It was manifested somewhat differently in prose in John Lyly's *Euphues* published the previous year, and in the entertaining and witty novella collections of Pettie (1576) and Riche (1581) that had succeeded the moralistic collections of Painter

(1566) and Fenton (1567). Among its traits were a renewed emphasis on connecting with the Greco-Roman classical tradition, re-creating their genres such as pastoral and epic in English, and an insistence on the fictional nature of literature—theoretically in Sidney's treatise *A Defence of Poesie* (ca. 1580) which defines poetry as nothing but fiction, practically in creating fictional speakers for poems (Spenser's cast of shepherds, Sidney's "Astrophil"). It pursued a conscious aesthetic goal of variety, so that unity arises from creating a relation among the diverse. Examples are the thematic unity that binds each of the four sets of "Eclogues" together in Sidney's *Arcadia,* that of sonnet sequences like those of Sidney, Daniel, Drayton, or that of *The Shepheardes Calender* itself with its three different kinds of moral, plaintive, and recreative eclogues all bound together by the rhythm of the seasons. E. K. announced this aesthetic in his prefatory epistle to Spenser's collection, drawing analogies with painting where "the daintie lineaments of beautye" are shadowed with "rude thickets and craggy clifts," or music wherein "oftentimes a dischorde . . . maketh a comely concordance."[2] Perhaps most importantly, it was a poetry of figure rather than literal statement, designed less to convey information than to evoke feelings in the reader by such devices as image or metaphor. As such, it derived much from the continental vogue of Petrarch and the sonnet.

The primary form this goal of evocation first took in Sidney and Spenser's "reform" was a ceremonial poetry that leads a reader through an experience like celebration in the "April" eclogue of *The Shepheardes Calender* or purgation of love pangs in the "August" eclogue or grief in the double sestina "Ye gote-heard gods" in Sidney's *Old Arcadia.* Ceremony continued to be Spenser's main mode, and he deepened it in *Amoretti, Epithalamion,* and *Fowre Hymnes.* Sidney, however, was to turn away from it toward another form of evocative poetry, the sort of dramatic poetry stating little but exhibiting the mind in a state of movement, as in *Astrophil and Stella*—for example, sonnet 31:

> With how sad steps, o Moone, thou climb'st the skies,
>> How silently, and with how wanne a face,
>> What, may it be that even in heav'nly place
> That busie archer his sharp arrowes tries?
> Sure, if that long with *Love* acquainted eyes
>> Can judge of *Love,* thou feel'st a Lover's case;
>> I reade it in thy lookes, thy languisht grace,

> To me that feele the like, thy state descries.
>   Then ev'n of fellowship, o Moone, tell me
> Is constant *Love* deem'd there but want of wit?
> Are Beauties there as proud as here they be?
> Do they above love to be lov'd, and yet
>   Those Lovers scorne whom that *Love* doth possesse?
>   Do they call *Vertue* there ungratefulness?[3]

This was the sort of poetry, with its combination of deep emotion and wit projected into a fictional myth, that was being written and circulated in manuscript in the 1580s when Campion was a student at Cambridge and then at Gray's Inn. It entered the public domain in print with sudden rapidity with the publication of *Arcadia* and books 1–3 of *The Faerie Queene* in 1590, *Astrophil and Stella* in 1591, the rest of Spenser's poetic output, and the appearance in print of disciples in sonnet and pastoral like Daniel and Drayton before the turn of the century. But print speeded up stylistic change, and beginning about 1595 when Campion started to publish there occurred a turn away from the "new poetry" toward a more "realistic" orientation of the art that was to eventuate in the "metaphysical" and "neoclassic" styles of the new reign of James I.

The well-known contrast between Marlowe's "The Passionate Shepherd to His Love" and Ralegh's "The Nymphs Reply to the Shepherd" indicates the changes that were taking place. Marlowe's song is rhetorical, a fiction of persuasion; it tries to involve the beloved in a total fictional world, or myth, whose outlines are indicated both by elements of the pastoral convention and by hyperbolic citation of a set of rich images. Ralegh's reply is not simply a point-by-point denial of Marlowe's song, it comes from a whole new poetic; instead of countermyth, it intends to destroy myth by laconic statements (rather than evocations) about reality, about shepherd's lies, and especially about the pressure of time and death. It is a poem where ideas are stated rather than implied; it tries to delineate the actual world, and instead of lush imagery ("beds of roses" and such) it attempts tight aphorisms, such as "fancy's spring, but sorrows fall."

A set of new genres sprang up which, eschewing myth and fiction, espoused realism and a plain unadorned style. The erotic elegy as practiced by Donne and Jonson ran counter to the sonnet sequences: the focus was not on the mistress in a mythic context but on the half-amused self-observation of the lover in a social context, and it was direct erotic experience rather than its transcendence that was celebrated. The self-proclaimed originality of verse satire by Hall (1597), Marston (1598), and others featured the addressing of actual social abuses of the time instead of a mythic past (and among such abuses was love as celebrated by the sonneteers of the preceding decade), and in a rough, plain, and frequently scurrile style. The verse epistle with its minimalist fiction of the poem as actual letter to an acquaintance appeared under the authorship of Lodge (1595), Drayton (1597), Daniel (1603), Donne, and others. The philosophical poem, asserting direct argument—often skeptical in its nature—about the facts of life, in a plain style, reappeared, as in Davies's *Nosce Teipsum,* Daniel's *Musophilus,* and the various verse "treatises" of Fulke Greville which pursued "Images of Life" (rather than "Images of Wit" as Sidney had) through a range of subjects such as human learning, fame, and war.[4]

These new genres owed something to the skeptical empiricism of Bacon and other thinkers, and were also related to the new curt or expressive style in prose and the new short prose genres like Bacon's *Essays* of 1597 and the prose "character." Finally, the 1590s were the heyday of the epigram, which treated actual city life, the London scene, with amusement, wit, satire, and a plain style. If we follow its history from Weever (1599) and Davies (1600) to Donne and Jonson, we will discover a growth in brevity and wit.

Several poets changed their styles, either in response to new fashions or in natural developments that helped create them. Sir John Davies was one: his *Orchestra* (1594) is an exercise in amplification, an oration in praise of dancing full of myth, put into the cunning mouth of the fictional persona Antinuous; his *Nosce Teipsum* of five years later is spoken in his own voice in a plain unfigured style that proceeds by statement, proof, objection, and answer in the manner of a prose treatise. In *Musophilus* (1598) Samuel Daniel turned from writing sonnets to a philosophical poem on the value of poetry, announcing it as "a new function of a *Poem,* to discourse," and appealing to Fulke Greville as typifying that mode—Greville, who had been developing a tight plain style from older poets like Gascoigne since the mid-1580s.[5] That inveterate reviser Michael Drayton, in the twenty-five years between *Ideas Mirrour* (1594) and its final form *Idea* (1619), turned the sonnet sequence from a hieratic celebration of the mistress into wry social comedy.[6] Campion, as we shall see, also made dramatic changes in his style.

The old "new poetry" and the newer "realistic" poetry meet in the volume of 1598 containing Marlowe's incomplete *Hero and Leander*

and George Chapman's so-called continuation of it. Whereas Marlowe's interest centered in the love story enshrined in a heady atmosphere of myth, Chapman's centered in the themes of order and
marriage in a social context, and the psychology of the lovers in the
face of such necessities. Chapman is almost satiric of the lovers, and
his rather knotty didactic style that reminds some readers of the
metaphysical poets takes the reader again and again away from the
Hellspont to the Thames and contemporary London. Such a movement establishes the vectors of Campion's various changes of focus
during his career as a lyric poet.

Sidney's Disciple

Campion's first published verse was a set of five songs signed "Content" gathered together with work by Samuel Daniel and Fulke Greville and included in *Poems and Sonets of Sundrie Other Noblemen and
Gentlemen* appended to Thomas Newman's surreptitious quarto of *Astrophil and Stella,* complete with a bumptious preface by Thomas
Nashe, in 1591. The first of them, "Canto Primo," is a complex imitation, as we can see in its first strophe:

> Harke, all you Ladies that doo sleepe:
> The Fairie Queene *Proserpina*
> Bids you awake, and pitie them that weepe:
>> You may doo in the darke
>> What the day doth forbid:
>> Feare not the doggs that barke,
>> Night will have all hid.
>> (D, 5)

"The Fairie Queene *Proserpina*" is an open allusion to Spenser, though
Campion immediately assimilates her to the classical myth of the
queen of darkness. The song is evocative in the manner of the "new
poetry"; it creates a world of darkness and freedom in love, and it acts
as ceremony, an invitation to the audience to enter into an action by
means of outlining prospectively that action (like *Epithalamion* or
much later Herrick's "Corinnas Going A-Maying"). When this song
was republished with its music in *A Booke of Ayres* in 1601, the last
four lines of each strophe were set to a haunting sequence that fell
into a regular quantitative scansion approaching a kind of Sapphic

strophe like Sidney's "If mine eyes can speake," especially in the Adonic last line: "Night will have all hid."[7] Finally, the complex classicism of the whole song is indicated not only by its approach to Sidney's programmatic quantitative experiments but also by the fact that it is an expansion of the late Latin spring song *Pervigilium Veneris,* with it refrain "*cras amet qui nunquam amavit, quique amavit cras amet*" (tomorrow he will love who has never loved before, and he who has loved will love tomorrow).

"Canto Secundo," "What faire pompe have I spide of glittering Ladies," is a vision of knights and ladies dancing in a romantic grove; it is very close to Sidney, its curious meter of rhymed quantitative Asclepiadics after Sidney's "O sweet woods the delight of solitariness" in *Arcadia.*[8] "Canto Tertio," "My love bound me with a kisse," is a short epigram, as is "Canto Quarto," "Love whets the dullest wittes."[9] Finally, "Canto Quinto" celebrates the moment of contentment the five songs outline, in a verse form of several complexities, among which is the "heel-treading" verse like Sidney's, wherein the first words of each line repeat the last words of the preceding.[10] The five songs may come from masque, and they outline a frequent masque situation wherein ladies awaken to love in the first song, appear to the forsaken knights in the second (which itself reads like a presenter's speech), and free them from enchantment by their love—celebrated in the two epigrams, which read like lyrics attached to dances—the whole ending with the last song celebrating the brilliance of the moment represented by the masque.[11] That last song is an explicit comment on the exaltation of life to mythic status we saw in the new poetry and will see more fully in one of its key products, the court masque.

The seeds of much of Campion's subsequent work lie here—his work in the masque, his pursuit of classical meters in the *Observations,* his embracing of the epigrammatic in *A Booke of Ayres.* But the context of the 1591 quarto—the context of the moment—is also important. The appendix consists of twenty-eight of the fifty sonnets Daniel was to publish as *Delia* in the next year, Campion's five songs, sonnet 29 of Greville's *Caelica,* and an anonymous song, "If flouds of teares," later set to music by John Dowland. Newman's quarto printed 107 sonnets of *Astrophil and Stella* (omitting the controversial sonnet 37) and then ten of the eleven songs separately, at the end (unlike the authorized later edition, which placed the songs here and there among the sonnets, where they fit to advance movement). Therefore, Daniel's suite of sonnets followed by Campion's songs imitate Sidney's sequence in miniature, perhaps doing so in an elaborate compliment to Sidney. If we compare the debuts of these two poets—Daniel was twenty-nine, Campion twenty-four—we see them developing different sorts of strength from Sidney's example. Daniel from the first was an expert in tonal unity: his sonnets lack Sidney's trick of dramatic contrast between octave and sestet, and instead pursue a single emotional effect through three quatrains and a couplet. And while he develops certain themes from Sidney—loss of self, living in love's slavery, hope leading to despair, the ironies of dream and waking—what is striking is his individual development of the sense of love's tragic irony ("the Prologue hope, the Epilogue despair," as Nashe put it in his preface)[12] in "If this be love" or "Look on my griefs." Campion does not share Sidney's vision at all: seeming to be a much more sunny spirit, he imitates the formal experiments of Sidney and his wit—as in "My love bound me with a kisse," which reads like a compressed epigrammatic reworking of some of Sidney's witty "baiser" sonnets, like sonnets 79 or 81 of *Astrophil and Stella.*

At this point Campion was operating as a poet, not yet as a song writer. He was to burn through his obsession with classical meters in spoken poetry in the *Observations* (published 1602 but written much earlier) and to work out some of the Spenserian fascination with myth in Latin poems like "Ad Thamesin" and "Umbra" of 1595 (a fascination he later channeled into the symbolic myths of the court masques produced between 1607 and 1613). With his appearance as a song-writer alongside Philip Rosseter in *A Booke of Ayres* in 1601, he had developed his own style, and had solidified in it his response to the poetic movements of the 1590s.

A Booke of Ayres

What strikes a reader or listener coming to *A Booke of Ayres* from other song books of the same era is, first, a distinctly *literary* quality: it is not merely the fact that Campion is known to have written his own lyrics that places his songbooks alone in the history of literature. A main element in this is the classical note struck by his songs. David Greer notes that "Campion tends to place songs that are in some way out-of-the-ordinary at the very beginning or end of a collection," thus foregrounding his originality.[13] In this case, his collection begins with an amplified version of Catullus's *Vivamus mea Lesbia* set to music, and ends with Campion's own creation of a Greco-Roman lyric in English quantitative Sapphic meter—and it is a Christian song at that, "Come let us sound with melody the praises." In between, the classical note is struck by such songs as "Harke, al you ladies" in imitation of the *Pervigilium Veneris* with a quantitative ending, "The man of life upright" which is a free paraphrase of Horace's *Integer vitae* ode, "Turne backe, you wanton flyer," with its echoes of Catullus, and "When thou must home," with its depiction of the classical underworld with Iope and Helen and its foundation in Propertius. But it is not merely a self-conscious classicism that raises literary interest in these songs; it is also their density of effect, their greater line-by-line interest that results from a reduction of repetition and an increase in wit. His themes are not so much different from those of Robert Jones, Thomas Morley, and John Dowland—invitations to love, celebration of beauty, yearning, despair over unfulfilled love, complaint—but, clothed as they are in the styles of the sonneteers and the classical poets, they show a much greater tonal variety and quickness of wit. For example, the light mockery with which he treats the old Cupid myth in "Blame not my cheeks," "When the God of merrie love," or "Mistris, since you so much desire" is of a piece with the turn toward satire of such motifs we find in Greville's *Caelica,* sonnets 12–13, 20, or 25, or in Drayton's late version of *Idea* (1619), sonnets 7, 22, 36, or 59.

His songs are also more compressed than those of his fellow composers. Dowland and the others were still writing—or using—texts of the old "copie" style of leisurely restatement like "Tichborne's Lament." Here, for instance, is the first half of John Dowland's "Shall I sue":

> Shall I sue shall I seeke for grace?
>   Shall I pray shall I proue?
> Shall I striue to a heauenly Ioy,
>   with an earthy loue?
> Shall I think that a bleeding hart
>   or a wounded eie,
> Or a sigh can ascend the cloudes
>   to attaine so hie.
>
>
> Silly wretch forsake these dreames,
>   of a vaine desire,

O bethinke what hie regard,
    holy hopes doe require.
Fauour is as faire as things are,
    treasure is not bought,
Fauour is not wonne with words,
    nor the wish of a thought.[14]

It is aggregative, it layers effect on effect by repetition or amplification, stating rather than evoking, so as to create a unified tone; the other two strophes likewise tend to repeat a single concept, usually four times per strophe. Campion took the loose and repetitive lyric form of his time and disciplined it by argumentative and logical means. He did so, as we saw extensively in the previous chapter, by utilizing the style of the epigram.

The epigram had its roots in culture, in a fashion for brevity in all things that overtook England in the 1590s. Thomas Nashe, for instance, complained as early as 1589 of "a new fashion amongst our Nation, to vaunt the pride of contraction in every . . . action; insomuch that the *Pater noster,* which was wont to fill a sheete of Paper, is written in the compasse of a pennie," and Lancelot Andrewes echoed him, in 1594, "In coins, they that in smallest compass contain greatest value, are best esteemed; and in sentences, those that in fewest words comprise most matter, are most praised."[15] This fashion was reflected in painting by Nicholas Hilliard and the miniaturists, in literary prose by the new "curt" or "Senecan" style with its short disconnected phrases, of which Bacon's 1597 *Essays* is a good example, with its favorite transitional phrase "in brief" (which Campion in the prose of his prefaces and treatises was so fond of). The new prose genres of essay and character stressing image—"a shorte Embleme; in little comprehending much" was Overbury's characterization—became popular.[16] In fact, there is evidence to suggest that by the end of the first decade of the seventeenth century, manuscript collections of short forms like epigram and character had become as widespread as had collections of sonnets twenty years before.[17] In the verse epigram that flourished in the 1590s, we see not only a growth of compression as we move from Davies to Ben Jonson, but also such an expansion of subject matter away from the satiric toward not only the complimentary but the elegaic, that Jonson could assert that his epigrams were the finest fruits of his labors. His "Epitaph on Elizabeth, L. H." is a display piece celebrating the aesthetic of the epigram by pulling much of a life into it:

> Would'st thou heare, what man can say
> In a little? Reader, stay.
> Under-neath this stone doth lye
> As much beautie, as could dye:
> Which in life did harbour give
> To more vertue, then doth live.
> If, at all, shee had a fault,
> Leave it buryed in this vault.
> One name was Elizabeth,
> Th' other let it sleepe with death:
> Fitter, where it dyed, to tell,
> Then that it liv'd at all. Farewell.[18]

No longer the disciple of Sidney, Campion is moving in a parallel path to Jonson at this time in his career. In his espousal of epigram in print, he preceded Jonson by several years (his Latin epigrams having seen print in 1595, this collection of ayres in 1601, whereas Johnson's epigrams did not see print till his folio of 1616) and his adaptation of Catullus's *Vivamus mea Lesbia* preceeded Jonson's printing of his "Come my Celia" in *Volpone* in 1605. On the other hand, Jonson led the way in the court masque, having begun as a dramatist, and produced his first masque at court in 1605, two years before Campion began. Of course, Jonson had been writing epigrams in the 1590s, and Campion had been involved in the masque perhaps as early as 1591. What their interlaced careers had in common was a goal: to bring the classical note into English, no longer in the form of verse that sounded vaguely like Latin meters and employed lush mythological effects, but rather in poetry that followed the main lines of the Greco-Roman aesthetic of compression and dry-eyed realism.

Campion did not aspire to the compression of Jonson in his ayres—because of course they did not have the subject or tone of the epigram and its drive toward definition—but utilized its techniques for love poetry, to produce epigrammatic lyric. As we saw at length in the previous chapter, Campion adopted techniques such as brevity, economy, compression, spare ornamentation, and the logical rather than associative structure that led toward a surprising reversal and strong closure. And we saw how—in examples of epigrammatic lyric from

A Book of Ayres like "When to her lute," "When thou must home," and "Blame not my cheekes"—he was interested in tracing tonal change. In adopting the witty and intellectual epigram to lyric, he expanded it somewhat in order to obtain room for the turns of feeling that are paramount in music. Indeed, there was a kind of wit in the adaptation, for epigram above all other forms of poetry had behind it a tradition of the written rather than the spoken, of engraving in fact (as Jonson made clear in his epitaphs on his son, on his daughter, on Salomon Pavey the child actor), and Campion was making it the basis not only of spoken poetry but of song. A good example of the amalgam of the incised and vocalized, the intellectual form turned to trace feeling, is "Thou art not faire":

> Thou art not faire, for all thy red and white,
> For all those rosie ornaments in thee;
> Thou art not sweet, though made of meer delight,
> Nor faire nor sweet, unlesse thou pitie mee.
> I will not sooth thy fancies: thou shalt prove
> That beauty is no beautie without love.
>
> Yet love me not, nor seeke thou to allure
> My thoughts with beautie, were it more devine;
> Thy smiles and kisses I cannot endure,
> I'le not be wrapt up in those armes of thine.
> Now shew it, if thou be a woman right:
> Embrace, and kisse, and love me, in despight.
>   (*A Booke*, 1:12)

The first strophe is more like the traditional epigram, visual in orientation at the start; it exhibits a neat tie in line 4 that is followed by the aphorism of line 6. The second strophe moves it from the lapidary to the experiential: we have a sense of their interaction at the moment, and the final turn shows the man's amusement as well as his desire, both couched in general satire. We have seen how Campion used melodic and rhythmic motifs in the music to songs like this one to point up epigrammatic effects. Campion's ayres of 1601 carried the fashion of brevity into music. Overbury's characterization of the "character" applies to Campion's music: "It is a quicke and softe touch of many strings, all shutting up in one musicall close."[19]

In brief, we have already examined *A Booke of Ayres,* since most of our examples in the previous chapter came from this volume. But one overall impression deserves mention: the self-conscious variety of the volume. There are doleful mood-pieces like "Followe thy faire sunne" (1.4) or "The Sypres curten of the night" (1.9), and there are light-hearted conceits of lovers like "Turne backe, you wanton flyer" (1.7) or "Your faire lookes enflame my desire" (1.17). There are classical songs, songs cultivating a refined courtly sentiment like "Follow your Saint" (1.10) and "See where she flies" (1.13), and sensuous and humorous country ballads like "I care not for these Ladies (1.3), "My love hath vow'd (1.5), and "It fell on a summers day" (1.8). There are songs that envelop the human love experience in a heady aura of myth like "My sweetest Lesbia" (1.1), "Harke, al you ladies" (1.19), and "When thou must home" (1.20), and there are divine and moral songs, that move us away from the quotidian, toward the end of the volume, like "The man of life upright" (1.18) and the final "Come, let us sound" (1.21) with its muted music pacing toward silence. Such variety bespeaks a vivid sense of the copiousness of human experience.

Two Bookes of Ayres

Campion's next book of songs after a dozen years' silence, *Two Bookes of Ayres: The First Contayning Divine and Morall Songs: The Second, Light Conceits of Lovers* (ca. 1613), develops contrast instead of variety, and that difference involves history of aesthetics. H. V. S. Ogden has shown how frequently variety and contrast occur as complementary terms in sixteenth- and seventeenth-century discussions of art. Basically, variety, or the presentation of a multiplicity of parts or of details coexisting, was considered to be a representation of God's creation as it was conceived by "Christian optimism," its plenitude, its complexity set out for the delight and use of mankind. Contrast was a simplification of variety to the terms of dramatic conflict; it was concerned with establishment of mood, with limit.[20] Variety was a response to the world and its wonder; it presumed a mysterious but benevolent author, and it assumed that art was an analogue of nature so conceived. Contrast was the way an individual saw the world; it was a willed simplification, a principle of intelligibility that owed more to art and the products of the mind than to nature. Variety was itself the keynote of the "new poetry," and so it is no surprise to find expressions of it like this in Sidney's *Arcadia:* "Do you not see how everything conspires together to make this place a heavenly dwelling?

Do you not see the grass, how in colour they excel the emeralds, everyone striving to pass his fellow—and yet they are all kept in an equal height? And see you not the rest of all these beautiful flowers, each of which would require a man's wit to know, and his life to express? . . . Is not every echo here a perfect music? And these fresh and delightful brooks, how slowly they slide away, as loath to leave the company of so many things united in perfection!"[21] Its monuments are the *Arcadia,* the various sonnet sequences, and of course *The Faerie Queene* with its multiple interwoven plots. There is a shift toward contrast in the early seventeenth century. We find the following expression and exemplification of it as an aesthetic principle in that poem that influenced two generations, Sir John Denham's "Cooper's Hill" (1642): "Though deep, yet clear, though gentle, yet not dull, / Strong without rage, without ore-flowing full."[22] The lines themselves show how couplet-rhetoric with its balance and antithesis was dependent on the aesthetic of contrast. So, too, Milton was conceived to make block contrasts of high and low, light and dark, in *Paradise Lost,* or in that striking two-panel composition using contrast to emphasize states of mind, "L'Allegro" and "Il Penseroso." We can see it beginning in Jonson, in his development of the antimasque as contrast to the main masque, and in the couplet-rhetoric that literary historians are fond of suggesting is a precursor of that developed by Denham, Dryden, and Pope.

When Campion was moved to make a clear large contrast the principle of his second collection of ayres, he was moving from celebrating the world to exploring the mind and the ways it knows and feels. That was to lead to several other new directions. He was not only self-conscious about creating a large overall contrast in this volume, but was downright defensive about it, in his sense of its novelty, for he wrote in "To the Reader":

> That Holy Hymns with Lovers cares are knit
> Both in one Quire here, thou maist think't unfit;
> Why do'st not blame the Stationer as well
> Who in the same Shop sets all sorts to sell?
>   (D, 85)

And by dedicating *The First Booke* to Francis, earl of Cumberland, and the *Second* to his son Henry, Lord Clifford, he intensified the contrast, linking age to the sacred and youth to the secular:

> Pure Hymnes, such as the seaventh day loves, doe leade;
> Grave age did justly chalenge those of mee:
> These weeke-day workes, in order that succeede,
> Your youth best fits, and yours, yong Lord, they be.
>
> (*D*, 84)

The contrast involves different ways of seeing life; and, as we shall see, loosely linked to that topic are developments like rhythms of evaluation and reevaluation, the cultivation of perspective, and a rhetoric of antithesis.

The First Booke is central for his career: the first English collection of sacred ayres to proceed from the new lutenist school, it let a whole new dimension into Campion's world view. Gone is the Greco-Roman classicism of *A Booke of Ayres* that threatened to supply a new myth for life at the accession of James I; instead we have reflections of the life of Campion's day. Within *The First Booke* we have some variety, a mixture of the general and timeless with the specific and contemporary. There is general moral verse in the Horatian manner, like the reprinted "The man of life upright" (2) or "*Jacke* and *Jone*" on the simple life (20), but put in terms of English country living complete with reference to the depredations of noble hunts; and then there are political hymns referring directly to contemporary events like the Gunpowder Plot (6) or the death of Prince Henry (21). There are several pieces in the "witty" tradition of Latin hymnody like "View mee, Lord" (5) and "Tune thy Musicke" (8), and on the other hand there are several paraphrases of psalms that recall their usage in church service—"Out of my soules deapth" from Psalm 130 (4), "As by the streames of *Babilon*" from Psalm 137 (14), and "Sing a song of joy" from Psalm 104 (15).

What predominates in *The First Booke* and ties these different sorts of religious verse together is a plain style of pithy literal statement (perhaps encouraged by the tradition of paraphrasing psalms), a style that eschews metaphor and incorporates a nonsensuous diction consisting for the most part of abstract but specific nouns—whether they be the standard terms of religious discourse like "grace" or "Patience,' or not, as in "Making trouble their content" (10). Campion begins here his habit of inserting short aphorisms into his texts: "All their pleasure is content" or "Make the hedge, which others breake" (20), "In faire disguise blacke dangers be" (13), or "The man that nothing doth is dead" (19). "Wise men patience never want" (10) is especially interesting in this regard, since it pulls an extensive series of neatly phrased moral aphorisms into direct contact with the times when kindness grows cold and law becomes an art. Campion begins to concentrate on rhetorical schemes for relating precise terms concisely, as in lines like these: "'The Lord exceedes in mercy as in might; / His ruth is greater, though thy crimes be great" (12). Within this mode, Campion sometimes cultivates a real intellectual wit, as in the turn the second strophe of "Come, chearfull day" (17) takes, or the turn on the repeated "part of my life" in the first strophe. And there is an occasional knotty "strong line" like "So ev'ry day we live, a day wee dye" or "Thy tracks to endlesse joy or paine / Yeelds but the modell of a span" (16).

As befits religious verse, old age, and even the analogous concept of the sabboth, *The First Booke* as a whole lays down a thematic action of reevaluation of the earthly life and its claims. This comes out saliently in an interesting allegorical vision that centers on the eyes. "Loe when backe mine eye" (13) begins with the clearing of the eyesight after a person has passed through dangers, thus starting with a life-context. This leads to his reevaluating the world, setting aside appearances:

> Straight the caves of hell
>   Drest with flowres I see,
> Wherein false pleasures dwell,
> That, winning most, most deadly be.
>
> Throngs of masked Feinds,
>   Wing'd like Angels, flye,
> Ev'n in the gates of Friends;
> In faire disguise blacke dangers lye.

It ends with his casting his eyes heavenward and praying for guidance henceforth so as not to mis-see and fall into the snares he has seen. Many of the songs in this portion of the book exhort the listener to such a conversion and true ways of seeing, like "Lift up to heav'n, sad wretch, thy heavy spright" (12) or "Awake, awake, thou heavy spright" (16) or "Lighten, heavy hart, thy spright" (19); all center on the world as heavy and dark, heaven as weightless and light. It implies a revaluation of Campion's light-dark imagery as we saw it in the 1601 volume. "Seeke the Lord" (18) is about giving up the world, and intensifies the vision of "Loe when backe mine eye":

> Farewell, World, thou masse of meere confusion,
> False light with many shadowes dimm'd,
> Old Witch with new foyles trimm'd,
> Thou deadly sleepe of soule, and charm'd illusion.

Incidentally, the fact that this song is set to the music created for the Petrarchan love lament "Follow thy faire sunne" in *A Booke of Ayres* may introduce a touch of sacred parody, a song about joyful giving up the world set to the music used before for a very worldly song of despair. This song also rounds out what we can perceive to be a sequence on giving up the world and longing for heaven at the center of the book, starting with "Never weather-beaten Saile" (11) and ending with the next song to this one, "Lighten, heavy hart, thy spright" (19). Reevaluation governs not only the individual song, it pulls several of them into relation with one another.

In the best of these songs, reevaluation reveals an impression of fullness of response to a situation. "Where are all thy beauties now" (3) begins as a harsh indictment of a dead woman's vanity; it seems to be addressed to her body lying in state, and it may be glancing at the recently dead Elizabeth I (which of course illustrates once again the book's dedication to explore the contemporary world). The second strophe intensifies this tone:

> Thy rich state of twisted gold to Bayes is turned;
> Cold as thou art, are they loves that so much burned:
> Who dye in flatt'rers armes are seldom mourned.

Then the song takes a surprising turn: it suddenly places the condemnation the singer has been voicing in the mouths of specific other people who blame her—thus relativizing it—and establishes distance by projecting into the future, when all this will seem part of the past:

> Yet, in spight of envie, this be still proclaymed,
> That none worthyer then thy selfe thy worth hath blamed:
> When their poore names are lost, thou shalt live famed.

The song cannot rest content with simplistic pious rebuke, even rebuke of the egregious; the fineness of tone with which Campion conceived it dictates that it ends with full justice, with recognition of her genuine accomplishment as well as faults, and with honest respect for her in spite of the scorn, and it does so by a sweep into the distant future that redefines the situation as a story:

> When thy story, long time hence, shall be perused,
> Let the blemish of thy rule be thus excused:
> None ever liv'd more just, none more abused.

The sense of a full view of things and measured judgment that *The First Booke* achieves by taking up the religious perspective carries over into *The Second Booke*. Its very first song, "Vaine men whose follies make a God of Love," is a recantation of erotic idolatry, and as such deserves comparison with Donne's "Loves Deity." Its first strophe is aphoristic, urging men to "Prayse not what you desire, but what you prove." The second strophe continues this strategy, poising appearances at the start with reality at the end, and it pulls in personal experience in so doing: "Shee seem'd a Saint, that brake her faith with mee, / But prov'd a woman, as all other be." One suggestion that arises from this detail is that what could have been a song of personal disenchantment has achieved perspective by merging in generalities. But then, as in *The First Booke,* judgment is not allowed to remain simplistic, and the song must end by ruefully accepting the reality:

> So bitter is their sweet, that true content
> Unhappy men in them may never finde;
> Ah, but without them, none; both must consent,
> Else uncouth are the joyes of eyther kinde.
> Let us then prayse their good, forget their ill:
> Men must be men, and women women still.

As the final lines show, the song resists the idolatry of exalting its own judgment and enacts its theme of stripping away idolatry to reveal a human emotional situation for the limited yet necessary and valuable thing it is in fact: "Men must be men, and women women still." "Sweet, exclude mee not" (11) assays a similar complexity of tone in a lighter vein. A plea of a lover to his fiancée to let him into bed, he constructs a witty argument by analogy in the second strophe, and then quickly shifts in self-consciousness to beg her not to laugh at him (not to laugh at the overingenious analogy itself, perhaps):

> Tenants, to fulfill their Land-lords pleasure,
>   Pay their rent before the quarter:
> 'Tis my case, if you it rightly measure;
>   Put mee not then off with laughter.
> Consider then a little more:
>   Here's the way to all my store.

Finally, he assays another turn of wit, inviting her indirectly to enter a compact of deceit:

> Women are most apt to be surprised
> Sleeping, or sleepe wisely fayning.
> Then grace me yet a little more:
> Here's the way, barre not the dore.

By way of analogy with the reevaluation of *The First Booke*, what we have here is the taking of new perspectives. Surprisingly, many of these songs are meant to be sung by women. "Good men, shew, if you can tell" (9) is the lament of a naive young maiden who has been abandoned by her fickle lover; "So many loves have I neglected" (15) is about a woman caught in the love game, a courtly woman who regrets playing coy now that it has left her alone, without a lover; and "A secret love or two, I must confesse" (19) is the candid confession of a woman who indulges in courtly love affairs while still, she insists, loving her husband. As "A secret love" suggests, the female perspectives achieved in these songs frequently criticize the courtly love game. "Though your strangenesse frets my hart" (16), as we saw before, decimates the whole business by incorporating the tired clichés of a woman who is a seasoned player into the man's sardonic presentation alongside his own words and interpretations. The songs of *A Book of Ayres* were counters in the love game, persuasions to love, complaints, celebrations. Here the love songs operate at a distance; they put the love game into perspective and take a stance toward it. Campion achieved a new contemporaneity and realism by showing love and its problems of courtship, marriage, and adultery in a social context (rather than ideationally or abstractly), and by intensifying his psychological focus. The pleading lover in these songs is not the abject sufferer of "Follow your Saint," but a real person, the recognizable cynic or the disabused or the man of wit offering argument.

The dual development in *Two Bookes of Ayres* constitutes a further realization of the power of the epigrammatic mode in lyric that was announced in the previous volume and reiterated in the preface to this one. For, as Martial had been the first to show, the epigram's immediacy of effect was due not only to its brevity and related quick stylistic effects but also to its direct confrontation of the reader as an epistle in the plain style concerning his own quotidian life instead of remote romantic myth.[23] "Realism" of many sorts abounds in this book.

Songs of Mourning

Published between *Two Bookes of Ayres* (ca. 1613) and *The Third and Fourth Bookes of Ayres* (ca. 1617) was Campion's set of elegies on Prince Henry, who had died on 6 November 1612 of typhoid fever aggravated by overindulgence in exercise. Prince Henry's popularity and virtues combined with the usual romantic aura about the death of the young to produce a flood of elegies of him by the major and minor poets of the age, including John Donne and his friends the strong-lined speculative metaphysical poets Sir Edward Herbert, Henry King, and Sir Henry Goodyere; Spenserians like William Drummond, Giles Fletcher, and William Browne, who usually channeled their laments into pastoral elegy; and other important poets like George Chapman, Cyril Tourneur, John Webster, and Sir John Davies. Not the least of these elegies was *Songs of Mourning* (1613), "worded" by Thomas Campion and set to music by the prince's music tutor Giovanni Coperario. Campion's contribution is unique in at least two ways we would expect of the author of *Two Bookes of Ayres:* in its concrete historical treatment of Prince Henry and in its use of the structure of religious meditation.

Both the Spenserians and the metaphysicals attempted to relate this particular event to the most general of concerns, the former by involving the fate of mankind in the individual's death by means of myth (as Drummond did in *Teares on the Death of Moeliades,* celebrating "A second Adons death"), the latter by using the death of the individual as the basis for speculations into metaphysics (as Donne and Herbert did).[24] Campion chose instead to remain entirely within the realm of the particular and factual, by first stressing Prince Henry's individual virtues and exploits, and then by exploring his meaning for the people close to him—father, mother, brother, sister, brother-in-law—in personal rather than ideational terms. By opening out to Great Britain and the world in the last two songs, the series achieves some universality of compass; but even here what is stressed is particular history (the East India venture, for example), and the politically general has been reached by accretion rather than assimilation.

The truly universal dimensions of Henry's death lie, for Campion, in the common emotions aroused by it. For he conceived of his song cycle as modeled on meditative exercise of the sort we find in Joseph Hall; he casts himself as a priest (as the first six lines of the *Elegie* show), his purpose to move his audience to cleansing grief by means of a spoken prelude and a body of seven songs. The *Elegie,* by stressing Henry's accomplishments and using the relation between Fate and Providence as a frame, is addressed to the audience's understanding. The seven linked songs that follow are to use this understanding as the basis of a cathartic act involving the emotions, at first indirectly by leading the audience to identify with those most deeply affected, then directly by addressing the people of England and Europe themselves as those most broadly affected by Henry's death.

Songs of Mourning intensifies the religious strains Campion developed in *The First Booke of Ayres* by making religious verse into meditative exercises for the listener, so that the listener responds instead of simply taking in an address. He also proceeded in this volume to stress the conditions of this world, to cultivate realism and a social context while attempting a deep approach. This volume is, whatever its faults, totally original: from this point onward in his career, he seems to owe nothing to anybody.

The Third and Fourth Bookes of Ayres

A revision provides a good introduction to Campion's mature manner in *The Third and Fourth Bookes of Ayres* (ca. 1617). Here is the text of "Your faire lookes enflame my desire" as published in *A Book of Ayres* (1601):

> Your faire lookes enflame my desire:
>   Quench it againe with love.
> Stay, O strive not still to retire,
>   Doe not inhumane prove.
> If love may perswade,
>   Loves pleasures, deere, denie not;
> Heere is a silent grovie shade:
>   O tarrie then, and flie not.
>
> Have I seaz'd my heavenly delight
>   In this unhaunted grove?
> Time shall now her furie requite
>   With the revenge of love.
> Then come, sweetest, come,
>   My lips with kisses gracing:
> Here let us harbour all alone,
>   Die, die in sweete embracing.

Will you now so timely depart,
    And not returne againe?
Your sight lends such life to my hart
    That to depart is paine.
Feare yeelds no delay,
    Securenes helpeth pleasure:
Then, till the time gives safer stay,
    O farewell, my lives treasure!
                                    (*A Booke*, 1.17)

"If love may perswade": it falls into the category of persuasions to love; it is dramatic, it presents itself as a moment in the love game, and it shows the young man's sexual excitement. In fact, it reenacts his excitement, for what is notable here is the implication that things have happened between strophes (in the manner of Wyatt's "And wilt thou leave me thus?"): we realize that they have entered the grove together between the first and second strophes, and that between the second and third they have actually made love. In 1617 Campion published an extensive revision of this song, the vocal line only slightly changed, but with a new lute accompaniment. In the first strophe he revised; but in the second and third he took a new direction:

Your faire lookes urge my desire:
    Calme it, sweet, with love.
Stay, o why will you retire?
    Can you churlish prove?
If love may perswade,
    Loves pleasures, deare, deny not:
Here is a grove secur'd with shade;
    O then be wise, and flye not.

Harke, the Birds delighted sing,
    Yet our pleasure sleepes.
Wealth to none can profit bring,
    Which the miser keepes:
O come, while we may,
    Let's chayne Love with embraces;
Wee have not all times time to stay,
    Nor safety in all places.

What ill finde you now in this?
    Or who can complaine?

> There is nothing done amisse,
>   That breedes no man payne.
> 'Tis now flowry *May,*
>   But ev'n in cold *December,*
> When all these leaves are blowne away,
>   This place shall I remember.
>   (*Fourth Booke,* 23)

He has shortened the first four lines of each strophe by a syllable, thus giving a more commanding and direct feel to the song by strong trochaic beginnings (as Jonson did when he translated his version of Catullus as "Come my Celia, let us prove"). It is still persuasive, but instead of expressing his excitement and trying to arouse hers by that means, it dwells on their common interests. It is calmer and proceeds strophe by strophe in an argument instead of suggesting action by an interrupted movement, and instead of reenacting a dramatic moment it develops a scene for their common delight. As Joan Hart writes, "the scene has been repainted in colours at once stronger and more subtle"[25] and it has become the center of interest, with added details like the birds and tonal characterizations like "secur'd" and "safety." The erotic clichés in the first version have given way to sharp aphorisms like "Wealth to none can profit bring / Which the miser keepes," "Wee have not all times time to stay," and "There is nothing done amisse, / That breedes no man payne."[26] These aphorisms not only contribute a sententious tone to the whole song, but they also expand its context since they are generalities "imported" from areas of experience outside the situation itself; they are devices of compression and make the song contain, in its reference, more of life. The expanded context so created comes to the fore in the new ending, which Hart finds especially strong; she writes, "the later version is strengthened by the tension between the young man's experience and the older man's reflection upon it."[27] In sum, Campion moved in this song toward calm unity of effect, aphoristic sharpness, compression, and the reflective.

The songs of his late manner are terse: that is, they are not only briefer than the previous songs on an average, but they are compressed. The devices of compression are largely those foregrounding the relationships among individual weighty words developed in the plain style of *The First Booke,* but the lines are drawn more tightly. Often single significant words are repeated or varied in order to bring out all their implications and the relations among them. Frequently a song revolves around such a word, so that "simple" becomes the key-word of "Maydes are simple, some men say" (*Third Booke,* 4), or "good" in its many meanings ("valuable," "morally upright," "chattel") governs "Why presumes thy pride on that" (*Third Booke,* 6), or the relation between "faith," "hope," and "love" outlines the action of "Shall I then hope when faith is fled?" (*Third Booke,* 29). Frequently Campion achieves a couplet rhetoric of turn, balance, and antithesis such as Jonson was exploring, as in "Poore in desert, in name rich, proud of shame" ("O griefe, o spight," *Third Booke,* 8) or in the complexly balanced line "Bad with bad in ill sute well, but good with good live blessed" ("What is it that all men possesse," *Third Booke,* 14). He uses extensively the device of the aphorism, whereby, as we have seen above, distillations of general experience in diverse aspects of life are let into a song in order to extend its scope in a compressed manner, such as "Friendship is the glasse of Truth" ("Were my hart as some mens are," *Third Booke,* 3), "Poorely hee lives, that can love none" ("Shall I then hope," *Third Booke,* 29), or the more tonally loaded "Little knowes he how to love that never was deceived" ("Silly boy," *Third Booke,* 26).

These mature songs are plain in style, approaching their subjects directly and literally; in them, imagery is limited to illustration of a stated argument, and metaphorical diction is almost completely banished, in completion of a tendency we have seen operating all through his work. In "So tyr'd are all my thoughts" (*Third Booke,* 5) the singer tells forth fully and directly what he feels—and with some difficulty, which is itself dramatized—instead of letting it emerge through a fiction. "O griefe, O spight" (*Third Booke,* 8) is a direct lament on the times, including criticism of the purchases of knighthood under James I, more like a satire than a song, and celebrating its own "true wisedome that is just and *plaine*" (my italics). "Be thou then my beauty named" (*Third Booke* 19) is interesting in this regard, because it is in fact a critique of metaphor:

> Be thou then my beauty named,
> Since thy will is to be mine:
> For by that am I enflamed,
> Which on all alike doth shine.
> Others may the light admire,
> I onely truely feele the fire.

> But, if lofty titles move thee,
> Challenge then a Sov'raignes place:
>   Say I honour when I love thee,
> Let me call thy kindnesse grace.
>   State and Love things divers bee,
>   Yet will we teach them to agree.
>
>
>   Or, if this be not sufficing,
> Be thou stil'd my Goddesse then:
>   I will love thee sacrificing,
> In thine honour Hymnes Ile pen.
>   To be thine, what canst thou more?
>   Ile love thee, serve thee, and adore.

The singer quotes tongue-in-cheek the stylish metaphors she demands
of him—the sovereignty of the courtly love tradition ("honour,"
"grace") and then its idolotry ("Goddesse," "sacrificing," "Hymnes")—
and he does so in a way that makes the disparity between vehicle and
tenor witty and self-conscious (brought to light in the witty couplet
of the second strophe, where he names her method plainly). It is a
witty bargaining song that mocks her for her sexual ambition and
even her preference of fame over fact (especially in the first strophe)
and then mocks his own unscrupulousness (in the last). Taken together, their cynical but playful bargain creates a cutting critique of
the love game where words are more important than feelings, and at
the same time shows how intelligent people can navigate such waters.

It comes as a surprise that, contrary to the whole lutenist song tradition, many of these are not love songs at all. Two of them are about
the nature and significance of music—"Awake, thou spring of speaking grace" (*Third Booke,* 13) and "To his sweet Lute *Apollo* sang the
motions of the Spheares" on the contest between Apollo and Pan
(*Fourth Booke,* 8). One is about social entertainment—"Now winter
nights" (*Third Booke,* 12). One is a satirical lament on the times—
"O griefe, O spight" (*Third Booke,* 8). And two of them are especially
unusual in that they explore a deep state of psychotic depression (totally unrelated to love, by the way, which was the usual cause cited
for such predicaments)—"Could my heart more tongues imploy"
(*Third Booke,* 24) and "So tyr'd are all my thoughts" (*Third Booke,* 5):

So tyr'd are all my thoughts, that sence and spirits faile;
Mourning I pine, and know not what I ayle.
O what can yeeld ease to a minde,
        Joy in nothing that can finde?

How are all my powres fore-spoke? what strange distaste is this?
Hence, cruell hate of that which sweetest is:
Come, come delight, make my dull braine
        Feele once heate of joy againe.

The lovers teares are sweet, their mover makes them so;
Proud of a wound the bleeding Souldiers grow:
Poore I alone, dreaming, endure
        Griefe that knowes nor cause, nor cure.

And whence can all this grow? even from an idle minde,
That no delight in any good can finde.
Action alone makes the soule blest:
        Vertue dyes with too much rest.

It is not until Coleridge's "Dejection: an Ode" that we will see the
like in English verse again. It enacts the struggle to understand, the
difficulty of finding what we moderns might call an "objective correlative" that will express his state to himself. He knows the psychology
of depression, recognizes the link between thought, sense, and spirit,
senses joy as a kind of warmth within, and can contrast his case with
others; but it remains resistant to definition and understanding, and
all he can do at the end is recommend a cure of the symptoms.
Clearly, Campion's scope is expanded by such songs as this in this
volume—beyond that of the lutenist song books and beyond that of
many of his contemporaries in any genre.
    Those of the late songs that are love songs are not conceived as dra-
matic moments in the love game where the lover laments or tries to
persuade his mistress to grant his desires, but rather they are reflective and try to achieve definition of a given concept or stance clearly
and in all its specificity. As such, they are realistic, and they usually
relate love to contexts larger than the romantic, such as those supplied by society, nature, or even theology. "Shall I then hope" (*Third
Booke*, 29) is such a reflective love lyric:

Shall I then hope when faith is fled?
Can I seeke love when hope is gone?
Or can I live, when Love is dead?
Poorely hee lives, that can love none.
    Her vowes are broke, and I am free;
    Shee lost her faith in loosing mee.

When I compare mine owne events,
When I weigh others like annoy,
All doe but heape up discontents
That on a beauty build their joy.
    Thus I of all complaine, since shee
    All faith hath lost in loosing mee.

So my deare freedome have I gain'd
Through her unkindnesse and disgrace;
Yet could I ever live enchain'd,
As shee my service did embrace.
    But shee is chang'd, and I am free:
    Faith failing her, Love dyed in mee.

The singer interweaves the three theological virtues to show their interactions, the dependence of hope on faith, the dependence of love on hope, the interdependence of love and faith in her and then in himself. The continued comparison of the love affair with Christian virtue gives it a broad ideational context, and the comparisons in the second strophe give it a social context as well. The virtues provide a model for humans affecting each other; her violation has hurt him and deflated his life, but it has also provided an ironic freedom for him. They provide a standard of judgment: she lost *all* faith in breaking her faith to him. And they allow a variety of attitudes to circulate— irony, regret, a moment of hope, relief. The song as a whole is about their adjustment: it concerns the singer's curve of emotion, and it comes to rest in bitter understanding and definition.

These late songs eschew romance for naturalism and even the doggedly empirical. They are realistic. They use naturalistic and societal details freely, and they contain many allusions to specific situations and persons that their frequently occasional nature (as established in the verse epistle to Sir Thomas Monson) demands. They seek viable solutions to emotional and other problems, or at the least illuminating definitions of them. Their most distinctive trait is their concern with tone and tonal modulation—with the civilized art of taking a wide range of possible attitudes toward a situation and creating some adjustment among them, rather than simply discarding some and cultivating others. This concern appears first in the way emotions are compared and modified in the epistle to Monson; then in the complex voice of "Breake now my heart and dye" (*Third Booke,* 10), which we have examined before; or in the adjustment of lightly cynical, heavily sarcastic, and finally laudatory attitudes in "Silly boy" (*Third Booke,* 26). Songs like "Shall I then hope," "Thus I resolve" (*Third Booke,* 22), and, especially, "Were my hart as some mens are" (*Third Booke,* 3), which we examined in the previous chapter, are especially concerned with establishing and exploring viable attitudes, usually by indicating a delicate combination of diverse responses.

Most of our illustrations of Campion's mature mode come from *The Third Booke of Ayres,* because *The Fourth Booke* is a retrospective volume. Two of the songs—"Beauty, since you so much desire" (22) and "Your faire lookes urge my desire" (23)—are revisions of songs in *A Booke of Ayres.* At least four—"There is a Garden in her face" (7), "Young and simple though I am" (9), "I must complain" (17), and "Thinks't thou to seduce me then" (18)—had been circulating for some time and had been published by other song writers with their own music as much as a decade previously; and several others seem like early work set forth anew.

Campion in this publication followed his practice in *Two Bookes of Ayres* in dedicating his two books to father and son, respectively, to Sir Thomas Monson his old friend who had recently been released from jail, and to Monson's son John. But the difference between the two is not a direct contrast like that between sacred and secular but rather a distinction in tone, between rather bitter and hard-headed songs on the one hand and lighter frothy ones on the other. Youth and age here signify innocence and experience. Surely one reason for the peculiar form of the distinction is that these two books are occasional in a way that none of the other songbooks are: they turn their faces toward special people and situations. In his epistle, Campion is at great pains to specify the way he feels about Monson, his recent disgrace, and the way he himself defines his relationship to him; hence, certain of the songs (for instance, "O greife, O spight") seem to allude directly to Monson's circumstances and experience. And as in any good occasional verse that does not shy away from the particularity of the occasion, specificity of situation and complexity of tone result.

It was Campion's hope that *The Third Book* would cheer Sir Thomas; he wrote in his dedication,

> But how shall I this worke of fame expresse?
> How can I better, after pensivenesse,
> Then with light straynes of Musicke, made to move
> Sweetly with the wide-spreading plumes of love?
>
> (D, 133)

The curative function he assigned to the book determined its arrangement, for it takes Monson and the reader through a definite tonal progression from grief to lightheartedness. The first half is dark: its dominant emotions are negative ones (which the reiterated word "distaste" implies), such as complaint, disappointment, anger, and cynical disenchantment. Suddenly, with "Now winter nights enlarge" (12), the tone rises to conviviality, a tone that is sustained through most of the rest of the volume, where, if cynicism exists, it is the gay cynicism of the coquettes who sing "Silly boy," "If thou longst," or "So quicke, so hot, so mad," or where male disenchantment is spiced with comic acceptance.

The Fourth Booke has no such progression, but it does have a thread of unity that centers in—of all people—Geoffrey Chaucer. Campion writes in his preface in defense of some slightly salacious songs, "But if any squeamish stomackes shall checke at two or three vaine Ditties in the end of this Booke, let them powre off the clearest, and leave those as dregs in the bottome. Howsoever, if they be but conferred with the *Canterbury Tales* of that venerable Poet *Chaucer*, they will then appeare toothsome enough" (D, 168). One of the songs he refers to is "If any hath the heart to kill" (21), a lament over sexual impotence that should be compared to its only predecessor "Pin'd I am" (*Second Booke*, 14) focusing on the male member ("Some puts it daily in my hand, / To interrupt my muse"). Another is "Beauty, since you so much desire" (22):

> Beauty, since you so much desire
> To know the place of *Cupids* fire:
> About you somewhere doth it rest,
> Yet never harbour'd in your brest,

> Nor gout-like in your heele or toe;
> What foole would seeke Loves flame so low?
> But a little higher, but a little higher,
> There, there, o there lyes *Cupids* fire.

The song not only is explicit (with its music underlining its innuen-dos)[28] but it gathers humor from the fact that it is a revision—or par-ody, rather—of his own early song, "Mistris, since you so much desire" (*A Booke of Ayres,* 1:16) where "a little higher" meant the eyes, in good Platonic or Petrarchan fashion. Campion has moved to parody courtly love and its games, and also his own earlier involve-ment in it. A third song that he fears may breed offense is "Faine would I wed a faire yong man that day and night could please mee" (24) on female sexual desire, where the Chaucerian reference seems most apt; the singer is of the same mind as the Wife of Bath, the meter takes us back to old-fashioned fourteeners set out in couplets, and as a matter of fact there is a touch here and there of medieval Roman Catholicism: "If to love be sinne in mee, that sinne is soone absolved. / Sure, I thinke I shall at last flye to some Holy Order." Related to this strain are the songs of psychological cunning like "Vaile, love, mine eyes" (4) on a man's wilfull ignorance of his be-loved's infidelities (compare *Third Booke,* 22), ending with the gener-ality, "Hee that a true embrace will finde / To beauties faults must still be blinde." Also the rather cynical "I must complain" (17) ends by welcoming jealousy because it will excite the jaded lover.

The depiction of this sort of cunning centers in the full comple-ment of seven songs in *The Third and Fourth Bookes* that are given to female singers. Three of these women are naive maidens—the girl of "Maydes are simple" (*Third Booke,* 4) on her guard against male de-ceit, the girl in "Young and simple though I am" (*Fourth Booke,* 9) whose self-knowledge ruefully leaves a loophole ("This I know, who ere hee be / Love hee must, or flatter me"), and the tormented maiden of "Faine would I wed a faire young man." One is an experi-enced and rather jaded woman who gives younger women the advice, "Never love unlesse you can / Beare with all the faults of man" (*Third Booke,* 27). Two are experienced coquettes: the woman of "Silly boy, 'tis full Moone yet, the night as day shines clearely" (*Third Booke,* 26) is initiating her naive young lover into the perilous ways of love where "each *Troylus* hath his *Cresseid,*" in fact both warning him against her own infidelity and leaving the possibility hovering that his constancy may "beget a wonder" and make her constant too. In

"If thou longst so much to learne (sweet boy) what 'tis to love" (*Third Booke*, 16), the half-amused coquette leads her lover through the coming love affair, showing him how she will first lead him into a garden of delight but then prove unfaithful at the height of the affair, leaving him enraged but powerless to escape. These songs are much like the gallant style of John Donne in such poems as "The Baite" or "Womans Constancie." Finally, in the woman of "So quicke, so hot, so mad is thy fond sute" (*Third Booke*, 28) we come upon a prankster: what she says to her impassioned lover is that fear prevents her from keeping a tryst with him at any of the places he urges on her, but what comes out plainly at the end is that all along she has been amusing herself at his expense: "Since then I can on earth no fit roome finde, / In heaven I am resolv'd with you to meete." There was one woman's song in *A Booke of Ayres,* and three in *The Second Booke.* Not only have they doubled in volume in *The Third and Fourth Bookes of Ayres,* but their focus has shifted. The women in this last book are fully characterized—surprisingly, much more specifically characterized than the male singers—and the emphasis lies on the sense of character we get from them, the witty coquette of two minds about constancy, the jesting mistress putting off her suitor, the maid who is naive but knows it and yet sees plainly how prone she is to flattery. This is a new focus for Campion, and it takes him even further from his earlier mode of rhetoric, persuasion to love, and such, to a mode where revelation of the nature of the singer's mind rather than her or his effect on the listener is central. Definition is the center of attention, laying bare the self within.

Campion has embraced several new topics in his last volume—most of them lying quite outside the tradition of the lute song—including social and political commentary (often satiric), obscenity, depression, and the nature of female psychology. Much of his focus is now on the nature of the human mind and heart, something evanescent, hard to present directly. Many of these songs therefore reach beyond their surface statements, for what the listener is to grasp in them is not what the singer says—that is the correlative of feeling—so much as who she or he is. In the songs expressing psychotic depression this groping is especially salient, for such a state is hard if not impossible to express or analyze, and it is the very dramatizing of the art of groping for expression that comes as close as anything can to showing what it is that needs to be expressed. All of these elements are part of Campion's continuing change of emphasis from *persuasion* to *definition.*[29] The act of definition becomes the burden of some of the songs, most directly in his attempt at the philosophical love lyric "Are you what your faire lookes expresse?" (*Fourth Booke*, 15: "Thou joy'st, fond boy," *Fourth Booke*, 2, is a companion piece addressed to a young man). Behind this song lies the more weighty tradition of the *canzoni d'amore* from Cavalcanti to Spenser's *Fowre Hymnes*,[30] though Campion as is natural to him assays a lighter touch. The song is philosophically based, citing as it does terms like "Reason," "Soule," "substance," and "forme": "From law of Nature they digresse / Whose forme sutes not their minde." His focus is on appearance and reality, on working though the external image to define and evoke (if not to image) the mind—a difficult process that is indicated by taking the sensory inward:

> Love in the bosome is begot,
>   Not in the eyes;
> No beauty makes the eye more hot,
>   Her flames the spright surprise:
> Let our loving mindes then meete,
> For pure meetings are most sweet.

Campion's final songs, then, we have seen to be terse, plain, realistic, tonally complex, broad in scope, and always pressing toward definition. His spare plain style arises out of a heightened sense of the real and the necessity of confronting it directly; and this impulse involves both an attempt to define and evoke the real and an assumption of complex attitudes toward it, in the belief that only thus can human truth (instead of some standard unfeeling oversimplification) be reached. This was the task Campion set himself at the end of his career. His progress in the songs was toward a deepening complexity within a realistic vision. Within the mode of the epigrammatic, he worked to make the neat and graceful ayre, rich yet spare in its means, into the vehicle for a full and sententious exploration of reality.

It was his own mode he developed, a unique voice in English poetry. Throughout his career Campion maintained his own vision, adopting from others a technique or two rather than (like Daniel) a set of values. Within the endeavors of technique, he began as a disciple of Sidney, but soon became one of the innovators, developing alongside Ben Jonson the epigrammatic and plain styles. It was his own vision that led him from a glimpse of light to the inner torments and visceral joys of fire.

Chapter Four

Music

Madrigal and Ayre

In music, the big change came nine years after it had in poetry, with the first publication of Italian madrigals in Nicholas Yonge's *Musica Transalpina* in 1588, while Campion was at Gray's Inn and taking part in theatrical productions there. The situation as Yonge presented it was this:

since I first began to keepe house in this Citie, it hath beene no small comfort unto mee, that a great number of Gentlemen and Merchants of good accompt (as well of this realme as of forreine nations) have taken in good part such entertainment of pleasure, as my poore abilitie was able to affoord them, both by the exercise of Musicke daily used in my house, and by furnishing them with Bookes of that kinde yeerely sent me out of Italy and other places, which being for the most part Italian Songs, are for sweetness of Aire, verie well liked of all, but most in account with them that understand that language.[1]

Yonge was a musical amateur, a merchant like his guests; they loved Italian madrigals and Yonge was accustomed to import music books, as he imported mercantile goods, for their use. Eventually he was prevailed upon to collect what madrigals with texts translated into English he could, and publish them for others to use. This was a popular secular music, and it was intended for private performance, unlike the church music in the tradition moving from Thomas Tallis through William Byrd to Orlando Gibbons. This is a point it is hard to overemphasize: the pleasure to be derived from this music was one of participation rather than reception, and one should not think of hearing these pieces performed beautifully in a concert hall but of participating in them, as in a church choir singing part song, where each singer is consciously and intensely listening to himself intoning his own part while being less intensely aware of its fitting with other parts and deriving a kind of peripheral pleasure from that (the sort of thing that goes hilariously awry in Kingsley Amis's *Lucky Jim*).[2]

And it was Italian music, the latest thing. From time to time, since the death of the master of *la contenance anglois,* John Dunstable, in 1453, English music had lost touch with the Continent, and music lovers greeted with excitement what many of them conceived as the reconnection with Italy in the 1580s culminating in the publication of 1588. The Italian madrigal appeared, in contrast to the music of Byrd and his fellows, wild and inventive. Moreover, it bore evidence of a whole new musical idea. When Claudio Monteverdi published his *Scherzi musicali* in 1607, his brother Guilio Cesare saw fit to preface it with a "Declaration" in response to the attack on his brother Claudio by one Artusi, in which he assayed a bit of music history. He distinguished between the "old music" (what we now call "High Renaissance") of composers like Ockeghem, Josquin des Prez, and their followers, and the *seconda pratica* of madrigal composers like Cipriano de Rore and his brother's contemporaries Gaiches de Wert, Luca Marenzio, and Guilio Caccini, in terms of the relation between words and music: the earlier is "the one that turns on the perfection of the harmony, that is, the one that considers the harmony not commanded, but commanding, not the servant, but the mistress of the words," the later "the one that turns on the perfection of the melody, that is, the one that considers harmony not commanding, but commanded, and makes the words the mistress of the harmony" ("*l'oratione sia padrona del armonia e non serva*").[3] The new idea was that music followed the poetry.

Though Guilio Cesare Monteverdi mentions mainly composers contemporary with his brother, that idea had been the emphasis from the start. Howard Brown is quick to warn us that, though the early madrigal sounds, musically, much like the result of "the application of Franco-Flemish polyphonic technique to the native Italian frottola," it would be a mistake to leave it at that; rather, "the impulse to the madrigal seems to have come from poetic as well as musical circles," notably that of Pietro Bembo with his elevation of Petrarch.[4] We can, in fact, sketch a history of the Italian madrigal from Willaert to Monteverdi as its interests in literary expression come to supersede polyphonic and other musical considerations.

The English entered the picture when madrigal composition was at its peak, just before the genius of Monteverdi was to seize on it and make of it something new. Their idol was Luca Marenzio, the master of extravagant word-painting: it was his work they imitated, him they praised in prefaces.[5] *Musica Transalpina* contained ten of his most famous madrigals. The taste of Yonge and his friends was up-to-date but it was conservative, since few daring experiments such as chromaticism can be found in it (and they were at hand: it is notable that they passed by Marenzio's daring and popular "Doloroso martir"). The verse translations, it must be admitted, were wretched. *Musica Transalpina* did not introduce the madrigal into England but it did disseminate it, and in doing so it inaugurated what is clearly the "golden age" of English music. From 1588 to 1622 over forty volumes of original English madrigals were published, over thirty volumes of solo ayres, by masters such as William Byrd, Thomas Morley, Orlando Gibbons, Thomas Weelkes, John Wilbye, John Dowland, Thomas Campion, and John Danyel, and near masters like George Kirbye, John Ward, Giovanni Coperario, and Alfonso Ferrabosco the younger. It was of great variety and high accomplishment.

Yet the English madrigal had by no means the literary inspiration that the Italian had, and the relation of text to music was always problematic, a fact that caused revolt within the ranks by various musicians, especially virtuosi of the lute, at the turn of the century. Wilfrid Mellers describes the situation as something of a double pull, the "desire 'humanistically' to interpret a poetic text, largely through the expressive powers of dissonance," coexisting with "a supplementary desire to curb the turbulance of harmonic passion by means of dance rhythm."[6] At times this seems like a tension between confronting a text with expressive treatment and retreating from it in self-contained musical forms. And some contemporaries of the madrigalists saw it as a struggle in which the music won. After all, even the most scrupulous word-by-word treatment of a text in a thick polyphonic texture like Weelkes's can issue in a general sense of mood rather than a precise expression of a poem. That was the sense of things Thomas Campion was operating from, when he wrote, "But there are some, who to appeare the more deepe and singular in their judgement, will admit no Musicke but that which is long, intricate, bated with fuge, chaind with sincopation, and where the nature of everie word is precisely exprest in the Note. . . . Nevertheles, as in Poesie we give the preheminence to the Heroicall Poeme, so in Musicke we yeeld the chiefe place to the grave and well invented Motet, but not to every harsh and dull confused Fantasie, where in multitude of points the Harmonie is quite drowned" (*D*, 15–16). And many years later Samuel Pepys put the matter more radically: he noted that he was "more and more confirmed that singing with many voices is not singing but a sort of instrumental musique, the sense of the words being lost by not being heard, and especially when they set them with Fuges of words, one after another."[7] Campion was spearheading a revolt that has connections with the fashion for brevity and the turn of lyric toward epigram in the late 1590s, and it was to eventuate in the replacement of the madrigal by the new form of the solo ayre.

The shift indicates that it was the lutenist song-writers who were taking over and actually perfecting the new musical idea of text commanding music that Monteverdi had announced in the *secondo pratico*. It also implies that music was moving toward performance rather than participation. Edward Doughtie takes this view of it:

> In the English madrigal at least, the texts are often inconsequential as poetry because their main function was to provide syllables for singing, words simply naming a mood or action or emotion that the composer could exploit. Since the different voices were often singing different words simultaneously, the sense of the words was frequently obscured to all but the singers themselves. This is said not to condemn the madrigal but to define its appeal, which is mainly musical; like other chamber music, it was composed for performers rather than for audiences. The air, especially when performed as an accompanied solo, is more likely to be sung to an audience. It appeals to literary as well as musical interests because the music allows the words to be heard and understood, and because the words are frequently more satisfying as poetry than the madrigal verses.[8]

Another possibility is that the ayre—a solo voice singing to lute accompaniment—could be sung alone to one's self in privacy (as Wyatt had done much earlier); but whether sung alone or to an audience, the ayre is less of a social act than the madrigal in which, as often happened, all guests participated after a dinner party. The growing dominance of ayre over madrigal at the turn of the century, then, implies things about society (perhaps a preference for privacy, or a sense of personal isolation), about fashion (brevity and restraint replacing exuberance), about changes in poetry and about the growing dominance of poetry, with its increased expressiveness and dramatic quality, over music.

The vogue of the ayre spread as rapidly as had the changes in poetry in the 1590s. It was inaugurated by the maiden publication of the virtuoso lutenist John Dowland, *The First Booke of Songes or Ayres,* in 1597; the volume was enormously popular, running through five editions, in 1597, 1600, 1608, and 1613.[9] It was followed in 1598 by a collection by Michael Cavendish, and in 1600 by Dowland's own *Second Booke of Songs or Ayres,* which ran to the unusual release figure of 1,000 copies, as well as collections by Robert Jones and Thomas Morley. It was in 1601 that Campion and Rosseter published their twin volume with a cantankerous preface serving as manifesto of the new style, and the same year a second volume by Jones appeared. So it went on for the next dozen years, an average of two new collections appearing every year for a total of some twenty-eight. The year 1613 saw the appearance of Campion's *First and Second Bookes of Ayres* and the fifth edition of Dowland's *First Booke.* Then the vogue died out. Between 1613 and 1622 only two publications appeared, Campion's third and fourth sets and a new collection by John Attey. But before it died it had produced such a vast amount of fine songs, distinguished texts and compelling music—a new composer almost every year in its span of seventeen—that many of the old madrigalists like Morley and Pilkington hurried to switch over to the new style.

From their perspective as well as ours, the madrigal represented the old, its polyphonic textures developing out of the Renaissance mass, and the ayre the new, its expressive solo voice pointing toward opera. The madrigal was an unaccompanied polyphonic composition, classically for five or six voices of equal importance, in which great pains are taken to illustrate the emotional burdens of individual words or phrases. The ayre is not polyphonic, it is a song for solo voice with chordal instrumental accompaniment (usually a lute), often strophic; as the name implies, the tune or melody is the center of interest, and the melody is usually not broken up for the effects of individual words. The definition of the ayre is normative, because sometimes they were "through-composed" instead of strophic, and the accompaniment varied, even to the extent that some composers supplied parts for voices lower than the treble that carried the tune.[10] The verse fit for each was decidedly different. Madrigal verse is "suave and mellifluous" and "aims to express a general mood rather than particular and personal experience." Contrasts of mood are desirable because they suggest musical contrasts. Short antithetical phrases and striking isolated words rather than long developing units are also desirable, because of the frequent repetition of phrases in the polyphonic texture of the music, often shifting from voice to voice; for the same reason, refrains and interjections like "ay me" are appropriate.[11] The solo song dramatized its singer, and so the specific and personal are welcome as contributing to the total effect. Musical contrast is often as strong an element in the ayre as it is in the madrigal, but since the ayre strives for a total unified effect it often does not isolate phrases or striking words. Refrains and interjections are not common: it is "short and well seasoned," quick.

The norm in setting texts to music in the ayre is one note per syllable, and a song that is to last long enough to make a firm impression or sustain a mood must have many more words to it than a madrigal; usually composers used verse of several strophes, difference or contrast between them allowing a turn of emotion—and, in contrast to the madrigal's single effect, turns and changes were developed along with the dramatized role the singer took. The usual piece of madrigal verse was short, a single strophe often of six lines (of varying length) rhymed *ababcc*. To allow for musical expansion, it was "stichic" in inspiration, that is, it moved from one self-contained line with its own internal balances and structure to another. Ayres were strophic, accomplishing a single overall effect in a gathering of several lines bound together by rhyme—often a six-line strophe like that of the madrigal, with the rhyme-scheme repeated for two (in the concise ayres of Campion), three, or more strophes. Such organization exerted certain formal demands, usually in the case of "strophic equivalences" where the first line of the second strophe had to be metrically and rhetorically similar to the first (since it was to be set to the same musical phrase), and so on. Two strophes of Dowland's famous "lachrimae" (*Second Booke of Songs*, 2) provide a good example:

> Flow my teares fall from your springs,
> Exilde for euer: Let mee morne
> where nights black bird hir sad infamy sings,
> there let mee liue forlorne.
>
> Downe vaine lights shine you no more,
> No nights are dark enough for those
> that in dispaire their last fortuns deplore,
> light doth but shame disclose.[12]

The first and fifth lines, for instance, are not only parallel metrically and rhetorically, but are also analogous in idea, both expressing falling (the music to which they are both set consists of two descending phrases); and the two strophes together suggest an analogy between tears falling and light fading before darkness (of course there is a conceit here, the "vaine lights" being his eyes). The poetic and musical forms together thus create metaphor.

Strophic form, which involved much parallelism, naturally welcomed rhetorical schemes, and we frequently find anaphora, antithesis, anadiplosis, and climax. Edward Doughtie finds that the sort of wordplay and echoing such devices encourage lead to an overall form "best described as circular, or spiral or cumulative," an obvious example being Dowland's repetition of his opening line with its music at the end of "In darknesse let mee dwell."[13] Thus, many forces move the ayre to create an overall form in both verse and music that is polar to the madrigal's cultivation of momentary expressions piling up. As for general qualities of imagery and diction, an important practicing poet put it best:

The elements of the poetic vocabulary, therefore, which are best adapted for musical setting are those which require the least reflection to comprehend—its most dynamic and its most immediate. For example: interjections, which in one's mother tongue always sound onomatopoeic (fie, O, alas, adieu); imperatives; verbs of physical motion (going, coming, hasting, following, falling) or physical concomitants of emotions (laughing, weeping, frowning, sighing); adjectives denoting elementary qualities (bright, hard, green, sad); nouns denoting states of feeling (joy, love, rage, despair) or objects, the emotional associations of which are common to all, and strong (sea, night, moon, spring).[14]

Auden goes on to say that "complicated metaphors" or metaphysical conceits that take time to understand are unsuitable; and so it is, especially since the ayre is an auditory rather than visual form and cultivates the ear, rather than the eye with its images and metaphors. Yet frequently, as in the case of Dowland's "Flow my teares," the music makes its own metaphors.

Campion and Other Composers

In order to see or hear Campion's accomplishment in the solo song clearly, we should compare and contrast him—briefly—with a few of the other composers. Some of them seem little more than "reformed'" madrigalists, like Francis Pilkington (who reset Campion's "Now let her change" with a full complement of repeats and sequences, like a madrigal), Michael Cavendish, and Thomas Ford.[15] Morley in his ayres was as interested in purely musical effects modeled on dances or instrumental pieces as he had been in his madrigals. He was accustomed to begin his ayres with long preludes on the lute and to insert lengthy instrumental interludes between the vocal phrases (often making the lute interlude anticipate the next phrase in the vocal part, so that the lute leads), and to such an extent that a song like "A Painted tale" (*First Booke of Ayres,* 1) is 30 percent instrumental, according to David Greer's calculation.[16]

At the opposite end of the scale from the madrigalists are Campion's friends, the younger Ferrabosco and Coperario, the monodists of whom Pattison writes, "They were attracted by the recitative style, with its claims to follow the tones of the emotional speaking voice. They relied almost entirely on the voice and little on the accompaniment for their effects. Not only the rise and fall but also the speed of the declamation was regulated according to the sentiments of the words. Already they had some of the tricks of the Lawes brothers in the next generation of composers."[17] Coperario and Ferrabosco set up the poles for the lutenists: the old madrigal style with word-painting and purely musical considerations, and the new monodic style where the poetic text is everything, the music a mere coloring. Campion is more melodic than the latter, as well as much more concerned with text than the former.

Two composers nearer the center are Robert Jones and John Danyel. Jones presented himself as a singer rather than a lutenist,[18] and he seems to have regarded the function of song as serving the text completely.[19] He tends to set each line of verse but the last to an analogous musical phrase, the first few notes and the last few of each phrase corresponding (as Campion does frquently in *A Booke of Ayres*), and he pauses to interrupt that flow of analogues, as he is building to a climax, by frequent dialogue between the lute and the singer. He will usually effect a surprise by setting the final line of text to a totally new motif, as in "Now what is love" (*The Second Booke of Songs,* 9) and "Goe to bed sweet Muze" (*Ultimum Vale,* 3). This method is close to Campion's epigrammatic mode, but Jones is both more concerned to surprise and more leisurely in his accomplishment of it. He set five of Campion's texts. Edward Doughtie, in comparing Jones's setting of "Blame not my cheeks" with Campion's own, concludes that Jones in comparison "throws the balance of interest toward the music instead of the verse," often by creating "fantasies" on short phrases.[20] Campion, on the contrary, insists on "reining in the music when it threatens to distort the sense of the poem."[21]

If Jones did not fulfill his expressed purpose of caring more for the words than the music as well as Campion does, then John Danyel achieved his greatest successes by seeming not even to try, for he subjected the text to the music in such a way as to create a musico-poetic whole. His drive for expressiveness—making him the most chromatic of the song writers—is so great that he will repeat and rework lines emotively and will even override strophic form and set each strophe to its own music when the words or mood of a text seem to demand it, as in "Now the earth, the skies, the Aire" (*Songs for the Lute,* 20). He makes word-painting into high art, as in the setting of his brother Samuel's sonnet "Like as the lute" (4). His sense of musico-poetic form (which may owe something to the dance) leads him to bold strokes like creating extensive lute preludes and interludes for mood, or making suites of several individual songs, each with its own musical shape. "Can dolefull Notes" is one very expressive such suite that has a sophisticated version of the ABA form derived from dance, and is notable in that the words bind with the music only by becoming a commentary on it.[22]

Dowland and Campion are the two masters of the lute song. Both began as skillful melodists employing a form that, with its repetitions of the melody for each strophe, tends to foreground the tune or air. All of the texts in Dowland's *First Booke*—whether by known poets like Fulke Greville or Sir Henry Lea or by some anonymous writer (it is almost certain that Dowland did not write his own texts)[23]—are strophic. His work in the strophic ayre falls into two different manners. Ten of them are in the six-line strophe (usually pentameter) rhymed *ababcc* that seems to develop out of madrigal texts (or, behind them, the sestet of the sonnet). In setting them he usually tries to create analogy between the different melodies for the first four lines of text, and then explores a new melody of two lines for the couplet. Most of the other songs are dances, at least four of them being galliards, usually in twelve-line strophes. Here his manner approaches contrast as well as resemblance. "If my complaints" (4), which began as a lute dance and was eventually given the name "Captaine Digorie Piper his Galliard,"[24] is in the classic galliard form of three sections, the first and third corresponding in pace and line length while the middle section, in slightly shorter lines, forms a contrast.

All the songs in Campion's *A Booke of Ayres* are strophic too, and that will continue to be the case until the end of his career. Seven are in the six-line strophic form like Dowland's, but he tends, as we have seen before, to restrict the song to a pair of contrasting strophes with an epigrammatic effect. Less bound by a desire for regular musical form than Dowland, his practice in these six-line strophes varies: for

example, in "Blame not my cheeks" (14) analogous melodic motifs
bind the first two lines together, while in "My sweetest Lesbia" (1)
lines 1, 2, and 3 begin with a rhythmic motif which is dropped for
line 4 and then reestablished in line 5. He has a tendency to reflect
his opening at the close like that—"When to her lute" (6) and "Thou
art not faire" (12) each reflecting the melody of line 1 at line 5—thus
emphasizing the epigrammatic close by giving a sense that the song
is beginning again or being reconsidered. While most of Dowland's
songs that were not in this six-line form were dances, Campion's
other forms differ widely (as we shall see at more length below)—
four-line strophes bound by a rhythmic motif (2) or not (4), eight-
line stanzas, some dance tunes (7, 13), quantitative meters (21 and
part of 19). The dance is not part of Campion's musical vocabulary as
it is Dowland's (and as a matter of fact he lacks the rhythmic mastery
of the lutenist in general). He tends to use it as allusion—to make "I
care not for these Ladies" (3) a country dance, to express motion in
"See where she flies" (13)—and does not allow it to generate an overall contrastive form.

After their first volumes, Campion and Dowland part company.
And a radical departure it is, as Dowland's *Second Booke* shows. The
chromaticism he experimented with once in *The First Booke* becomes
frequent if not the rule, and he starts to experiment with the declamatory style of heightened speech in "Sorrow sorrow stay" (3) in seeking new modes of the expressive. It is in musical forms that his main
departures lie: he all but abandons the conventional fixed forms of
dance in favor of a free following of verbal rhythms wherein "each
phrase is lovingly allied to its most eloquent musical expression."[25]
He uses strophic form less frequently now, in only two thirds of the
songs, and even in those he will tend to override strophic form in his
settings. "I saw my Lady weepe" (1), for example, has no repeated
sections, and its melody is "carried through on the flow of thought
almost unhampered by the formal division of the lines."[26] It is but a
short step from this song to "Mourn, mourne, day is with darknesse
fled" (5), a single ten-line strophe which he through-composes completely (i.e., uses different music for each phrase, rather than repeating music in accord with a rhyme scheme). It is in "Shall I sue" (19)
that we first find a form of amplification whereby a single motif in
both text and music goes through several developments together, the
five repeated questions of the text each being set to variations of a
single scale-wise passage. There the text releases a musical impulse so

that the lover's reiterated pleading becomes a continually expanding piece of music, the whole being an "organic" form that involves text and music inseparably.[27] He was to pursue this idea of working and reworking a single musical motif until it reveals its final and most compelling form throughout his career; it was to cause him to mute contrasts in his dance-related songs, and finally to pursue it to its final form of theme and variation. We find that in vocal music in the variations of Job, David, and the cripple of John 5:1–6 on patience (*A Pilgrim's Solace* [1612], 14–16), in instrumental music in the *Lachrimae or Seven Teares figured in Seaven Passionate Pavans* (1605) which is variation on variation, each pavane varying its tune derived from the original "lachrimae" tune.

Dowland's musical vocabulary—as developed in his last volume, *A Pilgrim's Solace* of 1612, to include declamatory style, violin obbligato, solo and chorus—was more extensive than that of any of the other lutenist song-writers, and certainly much greater than Campion's. On the other hand his textual choices show a remarkable consistency. He was known far and wide as the composer of "Flow my teares," and he even signed himself "Jo. dolande de Lachrimae his owne hande" and referred again and again to himself as *Semper Douland semper Dolens*.[28] Sometimes his texts merge in one's memory, as "Flow not so fast ye fountaines" and "Weepe you no more sad fountaines" do, seeming like two strophes instead of two independent songs (*Third Booke*, 8 and 15). Imagery of tears, falling water, darkness, and the fall of light pervade his lyrics. Campion has much greater variety of mood and style in his texts. One reason why *A Booke of Ayres* seems so much more complex than Dowland's *First Booke* is that his texts are so various and demand so many different musical styles.[29]

As Campion's texts are so much more varied than Dowland's, so is his music. The one does not inevitably follow from the other, for it is possible to set a variety of texts one way only, as Robert Jones tended to do, or to use different texts to suggest musical ideas that have a structural principle like motivic expansion in common, as Dowland did. It is difficult to establish a clear taxonomy for *A Booke of Ayres* like the one we found in Dowland's first book. Campion's settings underline the implications of his texts precisely, economically, delicately; if there is considerable variety among the texts, several diffierent kinds of musical forms result. To name them is to go through the table of contents—the six-line strophe where the first three lines are held together by a rhythmic motif that is reiterated at the start of the couplet for unity ("My sweetest Lesbia"), the quite different isorhythmic four-line strophe proceeding line-by-line without contrast ("Though you are yoong"), the dance-tune with a trochaic "tornada" in the contrasting middle section leading into the refrain with its disjunctive dance rhythm, the whole having something of the ABA form characteristic of dances ("I care not for these Ladies"), the epigrammatic form wherein the ending takes us into surprisingly new motifs ("When to her lute").

There are three general points about Campion's songs that stand out in relief against Dowland's. First, there is less rhythmic interest—partly because the lute part so familiar to Dowland creates rhythm—and rhythm in general forms a less important part in creating musical design. This relates to the lesser interest Campion showed toward accompaniment in general. Second, Campion remains a strophic composer. Instead of Dowland's increasing tendency to override line-divisions and eventually through-compose, so that a strophe at best becomes a total undifferentiated unit, Campion conceived of the strophe as itself having an internal structure, combining units that taken together produce a whole. His musical thinking was linear (as was Robert Jones's), and pointed up the integrity of the line of text. That does not mean that his strophe lacked wholeness; on the contrary, it acquired a wholeness from the way individual lines fitted together. An example may make this clear. In "Followe thy faire sunne"[30] the first line begins with a three-note motif GDG descending and then ascending a fourth which then becomes the basis for a gentle rise and fall ending on "shaddowe." The second line is quite different, a long descending phrase from D to F-sharp, and the third line goes through a corresponding ascent back to D, chromatically. The fourth and last line is set to a skipping motion of intervals of a third and a fourth that recalls the opening of the song and then ends with a slow and delicately ornamented descending phrase on "unhappie shaddowe" where the notes over "-hap" and "shad-" echo the end of the first line. By composing the song line-by-line and at the same time creating relations of contrast and analogy between the lines, Campion makes the structure of the strophe (itself based on related movements in life) come forth in song.

Third, Campion works with contrast and balance, as we have just seen. Dowland tended to mute contrasts and even separations in his setting so as to pursue his motivic expansions. Campion, working with the line, is intent on pinpointing differences and resemblances within the line and between lines—so quickly that our attention is always being taxed. The first line of "When to her lute" is set to a slight rise and fall;[31] the second line begins with a rhythmic motif analogous to that of the beginning on "Her voice re-" but then moves into a rapid ornamentation expressing "revives" and a contrasting descent on "leaden stringes." "And doth in" is set to three notes analogous to the beginning, a fourth lower, and then rises an octave on "highest," while "echo clear" echoes "highest note" by being set to the same motif two notes higher. The first line of the couplet emphasizes the contrast within the text by beginning with an analogy, "But when she" recalling "When to her" but contrasting it by being set a fifth higher. The rest of the couplet proceeds with music that deliberately contrasts the quatrain, the rising sequence on "her sighes" countered by the fall of "the stringes do breake." But of course this contrasting couplet brings the song to rest, the suspense created by repeated inconclusive phrases reaching closure in the final G that repeats the opening notes. Form and expression come together here in contrast and balance. As we saw before in examining this and other songs, the adjustments of contrast and balance are in music what the art of the epigram is in poetry.[32]

It is no surprise that Campion had more concern for the integrity of his text than any of his fellow lutenist song-writers, even the monodists. His tendency more than the others to set one syllable to one note guarantees that every word will come forth clearly in the music. His musical vocabulary is more limited than most, whether that was due to his less rigorous musical training or to his program of brevity, simplicity, and lightness of texture. What he does pursue is economy of means, eschewing figuration in the accompaniment, repetitions of phrases, sequences, and the like. One way to see that is to notice how artful are his placing of rests, pauses that affect the movement of the text.[33] The drive for economy, according to David Greer, "led him to use straightforward repetition as the basis of his musical designs,"[34] creating rhythmic repetitions and repeating short motifs sequentially to give shape to a line, repeating individual lines within a strophe to produce forms like AAB, ABB, AABB, and AABCC.[35] While composers like Dowland and Danyel—and Morley in his different way—pursued a large unified melodic design in their compositions, Campion worked within a tight linear framework of contrasts and balances. His music is no less epigrammatic than his poetry.

A Booke of Ayres

Campion began his career as a melodist. So did Dowland. Campion's melodies seldom achieved the sweep of a Dowland song, and he did not seem to strive to create tunes that remain in the ear long after the words are forgotten; surely he did not want us to forget the words at all. But he did achieve most of his effects by melodic means, his accompaniments remaining simple, his rhythms basic. Another way of putting it is that he *used* melodies to create structures rather than trying to *create* melodies.

Most of the songs we have examined here and in chapter 2 are from *A Booke of Ayres*. They are among Campion's most tuneful, and the most often sung in performance. Looking—or listening—back over them, we can see that most of them achieved the musical effects we noticed by manipulating melodic motifs. When he uses word-painting he tends not to interrupt flow by local effects but to spread this device over the entire song so that its melodic curve becomes word-painting, as in "Followe thy faire sunne." When the music underlines the text's structure, it does so by repeated melodic motifs that carry us through an entire song, as in "My sweetest Lesbia" or "Follow your Saint." And the epigrammatic effects so often encountered are achieved by arousing, delaying, or even baffling, and then suddenly at the end fulfilling harmonic expectations that round out the melody, as in "When to her lute" and "Blame not my cheeks."

His typical method of musical structuring, as characterized by Gustave Reese, is this: "The melodies of most of the lighter ayres are based upon one or more phrase patterns. Usually only the rhythm of the pattern recurs, each time underlying a different pitch-series; occasionally, with the rhythm or instead of it, another element of the pattern, such as its general melodic contour, is retained. Often, such patterns are made up, in turn, of short recurrent motifs."[36] Reese's example is "Faire, if you expect admiring" (1.11), where a short rhythmic motif tending to monotone is repeated at various pitches at the beginnings of lines 1, 2, 4, 5, and 7, and a slightly descending melodic motif of five notes is repeated in the second half of all eight lines. This idiom of repeated motifs is what we heard earlier giving each line its integrity, and in so doing enforcing contrast and resemblance, too. In effect, it is rather like the keyboard variation form developed by Campion's contemporary John Bull, of whom Paula Johnson writes, "for Bull the segment is a separate and self-contained entity to be compared to adjacent segments, not the flexible rhythmic pulse that it was for Byrd."[37]

We entertained the speculation in our first chapter that Campion may have refined his musical techniques under the influence of his early associates and neighbors John Dowland and Philip Rosseter, and it is notable that both these composers—and Robert Jones, who took many of his texts from Campion, too—used this form of melodic repetition; good examples are Rosseter's "When Laura smiles" (*A Booke of Ayres,* 2.9) and Dowland's "Sleep, wayward thoughts" (*First Booke,* 14). But even in his first publication Campion has made such a form bear his own stamp. His concern for economy of means has caused him to opt for a much simpler accompaniment than Dowland's, and to reject long expressive held notes and repeated sequences that interrupt flow to the point at the end. This economy appears dramatically if we compare Rosseter's "When Laura smiles" to "When to her lute" which it resembles: Rosseter takes four strophes to reverse the tone from joy to sadness in contrast to Campion's one, and then of course Campion went on to make his first strophe a metaphor in the second. Also, Campion avoids the melismas and other ornamental writing Rosseter employed, preferring one note per syllable, by and large. In other words, Campion reduced musical interest in order to present his text clearly.

It was in *A Booke of Ayres* that he established the traits we have been claiming for him: concern for integrity of the text, economy of means, working with strophic form to create both linear integrity and contrast and balance between lines, in order to form a unified but varied whole. As David Greer writes, "Repetition on the largest and smallest scale—strophic, sectional, rhythmic, and sequential—was the principal means by which Campion achieved the simplicity he admired."[38]

Three cases require specific comment. "The man of life upright" (1.18) comprises six short run-on strophes, the first three forming one complete sentence, the last two another. The way Campion set this text is interesting: he established a short symmetrical melody in which the music of the second and third lines is analogous while the repeated melody of lines 1 and 4 frames them. This strict symmetry makes the melody operate like a short self-contained motif, and he repeated it as a kind of structural unit strophe-by-strophe in order to make a whole out of these parts. "Come let us sound" (1.21) is unique in its mode of repetition. It is the song in classical meters

Campion mentioned in his preface, "onely one song in Sapphicke verse" (*D*, 15). The music with a regular system of quarter-notes and half-notes outlines the quantitative meter thus (the long stress standing for half-notes, the short for quarter-notes): "Come, let us sound with melody the praises," a metrical shape repeated three times with the Adonic fourth line completing the strophe. The effect is like the isorhythmic "Though you are yoong," and here the identical repetition of the rhythmic motif allows the melody to range by itself, as in a through-composed song. Finally, with the concept of repeated melodic motifs in mind, we might look at the third line of "My sweetest Lesbia'" "Let us not way them: heav'ns great lampes doe dive." The syntax breaks in the middle of the line; demands for expression would require at least a rest between "them" and "heav'ns," especially since there is a sudden skip of an octave between them which allows for the establishment of a high D to become the basis for a descent in imitation of diving. But as we saw earlier, Campion was at pains to establish analogy between lines in this song, especially lines 1, 2, 3, and 5, in order to stress the internal coherence of the strophe.[39] And so he—for once—overrides his attention to the text in order to create a continuous melody for line 3—beginning as lines 1 and 2 did, and with an ending resembling theirs but naturally pitched lower on "dive"—in order to keep the total shape of contrast and balance moving.

Two Bookes of Ayres

The celebrated "Author of light," which has first place in the volume Campion designated as his first solo publication, shows how far he had come in the dozen years between 1601 and 1613. Wilfrid Mellers has analyzed the wealth of expressive effects of this song. As he pleasantly puts it, "the opening apostrophe to the divinity is set to the noble interval of a falling fifth—the most stable of all interval relationships after the octave—accompanied by a rising bass line to suggest the flooding of life and its revivifying effect."[40] Every phrase takes us into a new emotional effect—the syncopation of "My dying spright" over the bar-line to express the catch in the breath, the rising diatonic phrase for "Redeem it from the snares of," the hopeful rise of "Lord light me to thy blessed way," the cross-rhythms of "wander astray," the chromatic rise from uncertain "mists and darkness" to light accompanied by a descending bass line in the lute in contrary motion (indicating comparison and separating out). He concludes, "This, then, is a devotional song which preserves contact with the old liturgical tradition; yet it gives a much more comprehensive treatment of the technique of musical illustration that had been explored in the work of the fifteenth-century masters such as Ockeghem. Musical allegory becomes emotional realism."[41]

The song is almost through-composed in its pursuit of effect. One might say that the bones of the strophic idiom are visible—or audible—chiefly in the way in which the corresponding motifs to which "dying spright" and "confounding night" are set tie the first two lines of text together. By doing this, they allow the rest of the song to flow as a highly emotive expression of the particular case of the singer whose general case the first couplet established. Campion has become quite willing to break even melodic flow in order to express not only syntax but emotion. There is only one motivic recurrence in the rest of the song, where "Sun and Moone" recall the opening address to the author of light in a falling fifth that introduces the final couplet. This is a touch of beautiful fusion, both illustrative and structural,[42] since it reflects the nature of the author of light in introducing the lights that magnify him by comparison and bring the song to a close.

Campion reprinted "The man of life upright" in this volume (*First Booke,* 2) with few textual changes but with an entirely different musical setting. Gone is the symmetrical structure of 1601 that made a brace of melodies into a motif. Now in 1613 we have an open expressive structure, after the first line a slow ascent up the scale in paired notes moving from F on "cheerful" to G on "weight of" to A on "impious," ending on ornaments around D and E over "yoke of vanity." A slow harmonic sequence expressive of the life invoked, with minimal closure, replaces symmetry. There is an occasional through-composed song in this volume. "Her rosie cheekes" (*Second Booke,* 20) is after the manner of Dowland, since the overarching melodic curve takes its origin from a single motif. The rising scale with a falling note at the end of it over "Her rosie cheeks" is repeated and expanded for "her ever smiling eyes," and is then inverted over "Her rubine lips"; the original motif and its inversion then recur freely through the song while it develops other materials, such as the monotone over the phrase that introduces climax, "O that of other Creatures store."[43] The moving lament on Prince Henry, "All lookes be pale" (*First Booke,* 21) is likewise through-composed, and employs such effects as sudden falls of a diminished sixth or fifth, short declamatory sections, and a very effective chromatic sequence on the repeated refrain "weepe with mee."

In the chapter that rhymes with this one, we saw how Campion had expanded his poetic vocabulary in this volume, and we can now hear how his musical vocabulary has expanded, too. One element in that expansion is what we heard in "Author of light," a contact with liturgical tradition. That becomes especially active in three songs of *The First Booke* whose texts form variants of psalms: "Out of my soules deapth" (4) from Psalm 130, *De Profundis,* "As by the streames of *Babilon*" (16), a version of Psalm 137, *Super Flumina,* and "Sing a song of joy" (15) derived from Psalm 104, *Benedic, Anima Mea.* The music of these songs recalls the old version psalm tunes of their respective psalms, as set for voices and instruments in that volume Campion studied so carefully, Richard Alison's *The Psalms of David in Metre* (1559).[44] Campion is expanding his vocabulary by experimenting with musical allusion as composers did in the old "cantus firmus" masses. He is developing a talent for assimilation, and other voices than his own begin to enter his compositions. This element becomes important for him in secular as well as sacred music. One example is "The peacefull westerne winde" (*Second Booke,* 12) which incorporates the well-known traditional melody that John Taverner, Christopher Tye, and John Shepherd had taken as "cantus firmus" of their masses early in the sixteenth century. Sensing that tune in the first eight notes of the voice part, the listener hears along with Campion's song the mordant old words that give a new dimension to the text:

> Westron wynde when wyll thow blow
> the small rayne down can rayne
> Cryst if my love wer in my armys
> And I yn my bed agayne.

Similarly, when the London street-seller's cry, "Cherry-ripe, cherry-ripe," bursts into the musical refrain of "There is a Garden in her face" (*Fourth Booke,* 7), it breaks the solemn tone of the highly metaphorical song and totally revalues its previous portion. In one case he even indulges in "sacred parody": for "Seeke the Lord, and in his wayes perserver" (*First Booke,* 18) he used the music of "Followe thy faire sunne," by this musical allusion "reforming" or "baptizing" the doggedness of the earthly lover in order to apply it to a pursuit worthy his efforts.

Campion has developed beyond the melodist of *A Booke of Ayres,* and what he does with melody now is interesting: essentially, he breaks it loose from the text and the expression of each word so that it now has an independent existence, and it thus becomes an additional comment on the text. "Tune thy Musicke to thy hart" (*First Booke,* 8) exhibits the opposite sort of setting to "Author of light": instead of expressing each word, it is concerned with outlining a progression of repeated notes from C to G and back again. As we heard in chapter 2, the music works by establishing a desire in the listener for harmonic symmetry, for the return to C, by denying it and presenting a held B over "sorrow" instead, by starting over on G with "Devotion needes not Art" and finally—by the way of the rich borrowing from the poor which is a religious paradox (recalling a parable like that of the laborers in the vineyard of Matthew 20:1–16)—reaching the C. It is about tuning the self—tuning words to the tetrachord—and it reflects that subject by its melodic structure, independent of the verbal structure but inspired by it. So does "Come, chearfull day" (*First Booke,* 17), which we also inspected in chapter 2, where the text's complex series of reversals, expressing the complexity of life viewed from the religious perspective, generates an overall melodic structure of reversal piled on reversal to the point where the inverted motif becomes reinverted and in so doing takes the form of its original once more.

In "To musicke bent" (*First Booke,* 7) we find melodic form creating a comment by analogy on the mind of the singer rather than the nature of reality religiously considered. Here Campion puts his old strophic form under revision, for he makes a deliberate point of the fact that his desire to sing some "song of pleasure" in his first two lines of text is countered by the fact that "in vaine joys no comfort now I finde" in the third and fourth—and that both are set in jarring fashion to the same music. In other words, the strophic form is deliberately at variance with its text, and that is the point. As Joan Hart writes, "the poet discovers, in composing, that he is not after all in the mood for singing 'a song of pleasure,'"[45] and certain disquieting facts of the music—the uncommon progression from B to B-flat in the fifth bar of the lute part that the voice takes up on the next beat is one—indicate the lack of ease.[46] Hart goes on, "In the next line, 'Thy power O God, thy Mercies to record' with its hymn-like setting, both words and music ascend further heaven-wards. The setting of the final line of the stanza, 'Will sweeten ev'ry note, and ev'ry word,' is a kind of intensified reflection of the first line: formally satisfying and fused with the words, a crystallisation of what has preceded it."[47] Like "Tune thy musicke" and "Come, chearfull day," the music of this song exhibits a religious aesthetic, asserting that human desire comes to rest only in the hymn-tune dedicated to God.

The "light conceits of lovers" that fill *The Second Booke* exhibit some of *The First Booke's* experiments—in the musical allusion of "The peacefull westerne wind" (12), for example, or the through-composed ayres based on a germ motif that unfolds in "Her rosie cheekes" (20) or "There is none, O none but you" (13). But many of them, too, simply continue the mode of *A Booke of Ayres*. The contrast interested Campion here, and in keeping with the aesthetic of the religious songs we have examined, it is the sacred style that supplies the changes incorporated in the secular.

We have made much of the variety of texts and musical forms in *A Booke of Ayres*, and of the celebration of contrast in *Two Bookes of Ayres*. In the previous chapter we saw how variety, a response to a universe supposedly divinely ordered, yields to contrast, a principle of intelligibility based on the mind's ways of knowing. We saw poets working away from the former to the latter at the turn of the century, and we can see it in the other arts, too. Not only do we find this change in comparing a painter like Breughel to one like Claude Lorraine, but we can see it occurring within the careers of Flemish landscape painters like Gillis von Coninxloo (1544–1607) or Paul Brill (1559–1626) where crowded canvases give way to those conceived as closer up and presented in large contrasts of light and dark, near and far.[48] Almost any polyphonic mass with its voices weaving in and out celebrates variety (Johannes Ockeghem made that deliberate, for example), as does the madrigal; it is in baroque music where a single instrument is set against an orchestra in a concerto, or where movements of fast and slow are set together to form a suite, that we find contrast.

In the English music we have been studying, we can see the transition at close hand. The madrigal with its rich polyphonic texture had been dedicated to variety; the concept crops up again and again in Morley's writing, as when he writes, "for as you scholars say that love is full of hopes and fears so is the Madrigal, or lovers' music, full of diversity of passions and airs."[49] The lute song is a movement toward contrast, between treble and bass without intervening parts, between the melodic flow of voice and the rhythmic and chordal nature of the lute. Within the lute song we can see contrast opening out: when instead of a long flowing melody in the voice and a lute part that interacts polyphonically with the voice in Dowland, we have separate segments of melody that are to be compared and contrasted and a chordal lute part in "strong polarity" with the voice in Campion, for instance.[50] The composers of ayres that pushed music toward full-scale dramatic contrasts are Alfonso Ferrabosco the younger, Giovanni Coperario, and Nicholas Lanier.

These men are known as the English "monodists." They tried to domesticate the Italian monody developed by Caccini, Bardi, and others with its extreme fidelity to the text, its traits including "many repeated notes and narrow conjunct melodies that replace flowing melodic lines, . . . the clear cadences at the ends of lines of verse, breaking the whole into small units markedly different from the continuous web of polyphony, . . . and most important, the strict polarity of the melodic, rhythmically active treble over a rather stable and slow-moving bass line,"[51] a bass line that was to be taken from the lute with its tendency for interplay with the voice and located instead in the figured bass of harpsichord and viola da gamba unrelated to the voice. Ferrabosco's attempts were tentative, Coperario's more bold—as in his settings of *Songs of Mourning* where he seems intent to overgo Monteverdi.[52] Lanier settles into the monodic style with his setting of Campion's song "Bring away this sacred tree" from *The Lords' Masque* (1613), and he develops it to the full in his extensive dramatic monody "Hero and Leander" (ca. 1630).[53] These monodists are leading toward the music of Henry Lawes (whose "Adriadne" owes debts to Lanier's "Hero and Leander" as well as Monteverdi's *Arianna*)[54] and his generation, and beyond him to Henry Purcell. These are, in fact, the early stirrings of what we now call "the baroque" with its cultivation of the word and the dramatic, and "a harmonic polarity between bass and soprano, between harmonic support and a new type of melody dependent on such support," which gives the voice full declamation, the possibility of incorporating instrumental idioms, and so on.[55]

The Third and Fourth Bookes of Ayres

"You may finde here some three or four Songs that have been published before" (*D*, 168): in *The Third and Fourth Bookes of Ayres* Campion is taking account of other composers who set his texts. Jones had set four, Corkine one, Ferrabosco one, and Dowland one. Lanier had worked on his texts for masques and set three other poems.[56] The collaboration with Coperario was extensive: the theoretical treatises both wrote have much in common; Coperario worked on Campion's masques; and of course *Songs of Mourning* (1613) had been "Worded by Tho. Campion. And set forth to bee sung . . . By John Coprario." (*D*, 113). David Greer advances the suggestion that Campion's elegy on Prince Henry (*First Booke*, 21) had been modeled on Coperario's *Songs of Mourning* in its nervous monodic style.[57] If the melodists Dowland, Jones, and Rosseter are perhaps his early co-workers, then the monodists Coperario and Lanier are surely his later influences. In the 1613 volume we started to hear other voices beneath his own, in allusion; by 1617 we hear the pressure of other composers' voices.

So it was that the next stage—the ultimate one—was the expansion of his musical vocabulary by incorporating the new monodic techniques. The elegy on Prince Henry does in fact seem modeled on Coperario. In the latter's "How like a golden dreame" (*Songs of Mourning*, 5) he boldly begins with an octave sweep D to D that then settles on G and highlights the phrase by following it with a monotone motif on repeated A. Campion in setting his own music for his elegy creates likewise a sudden descent from high F to A on "Hally now is dead and gone" and follows by a repeated low F which becomes the basis of a slow rising motif on "Most sweet sight, All the earth late took delight." But whereas Coperario followed by more octave skipping, Campion proceeds to build a chromatic sequence on repeated "weepe with mee" in the second half of his song, and so the music acquires a melodic direction it lacks in Coperario.[58] This is partial imitation: it is in *The Third Booke* that we find him assimilating the style he was imitating in *The First*.

Typically it is the first song in the book that establishes the new: "Oft have I sigh'd" (*Third Booke*, 1) is through-composed, allowing the strophic structure to appear only in the analogous endings of lines 1, 2, and 4. Its style is declamatory rather than melodic and bears all the marks of monody: opening with four chords in the lute that prefigure the first vocal phrase, the voice entering on an off-beat, and declaiming short disjunct phrases interspersed with rests so as to break melodic movement and stress expressiveness. There is a movement toward melody in "Who absent hath both love and me forgot," but it is interrupted by more exclamations punctuated by rests in the repeated "O yet I languish still"—an example of the monodic theorist Guilio Caccini's *esclamazione più viva*[59]—that performs a slow chro-

matic descent from D to A and G, "languish" with its repeated notes
defining the descent D-C-G while the ligatures between phrases are
formed by the unusual chromatic movement of C-sharp to C-natural
and then B-natural to B-flat on the repeated "still, yet." "O sweet
delight" (*Third Booke,* 21) is more abrupt: little more than a series of
exclamations, its phrases are more disjunctive, its skips more frequent
and greater, and this style, characterized by David Greer as "repeated
notes, up-beat patterns following a strummed chord, halting rhythms
and rather angular contours,"[60] carries through to the end.

"O griefe, O spight" (*Third Booke,* 8) is more disjunctive still, its
text a compact set of outcries ranging over the conditions of virtue,
truth, art, vice, justice, power, and pity in the world! Not only are
the phrases short and interrupted constantly by rests, but there seems
behind them a desire to have no phrase resemble another. For example, "O griefe" is a syncopated monotone on G, "O spight" leaps to
C; then, after a double rest, we have a sudden descent of a diminished
sixth D to F-sharp, a slight melodic motif on "Truth far exil'd"
("exil'd" expressed by ornament) that emphasizes the brokenness of
the other phrases by contrast; then a rapid running-together of "False
arte lov'd, Vice ador'd" (with the increase from "love" to adoration
stressed) in a fall down the scale from E-flat to G. The last two
lines—which in the text draw a conclusion from outcry—establish a
short melody, beginning like the monodic treatment of "O grief"
over its echo "O who" but strengthening a melodic curve by analogous music between line 6 and line 5.

"O griefe, O spight" is interesting in that, at one and the same
time, it exaggerates the declamatory disjunctions of the monodic
style, and pulls it, at the end, into contact with the melodic style.
And when we speak of "assimilation" rather than simple imitation of
the monodists, this is the mode we find Campion developing. "Kinde
are her answeres" (7) is an excellent example of this characteristic
turn. The text itself concerns disjunction, "breaking time" or failing
to follow through, the major metaphor being the interrupted dance.
It begins with a syncopation, a sudden fall from C to F on "Kinde
are her answeres" that is followed, after a rest, by a contrasting monotone phrase centering on G. In a rather unusual procedure, these two
disjuctive motifs are repeated exactly for the next two lines; then line
5 begins with an echo of line 1 on "All her free favors" but here it
becomes the basis of a longer melodic phrase; and this is followed,
after a rest emphasizing a dramatic skip from G to C, by a two-phrase

melody that brings the song to a close. The general effect is of baffled cry followed by an intermediate resolution. The clustering of monodic devices in the first half of the text and following it by a melodic conclusion in the second half is characteristic of Campion's late mode.

"Breake now my heart and dye" (*Third Booke,* 10) is an interior dialogue with a structure of that sort. It begins with the despairing part of the mind in a sudden descent from G to low C on "Breake now my heart and dye"; this is countered by the hopeful part's uncertain expression in disjunctive phrases of "Oh no, oh no, she may relent," and the conflict is repeated with the same motifs in the second line. This is very effective, but Lowbury, Salter, and Young perhaps exaggerate when they find it "in style and pathos . . . comparable with Monteverdi recitative."[61] But then the whole mind—the judgment that comes between hope and despair—moves in with a melodic conclusion in three phrases (two identical and one analogous) that puts the case in a broad and somewhat humorous objective context.

This combination becomes the foundation of some of the most supple settings of the late songs. "Fire, fire" (*Third Booke,* 20), for example, runs a breathtaking emotional gamut from distress to humor to pathos. The song begins with monodic disjunctive treatment of the cry "Fire, fire" with its syncopations, long rests, and skips, and this slides into melody when the case becomes clarified in lines 3 to 5. But with the wild exaggeration of lines 6 and 7, the music suddenly changes to a dance-rhythm of regular thumping iambics perhaps imitative of the dancing of the waves and expressing invitation. When this moment yields to pathos in the last lines the music moves into a slow melodic descent.

The growth of Campion's expressive vocabulary by assimilating monodic techniques can be seen clearly if we compare two very tonally adroit songs, songs which take a complex tone toward the subject. We have looked at the texts before—"Where are all thy beauties now" (*First Booke,* 3) and "Were my hart as some mens are" (*Third Booke,* 3). The earlier song works by breaking the melodic nature it inherits from the early work of 1601, the first two of its three lines establishing a repeated melody, the third line introducing a leap to high F that falls rapidly to low F-sharp (a diminished octave) on "All fled; and thou alone," and then returns to the melody at the end. "Were my hart" is more like heightened speech: after a skip of a fourth from "Were my" to "hart" it stays in a monotone range around D for the rest of the line, then moves in the second line to similar work, in the third line departing only on the skip to "thing devine." It is intoned rather than melodic, calls little attention to musical changes, and allows the tone of voice within the words to come forth more clearly (as the only objects of our attention) than does the song composed four or five years previously.

The stress on character in the female songs we noticed in the previous chapter is relevant here as a spin-off of the monodic style, for the monodic impulse is a dramatic impulse, monodies like "Hero and Leander" and "Ariadne" asking the singer or reciter to don a persona as if in a play.[62] And the musical handling of the female songs is deliberately diverse therefore. "So quicke, so hot, so mad" (*Third Booke,* 28) sounds like an interrupted dance-tune,[63] and it is heavily ornamented with a repeated and very striking rhythm of a dotted quarter-note, two sixteenth-notes, and a quarter-note that produces an effect a little like a giggle interrupting each phrase of the teasing lady's reply. On the other hand, "Faine would I wed" (*Fourth Booke,* 24) ends the two-part volume with a striking experiment. The driving desire in the young woman's voice is expressed by creating different melodic motifs for each of its couplets, so that we get six different strains with general relationships of contrast and resemblance. But the same accompaniment, a striking eight-chord motif in the bass, is repeated twelve times through the whole piece while the melodies change, so that the song appears in the instrumental form of "divisions over a ground" or free variation in a treble part (by "dividing" long notes into short notes) of an ostinato bass line that supports it. That ground David Greer has identified as a dance, the *passamezzo antico*.[64] The song thus expresses desire by varied words and melodies over and over in the repeated division form, a kind of dancing "the olde daunce" which the text suggests. Also, in its clear separation and even polarization of bass line and vocal line, as well as its bold juxtaposition of instrumental form with vocal form, it approaches the early baroque.

In his poetry Campion was one of the pioneers: working out of a programmatic classicism like Jonson, he produced his own version of the lyric in the plain style, serious, supple in tone, spare in its means. In music he was influenced more by others than influential himself. His bent lay in assimilation: he produced his own kind of song and expanded his technique by incorporating the innovations of others. The same is true of Dowland, whose development parallels Campion's: in his small way like J. S. Bach, Dowland's genius was strongly individualistic and worked by assimilation and transformation of new ideas into his own established idiom. What we see in Campion's final volume is mastery. Along with the innovative songs there are several in his older mode, but they have a new economy and lightness of touch, as if the experimentation managed to work its way into that older mode and give it new life. Such a song is "So sweet is thy discourse" (*Fourth Booke*, 6) where melodic and monodic idioms blend completely. It would be hard to match anywhere the sheer simplicity and beauty of this piece, as readers may verify by listening to it as recorded by Glenda Simpson, her high and light expressive soprano voice poised against a spare and light lyra viol accompaniment.[65]

Chapter Five

Theory

Campion's songs are strikingly original: everything he borrowed he made his own, as did Dowland. But where he accomplished work in music which we might call innovative rather than original—where he brought something totally new into the picture—was in conceptualization. It was he who formed an apology and a program for the whole school of lutenist song-writers. These things he announced in his prefaces, and he pursued related matters like prosody in poetry and harmony in music in rather extensive prose treatises. In short, he was an intellectual—poet, musician, physician—and he had considerable talent as a theorist.

His theoretical interests put him into contact with the rich activity on the Continent in the field of poetry and its relation to music. There are two centers of development we should know something about. First is the Académie de poésie et de Musique founded in Paris under the influence of the Pléiade in 1570. Inspired in part by the ideas of Pierre de Ronsard, it sought to revive the lyricism of Greco-Roman music by setting *vers mesurés à l'antique* or French verse composed in the quantitative meters of Latin to music. Quantitative texts by Jean-Antoine de Baïf, Thibault de Courville, and others were put to rather severe homophonic settings with narrow melodic lines and unmetered rhythmic flow by such composers as Jacques Mauduit and Claude le Jeune.[1] The French tried to accomplish the remarriage of poetry and music by making poetry conform to the mensural nature of music. Theirs was a very learned and compelling theoretical position; it attracted Philip Sidney in England, among others, as a theory, but it did not produce great music.

The Italians went at the problem from the other end, as it were: instead of trying to create a poetry that would fit the nature of music, they tried to create a kind of music that would serve the poetry thoroughly. This was the Italian monody we inspected previously, its poetry free of restraints, its music designed to highlight the poetry by declamatory means, breaking with melody, imitating impassioned speech, using accompaniment as foundation only. This music was the result of the theoretical discussions of the Florentine Camerata, which flourished in the 1580s and after, and included thinkers like Count Giovanni Bardi and musicians like Vincenzo Galilei, father of the astronomer, Guilio Caccini, and Jacopo Peri. Like the French, their goal was to retrieve the union of poetry and music of Greco-Roman times, and especially to revive the ability of music to affect the various passions—the sort of thing John Dryden celebrated in "Alexander's Feast"—but unlike the French they emphasized the sentiments of poetry rather than its rhythms, because through them they thought to affect the life of the listener. Elise Jorgens writes of this movement, "Italian monodists . . . had two main goals: intelligibility of the text, and the rhetorical function of portrayal of the emotions in the text. These two goals were related in practice, for intelligibility was accomplished through a declamation that heightened the emotions, not through strictly musical means but dramatically, in such a way that the singer assumes the character of the poet's persona. Given these two goals, monody was the logical medium. The homophony of musique mesurée although it did provide intelligibility, was not so amenable to a dramatic portrayal of emotions."[2] Their work was enduring and various. They produced treatises, like Galilei's attack on counterpoint in *Dialogo . . . della musica antica e dell moderna* (1581) and collections of monodies with extensive explanatory prefaces like Caccini's *Nuove musiche* (1601), and of course they were moving toward opera. Around the turn of the century Peri and Caccini produced *Dafne* and *Euridice* with recitative and *basso continuo* or thorough-bass accompaniment (i.e., a continuous bass-line independent of the vocal part), and it was this that was taken up by the genius of Monteverdi.

Aesthetics of the Ayre

Campion, as Bruce Pattison reports, "was the only English composer who had something like a complete theory of the air."[3] In his expressions of that theory we can see traces here and there of both the French Académie and the Italian Camerata, the former in the theoretical position, the latter in practical musical considerations. The origin of the ayre he traces to antiquity, in the preface to *A Booke of Ayres,* but he sees it as the French saw it—poetic rhythm and musical rhythm coming together—rather than as the Italians did in the raising of the affections: "The Lyricke Poets among the Greekes and Latines were first inventers of Ayres, tying themselves strictly to the number and value of their sillables, of which sort, you shall find here onely one song in Saphicke verse; the rest are after the fascion of the time, eare-pleasing rimes without Arte" (*D*, 15). But when he inveighs against the madrigal and polyphony's obscuring of the text with its thick texture of music "long, intricate, bated with fuge, chaind with sincopation, and where the nature of everie word is precisely exprest in the Note," its preludes, rests, and word-painting, he seems to be echoing Vincenzo Galilei's *Dialogo* with its ridicule of devices Morley was to recommend with such enthusiasm, like rapid passages expressing "to flee" or descending passages expressing "He descended into hell," or expressing "This one aspires to the stars" by an ascent "to a height that no one shrieking for excessive pain, internal or external, has ever reached."[4]

When Campion goes on to recommend instead maintaining "in Notes, as in action, a manly cariage, gracing no word, but that which is eminent and emphaticall," there may be a slight echo of Galilei's concept of setting a text as the assumption of a dramatic persona: "When the ancient musician sang any poem whatsoever, he first considered very diligently the character of the person speaking . . . and these conceptions, previously clothed by the poet in chosen words suited to such a need, the musician then expressed in the tone and with the accents and gestures, the quantity and quality of sound, and the rhythm appropriate to that action and to such a person."[5] That Campion was aware that to sing a song is to take a part shows in his link of singing to comportment in life—"action," "a manly cariage"—and this dramatic basis was to grow stronger in his mind from book to book, the last being the most consciously histrionic.

Campion's originality in this preface lies in his location of the ayre within a general aesthetic rather than music theory, an aesthetic that had its roots in social fashion, dress, prose style, lyric style, and other elements of life in England during the late 1590s. "What Epigrams are in Poetrie, the same are Ayres in musicke, then in their chiefe perfection when they are short and well seasoned" (*D*, 15). We have explored the implications of this statement: it includes brevity, lack of ornamentation, stress on invention, compression, complexity, the great in the small. This concept governs the preface. It is what forbids polyphony and extended word-painting, since "a naked Ayre without guide or prop, or colour but his owne . . . requires so much the more invention to make it please." It relates the ayre to Greco-

Roman lyric, and it places it within a generic hierarchy, the ayre being a short and pleasing piece that does not aspire to "the grave and well invented Motet" just as the epigram sat below the epic or "Heroicall Poeme" (D, 15–16). It is important that Campion characterized his music by reference to poetry, for in doing so he created a musico-poetic aesthetic by means of joining musical practice to poetic theory. Neither the French Académie nor the Florentine Camerata had done that.

Though he wrote a treatise on music and another on prosody, his main interest when all was said and done lay not in these "sister arts" themselves so much as in their combination. In the preface to *Two Bookes of Ayres* he reiterates the musico-poetic comparison: "Short Ayres, if they be skillfully framed, and naturally exprest, are like quicke and good Epigrammes in Poesie, many of them shewing as much artifice, and breeding as great difficultie, as a larger Poeme" (D, 55). The art of the musical epigram lies in the combination, as he proceeds to outline it: "In these English Ayres, I have chiefely aymed to couple my Words and Notes lovingly together, which will be much for him to do that hath not power over both." The specific concern he goes on to mention and then drop is what poetry and music have in common, sound (which had so concerned him in the *Observations*): "The light of this will best appeare to him who hath pays'd our Monasyllables and Syllables combined, both which are so loaded with Consonants, as that they will hardly keepe company with swift Notes, or give the Vowell convenient liberty" (D, 55–56). This statement is the result of many years of weighing syllables and reckoning the effects of vowels and consonants, as we shall see in examining the *Observations*. His point is well taken: who can imagine setting to music (or even articulating) a line clogged with consonants like Matthew Arnold's "Who prop, thou ask'st, in these bad days, my mind?"[6]

His vision of the ayre is a sound, something founded on the syllables of words that give sound articulation and human meaning but going beyond them into pure feeling.[7] "So sweet is thy discourse to me" is an excellent example. In the prefatory note to *The Fourth Booke* he writes, "The Apothecaries have Bookes of Gold, whose leaves being opened are so light as that they are subject to be shaken with the least breath, yet, rightly handled, they serve both for ornament and use: such are light *Ayres*" (D, 168). It is a metaphor for his book: open its leaves, shake them with your breath, bring forth the meaning and pleasure in them. "Awake, thou spring of speaking grace"

(*Second Booke*, 13): to sing is to activate body and soul. By a pun he locates sound in climate: "But some there are who admit onely *French* or *Italian* Ayres, as if every Country had not his proper Ayre, which the people thereof naturally usurpe in their Musicke" (*D, 55*). The ayre originates in the air, the actual air so light we cannot see it but can feel it and hear it, the air that moves the leaves and comes through the window to touch our arms as we write, that enters our lungs and—when we express a thought such as this—gathers and issues out again in human sound.

Such is the musico-poetic aesthetic he sketches so briefly and suggestively in his prefaces. His two prose treatises—which we will now examine—did not directly contribute to this aesthetic, let alone produce it. Rather, they lie behind it. When he writes about weighing syllables we can hear the work on prosody behind it; when he inveighs against polyphony we can hear the treatise on harmony coming. They are both about sound, about the linear sound of poetry and the harmonic sound of music. The treatise on prosody is a result of Campion's meditations on concerns raised by Baïf and the French Académie. The treatise on contrapuntal harmony outlines a theory that gives voice to some assumptions contained in the practice of the Italian monodists and their English heirs.

Treatises on Composition

A New Way of Making Fowre Parts in Counter-point is really a collection of four little technical treatises on the scale, counterpoint, tonality, and the concords. But the last three of them find a point of unity in their overriding concern for harmonic sequence, and, beneath that, a new baroque concept of music as simultaneously vertical and linear, as the motion of chords.

It is eclectic. In the final treatise, on concords, Campion freely acknowledges that he is doing little more than translating Sethus Calvisius (1556–1615), a Thuringian mathematician, astronomer, and musician who served as musical director of St. Thomas Church, Leipzig (that was to be Bach's church) for most of his life and composed instrumental works, psalm-settings, and hymns. And his main treatise on counterpoint shares some examples and wording with a manuscript by his collaborator Giovanni Coperario.[8]

The first piece, by way of a preface wherein "the nature of the Scale is expressed, with a briefe Method teaching to Sing," is about notation. Campion begins with a discussion of the ambiguity of musical terms, noting that the word "Note" sometimes signifies the mark on the score, sometimes "the sound it signifies" (*D,* 324), sometimes the whole tune. His design is to reduce ambiguity by simplifying. Because in the old mediaeval "Gamut" scale the same note, D, could be vocalized as either *re* or *sol,* according to which part of the scale it was considered to belong to, Campion suggested replacing the old hexachord (six-note scale, ut-re-mi-fa-sol-la) by a four-note scale modeled on the Greek system; since he advised grouping tetrachords in pairs, he was prefiguring our modern octave system. In singing from a score so conceived, the main thing to keep in mind is the position of the semitones, and Campion suggests ways to do that.

The third piece, "a necessary discourse of *Keyes,* and their proper *Closes,*" is about tonality, the sense of what key a piece is in. It is Campion's attempt to solve the confusion (which also plagued Morley) resulting from the coexistence of both the medieval modes and some sense of the modern keys as the possible bases of tonality in his time. He tries to guide the musician toward consistency by establishing the cadences proper to the different keys. This is to define by motion, direction, or end, and it fitted in with his sense of composition as the progression of chords. In the process, he quotes two of his own songs, "Turne all thy thoughts" and "Young and simple though I am" (*Fourth Booke,* 20 and 9), and takes occasion to criticize the madrigalist George Kirbye.

In the fourth disourse of "the allowed passages of all *Concords,*" which he adapts from Calvisius (in the process inserting original material, like his own song "A secret love or two," *Second Booke,* 19), he is concerned with progression again, with what chords naturally follow others and what do not. He lists what two-part intervals may be used in succession: for example, the major sixth may be followed by another sixth, an octave, or a third, but seldom by a fifth, and so on.

It is the second part, the major treatise on counterpoint, that ties these others together, the discourses on tonality and the concords forming its appendixes. That he took great pride in it is obvious, for after outlining his system he avers, "If I should discover no more then this already deciphered . . . I had effected more in Counterpoint then any man before me hath ever attempted" (*D,* 332). His purpose is to teach the beginner how to compose note-against-note counterpoint in four parts, the essential trick being to preserve the triad of a third, a fifth, and an eighth that outlines the harmony while the bass line is in motion ascending or descending—how if the bass moves a third or a fourth the other parts line up over it. The spirit of this teacher is to reduce what our ears tell us to a single mathematical rule—"that you may perceive how cunning and how certaine nature is in all her operations" (*D,* 332)—digesting the whole into a simple table contained in a little box on the page. After setting out the fundamental principles of his rule, he lays out an eleven-note bass melody and then shows how to harmonize it (*D,* 331); he ends with a short hymn composed according to rule (*D,* 342) so that the student will have a sense of what is possible. While this treatise is set out as a manual intended for "young beginners" (in keeping with his presentation of himself as a simplifier throughout), it is really a revolutionary document.

M. C. Boyd and Lowbury, Salter, and Young give adequate explanation of the details of the treatise on counterpoint.[9] Two points are especially noteworthy for their innovation, the concepts of chords in sequence and of the use of the bass as foundation. The first has caused some confusion: both Vivian and Lowbury et al. assert that Campion's rules for progression of intervals were anticipated by Morley's *A Plaine and Easie Introduction to Practicall Musicke* (*V,* lxv).[10] They are quite wrong. What Morley did was to show how to write separate and unconnected chords, whereas Campion is telling us how to write progressions from one chord to another. Morley was starting to conceive the chord as an entity rather than the sometimes accidental meeting place of polyphonic parts, and so he insisted, for instance, that if the treble is in unison with the tenor, the bass must be a third under the tenor and the alto a fifth or sixth above the bass, and so on for each chord.[11] Campion is conceiving the movement from chord to chord as essential in music, and what he insists on is that the intervals between parts change in an ordered way to preserve the triad as the bass rises or descends: "If the Base shall ascend either a second, third, or fourth, that part which stands in the third or tenth above the Base shall fall into an eight, what which is a fift shall passe into a third, and that which is an eight shall remove into a fift" (*D,* 329), and so on. Campion's use of active verbs of motion instead of verbs of place is worth notice here.

For the second point: up through the time of Morley the tenor part in harmony had been the basis of composition. In a four-part polyphonic mass movement, for instance, the tenor voice might slowly intone the "cantus firmus" on which the piece was based (perhaps a plainchant motif like *In nomine* or a secular tune like *l'homme armé*)

and the bass, alto, and soprano voices would weave melodies derived
from it around it. Campion insists on doing it differently, and he
does so by putting the matter into a rich aesthetic context derived
from a cosmic one:

The parts of Musicke are in all but foure . . . These foure parts by the
learned are said to resemble the foure Elements; the Base expresseth the true
nature of the earth, who being the gravest and lowest of all the Elements, is
as a foundation to the rest. The Tenor is likened to the water, the Meane to
the Aire, and the Treble to the Fire. Moreover, by how much the water is
more light then the earth, by so much is the Aire lighter then the water,
and Fire then Aire. They have also in their native property every one place
above the other, the lighter uppermost, the waightiest in the bottome. Having now demonstrated that there are in all but foure parts, and that the Base
is the foundation of the other three, I assume that the true sight and judgement of the other three must proceed from the lowest, which is the Base,
and also I conclude that every part in nature doth affect his proper and naturall place as the elements doe.
    True it is that the auncient Musitions, who entended their Musicke onely
for the Church, tooke their sight from the Tenor, which was rather done out
of necessity then any respect to the true nature of Musicke: for it was usuall
with them to have a Tenor as a Theame, to which they were compelled to
adapt their other parts. But I will plainely convince by demonstration that
contrary to some opinions the Base containes in it both the Aire and true
judgement of the Key, expressing how any man at the first sight may view
in it all the other parts in their originall essence. (D, 327)

Once again we are seeing how cunning nature is. The bass of cadences
determines the key of a piece of music as we know, but what is important and new is that the movement of the tune is contained in the
sequence of bass notes rather than the tenor. "By drawing attention
to a formal bass as the foundation of everything," Kastendieck writes,
"Campion thus chains the other parts to a movement in accordance
with a definite scheme of intervals (of the third, the fifth, and eighth)
reckoned from the bass. Thus the idea of chordal progression based
on a succession of bass notes is established."[12] This is essentially the
system of modern contrapuntal harmonic technique, and both Kastendieck and Bukofzer consider Campion to have been the first originator
of what was established more magisterially later by Jean-Philippe Rameau's *Traité de l'Harmonie* in 1722.
    The implications of this move are many, though of course many of
them did not become operative until much later. Campion makes it

clear that he is detaching music from church tradition of the tenor (with a fixed repertory of tunes) that it had followed for centuries. He was probably not conscious that he was detaching music from the purely vocal: the tenor carried a tune, but the bass indicates the lower registers of a voice or instrument, indifferently. Up through the sixteenth century music had been basically vocal, instrumental music being comparatively undeveloped, often amounting to playing vocal parts on instruments or composing instrumental variations on a vocal tune like "lachrimae" or "Walsingham." After Campion's innovation it would become possible for instrumental pieces to develop independently of a vocal line, in suites, concerti, etc. Start with a tenor and you start with a melody to be embroidered in the voices above and below. But start with a bass that determines a chord and chordal progressions and you provide the bottom of a set of intervals, a limit, you carve out a "musical space," as it were. Your music can become more "abstract."

Campion's theoretical work was firmly embedded in contemporary theory, from which he drew his own conclusions, and in the practice of his time too, for he was drawing out in theory what underlay the practice of the monodists; as Elise Jorgens writes, "an understanding of harmonic thinking upward from the bass" is "an essential requirement for the continuo style of accompaniment that would distinguish the new songs musically from the old."[13] It is, in essence, baroque theory since it tries to establish chordal harmony by principles of tonality as Rameau later did.[14] Its essential importance to the development of English baroque is indicated by the fact that it alone of all Campion's works was current all through the seventeenth century. In 1655 it was incorporated, with annotations by Christopher Simpson, into John Playford's *Introduction to the Skill of Musick* (which also reprinted in a later edition a translation of the monodist Guilio Caccini's preface to *Nuove musiche*), there to remain, with some alterations, through the various editions until it was replaced in 1694 by a new section on descant written by that giant of the English baroque style Henry Purcell.

Musicologists have a high opinion of this treatise. Manfred Bukofzer calls it "original and radical," and says that Campion was "ahead of his time by more than a century," and Gustave Reese says that in it we can see that "the days of the polyphonic period were numbered."[15] But we must not claim too much. If Campion may be said to have laid down the harmonic principles of baroque music, yet

he had none of its spirit. Such principles may have guided his composition of alternate four-part contrapuntal versions of many of the ayres
in *The First Booke*[16] or may have governed his alterations of an old
dance tune for the ostinato bass of a song like "Faine would I wed a
faire young man." He was not a baroque composer, nor do his songs
show strong traces of those of his contemporaries who were moving
toward the baroque. But his theory pointed toward it.

Observations in the Art of English Poesie

"To break the pentameter, that was the first heave."[17] Campion felt
the same way about the tyranny of a single way of organizing sound
in verse, but for him it was rhymed iambic pentameter, and his emphasis fell on the rhyme because he felt it was responsible for slovenly
metrics: to crack open rhyme and pull out the line, that was the first
thrust.

Since Ezra Pound's day our situation in poetry has reversed itself,
and instead of a single domineering system we have such variety that
to some it seems chaotic. Consider the sounds in our ears today. We
have syllabic verse, where a fixed number of syllables without regard
to accent determines the line (Marianne Moore, Dylan Thomas,
Philip Levine), as against accentual verse like the Old English allitera-
tive verse of Gerard Manley Hopkins's "sprung rhythm" where a fixed
number of accents without regard to number of syllables is the deter-
minant. The traditional accentual-syllabic verse that has dominated
English certainly since the sixteenth century, probably since Chaucer,
is still with us (W. B. Yeats, Robert Frost, Seamus Heaney). Among
newer movements there is "projective verse" which though founded
on vocal lines seems designed more for the eye than the ear, as do
"Imagist" forms (Charles Olson, Robert Creeley). But in general we
have such a variety of free verse without theory that almost every
practicing poet today must create his or her own prosodic system.
This fact bothers some prosodists, like Paul Fussell who remains loyal
to the accentual-syllabic prosody of Robert Frost, or J. V. Cunningham who feels that poets today are caught between a moribund traditional accentual-syllabic system that is a meter by law and encourages
the fiction of a metrical norm and departures from it on the one hand,
and on the other hand what he terms "parasitic meter," in poets like
Eliot and Stevens, that operates by alluding to traditional meter as a
base here and there and then departing from it with lineated prose.[18]

Prosody is a matter of debate again for us as it was for Campion. While most poets around him were writing accentual-syllabic rhymed verse, its theory was uncertain, for while George Gascoigne instructed how to plod from one iamb to the next in order to complete a line, other theorists like George Puttenham advised attending to number of syllables only.[19] Campion's situation was more like Pound's than ours today. For him, rhymed accentual-syllabic meter had dominated European poetry since "the declining of the Roman Empire" (*D*, 293) and its collapse into barbarism. What was wrong with it? For one thing, it was "over-determined": that is, there were two different systems straightjacketing verse, one by both number and accent within the line, the other by sound-echoes between lines. It seemed like a man trying to keep his trousers up by both belt and suspenders. On the one hand, rhyme schemes in general, and especially fixed forms like the sonnet he so disliked (*D*, 295–96) "inforceth a man oftentimes to abjure his matter and extend a short conceit beyond all bounds of arte" (*D*, 295), making his thought expand or contract unnaturally, like the bed of Procrustes. Ben Jonson felt the same way, and wrote a comic "Fit of Rime Against Rime" to show his frustration at the way rhyme breaks up the flow of thought:

> Rime, the rack of finest wits,
> That expresseth but by fits,
> > True Conceipt, . . .
> Wresting words, from their true calling;
> Propping Verse, for feare of falling
> > To the ground,
> Joynting Syllabes, drowning Letters,
> Fastning Vowells, as with fetters
> > They were bound![20]

On the other hand, rhyme often takes the emphasis and allows the meter to go soft or slack. Here is a line, ostensibly iambic pentameter, from a staff of rhymed verse: "Was it my desteny, or dismall chaunce?" Campion scans it this way: "Was it my desteny, or dismall chaunce?" It has no metrical shape, since only the last two feet assert the iambic. It contains only four stresses. From Campion's view it is not even satisfying as syllabic verse, since he considered an accented syllable as longer than an unaccented, and so the line falls out short in time (*D*, 295); if we count an unstressed syllable as a unit and a stressed syllable as two, then an iambic pentameter line should be

fifteen units in length, whereas this line is fourteen—a real problem
for a musician.

There were other matters at stake. Campion defined rhyme this
way: "By Rime is understoode that which ends in the like sound, so
that verses in such maner composed yeeld but a continual repetition
of that Rhetoricall figure which we tearme *similiter desinentia,* . . . being but *figura verbi*" (*D,* 294). Here he entered a brief skirmish in the
war between rhetoric and poetic. Rhetoric aims at persuasion, and its
devices tend to emphasis within prose periods—stressing the beginning of a sentence by anaphora, parts of a sentence by "figures of
words" like antithesis or balance, endings by metrical cursus or the
"similar ending" of rhyme. Poetry is the art of expression—of the
self, of the harmony of the universe—and it demands an even flow,
proportion, every word having its own importance; only in the epigram do we tend to emphasize one part, the ending, at the expense
of others. Since the Middle Ages, rhetoric had invaded poetic again
and again,[21] and in Campion's time it still dominated many poetic
treatises, like George Puttenham's *The Arte of English Poetrie* (1589).
Also at stake was the attempt to return poetry to its status in antiquity, for the Greeks and Romans had neither rhyme nor accent, only
lines defined by regular systems of alternating long and short syllables
that were easily set to music. Here Campion joined hands with Baïf
and the French Académie. Finally, Campion was a musician, and for
a musician rhyme tended to dictate musical form—the monodists
strove against this, as did Dowland and Danyel—while accent was
not very relevant, since the measure of notes of different length—half-
notes, quarter-notes, and so forth—was more important than the beat
(*D,* 297).

Campion proposed to reform English prosody by substituting the
Greco-Roman system of quantitative verse that proceeds by long and
short syllables (a long syllable being double the length or quantity of
a short) for the accentual system of stressed and unstressed syllables.
As was his wont, he located his proposal in a general aesthetic context: "The world is made by Simmetry and proportion, and is in that
respect compared to Musick, and Musick to Poetry. . . . What musick can there be where there is no proportion observed?" (*D,* 293).
For Campion the musician, proportion meant measure or mensura-
tion, or "number," lines of equal length taking the same amount of
time to pronounce or sing. "The eare is a rationall sence and a chiefe
judge of proportion," he wrote, "but in our kind of riming what pro-

portion is there kept where there remaines such a confusd inequalitie of sillables?" (*D*, 294).

Practically, the problem was to translate an accentually conceived language into one that was quantitatively conceived. His solution was one of simple translation: "the first rule that is to be observed is the nature of the accent, which we must ever follow" (*D*, 313). He will not violate the nature of the English language, only regulate it: an accented syllable is a long syllable, an unaccented a short. This rule is modified by his only other rule, the familiar Latin rule of "position," whereby any vowel followed by two or more consonants —either within the word or between words—is always long (*D*, 313–14). This makes more sense in music than in recitation, where length gives a singer time to pronounce both consonants, and where the even flow of notes frequently makes one word slide into another (the main effect being a succession of vowels and consonants carrying meaning—"MysweetestLesbialetusliveandlove").

The result was to highlight the line. Instead of what he considered disordered lines tumbling together and held in check by rhyme, the line was to have its own proportion, its fixed length and internal sound structure. This comes out most clearly in what he called "compound numbers" where the line is compounded of a system of different sorts of feet. He may have learned this from Sidney, whose Asclepiadic meters he imitated in his first published verse, "Canto Secundo" of the *Astrophil and Stella* appendix. The Asclepiadic line is compounded of spondees and dactylls, so that it has its own internal sound structure: "Ō sweēt wōods the delīght of solĭtărĭnes! / Ō hōw much Ĭ dō līke your sŏlĭtărĭnes!"[22] The line, we may say, has "integrity" or internal coherence, defined not only by the certain length of time it takes to pronounce it but by a structure of long and short sounds that makes it distinctive, makes it have an impact on the ear—and that needs no rhyme or fixed scheme to give it a coherence it attains simply by being repeated. In examining the music of Campion's songs, we saw how important the internal structure of lines put together in a strophe was. In this treatise we can see him developing that skill.

Observations in the Art of English Poesie, dedicated to reason and brevity (*D*, 292), is organized into ten short chapters moving from the most general to the most specific. Campion starts with "Numbers in Generall" on proportion, number, and poetry, then proceeds to criticize accentual rhymed verse as lacking in proportion. In the third chapter he proposes his quantitative scheme, basing his metrics on the iamb that falls "so naturally in our toong" (D, 297), instead of the usual dactyll. In the fourth and fifth chapters he treats iambic verse either strict or varied, which he asserts is proper to epic and tragedy, in the sixth the trochaic proper to epigram (with a plethora of examples). He then proceeds to his compound meters, the elegiac for elegy (chapter 7), the anacreontic for madrigal (chapter 9), and the lyric for ditties, or song texts, and odes (chapter 8). His lyric forms derive from the Sapphic stanza; there are three of them, the second of which is examplified by this lovely verse:

> Rose-cheekt *Lawra*, come,
> Sing thou smoothly with thy beawties
> Silent musick, either other
>   Sweetly gracing.
> Lovely formes do flowe
> From concent devinely framed;
> Heav'n is musick, and thy beawties
>   Birth is heavenly.
> These dull notes we sing
> Discords neede for helps to grace them;
> Only beawty purely loving
>   Knowes no discord:
> But still mooves delight,
> Like cleare springs renu'd by flowing,
> Ever perfect, ever in them-
>   selves eternall.
>   (D, 310)[23]

His last chapter descends to particulars, giving directions for determining the quantity of accented syllables—"But above all the accent of our words is diligently to be observ'd, for chiefly by the accent in any language the true value of the sillables is to be measured" (D, 313), he reiterates—first by his two rules of accent and position, then by detailed annotations about exceptions and special cases, insisting, by the way, that pronunciation rather than spelling determine length.

The six chapters on the various kinds of verse are as much anthologies of quantitative verse as they are directions for making it, and several of these poems are quite interesting. Campion is especially careful to avoid bogus classicism and stay in his time, and so his subjects—

an occasion at Whitehall, sumptuary clothing, the cuckoldry of Barnabe Barnes, drunkenness, Puritans—and his names too are distinctly
sixteenth-century English. Moreover, because he bases quantity on accent, many of the poems can be read accentually by the modern
reader, with good effect. For example, the "English march" consists
of two feet and one odd syllable, which he would scan thus:

> Rāvīng | wārre, bĕgŏt
>
> Īn thĕ | thīrstўĕ | sānds
>
> Ōf thĕ | *Lȳbiăn* | Īlēs,
>
> Wāsts ŏur | ēmptўĕ | fīelds.
>   (*D*, 302)

But it could be just as easily scanned accentually, and when we do so
its fine imitation of a threatening drum-beat—three beats per line
and a pause—comes out in this antiwar poem:

> / ×   /   × /
> Raving warre, begot
>
> /   × / × /
> In the thirstye sands
>
> / × / × /
> Of the *Lybian* Iles,
>
> / × / × /
> Wasts our emptye fields.

Similarly his elegiac "Constant to none" is designed to imitate the
slightly falling effect of following a hexameter line with a pentameter
in Latin elegaic, according to Ovid's prescription "sex mihi surgat
opus numeris, in quinque residat" (in six measures let my work rise,
then fall again in five, *Amores*, 1.1.27):

> Cōnstānt | tŏ nōne, | bŭt ēvēr | fālsĕ | tŏ mē,
>
>   Trāitēr | stīll tŏ | lŏve || thrōugh thў | fāint dĕsīrēs
> ....
> That both he can regard thee, and refrain:
>   If grac't, firme he stands, if not, easely falls.
>   (*D*, 307)[24]

What stands out in these lines is the strong medial caesura that makes the first line seem to start with a choriambic beginning that, with the fifth syllable, moves "upward" in iambs, while the second line's sixth syllable moves it into a falling trochaic effect. A poet searching for new expressive sounds might in imitation of this come up with these verses:

> /   ×   × / ‖ × / ×   /   × /
> Bound with a kiss, the velvet hurts my sides:
> Face comes and goes, she dances and recedes,
> Just like the moon, the governess of tides,
> All of my life, blood's rise and fall she leads.

Campion's main accomplishment, as he saw it, was that he had produced eight new and interesting meters "agreeable with the nature of our sillables" for English poets to use (D, 312).

Historically considered, Campion's *Observations* comes at the very end of a twenty-year experiment. In the late 1570s and early 1580s Sidney had argued for classical meters and had given several examples in his *Old Arcadia*. That Sidney was Campion's master appears right at the opening dedication to Sackville, where he asserts that the function of poetry is "raysing the minde to a more high and lofty conceite" (D, 291), reflecting statements such as Sidney had made in the *Defence of Poesie:* "to lift up the minde from the dungeon of the bodie, to the enjoying his owne divine essence."[25] Behind Sidney were the experiments of the Pléiade and Baïf's Académie in *vers mesurée* and a few tentative essays by English classicists and Humanists.

It began with the humanist Roger Ascham's plea for quantitative meters and quotation of a few examples by himself and Thomas Watson in both *Toxophilus* (1545) and *The Scholemaster* (1570). Sidney took up the cause and became its great examplar. Encouraged by the arguments and simple rules of Thomas Drant, he produced many fine poems in a deliberate variety of classical meters in his original *Arcadia* as well as a persuasive argument for them as more easily set to music than accentual rhymes:

Dicus said that since verses had their chief ornament, if not end, in music, those which were just appropriated to music did best to obtain their end, or at least were the most adorned; but those must needs most agree with music, since music standing principally upon the sound and the quantity, to answer the sound they brought words, and to answer the quantity they brought measure. So that for every simibreve or minim, it had his syllable matched unto it with a long foot or a short foot, whereon they [the ancients] drew on certain names (as dactylus, spondeus, trocheus, etc.), and without wresting the word did as it were kindly accompany the time, so that either by the time a poet should straight know how every word should be measured unto it, or by the verse as soon find out the full quantity of the music. Besides that it hath in itself a kind (as a man may well call it) of secret music, since by the measure one may perceive some verses running with a high note fit for great matters, some with a light foot fit for no greater than amorous conceits.[26]

Sidney apparently led both Edmund Spenser and Gabriel Harvey to try similar experiments (in their *Correspondence* of 1579), and his example led William Webbe to include a section on classical meters in *A Discourse of English Poetry* (1586). Chief among the poems in these meters—most of them in hexameters—are Richard Stanyhurst's *The First Four Bookes of Virgil his Aeneis* (1582), Abraham Fraunce's *Amyntas* (1587), his *Countesse of Pembrokes Emanuel* (1591) and *Amyntas Dale* (1592), a few songs set by William Byrd in *Psalms, Sonets, and Songs* (1588), Richard Barnfield's *Hellens Rape* (1594), Francis Sabie's *Pans Pipe* (1595), and the anonymous *First Booke of the Preservation of King Henry VII* (1599). The last of them, several elegies on Sidney in Francis Davison's *Poetical Rhapsody*, appeared in the same year as Campion's treatise.

In almost all of these experiments, the main concern had been to reproduce classical meters in English as part of a self-conscious classicist program. It was the epic strain of dactyllic hexameter—Homer and Vergil—they were trying to domesticate, and frequently it caused great strain, as when Stanyhurst even coined dactyllic words like "bootless morglay." They were frequently met with derision, and Ben Jonson said that "Abraham Frauncis in his English Hexameters was a Foole."[27] Campion's uniqueness lay in his repudiation of the dream of classicism, his insistence on making classical meters English, giving his readers illustrative poems fitting to their tongues with familiar subject matter and names. Especially important was his insistence that quantity be established from the natural accent of English words as they were actually spoken, and that the iamb natural to English speech (rather than the Latin dactyl) be the basis of his metrics, so that his quantitative verse alone follows the normal auditory pattern of English speech.

Nevertheless, his arguments convinced nobody—finally not even himself. The next year Samuel Daniel attacked him in *A Defence of Ryme,* and literary historians feel that Daniel won. His attack is a piece of emotive discourse, his main effort to cut beneath Campion's specifics (as was his wont, for example, in *Musophilus*) in order to defend the medieval poetic tradition he rightly conceived Campion and other humanists to be attacking. His main specific point is that Campion is only juggling terms: "For what adoe haue we heere? what strange precepts of Arte about the framing of an Iambique verse in our language? which, when all is done, reaches not by a foote, but falleth out to be the plaine ancient verse, consisting of ten sillables or fiue feete, which hath euer beene vsed amongst vs time out of minde."[28] In his defense of the accentual-syllabic system, Daniel asserts that Campion's iambics are nothing more than iambic pentameter blank verse, his dimeter only half a line of such verse, his elegiacs "no other then our old accustomed measure of fiue feet: if there be any difference, it must be made in the reading."[29] There is some justice to Daniel's view, and in fact we might imagine that Campion would have expressed qualified agreement in principle (though Daniel's criticism is too simple and sweeping), because he was not trying to supplant native meters but to explain and regulate them. Derek Attridge's view of the case is that "by demonstrating that quantitative verse succeeds only when it is also accentual, Campion had undermined the whole enterprise" of classical meters while arguing its final defense.[30]

At any rate, Campion did not answer Daniel, and dropped the matter completely, producing only one poem in classical meter outside this treatise, that being the last song in Sapphics in the 1601 volume. The true importance of the *Observations* is for his own career. It is a youthful work; perhaps written as early as 1591, it represents the final point of his apprenticeship to Sidney, and in it he was performing experiments that would bear fruit in the song books.[31] His insistent drive for expressive metrical variety, coupled with his liberal use of a variety of sound effects to support scansion, is responsible for the unique sounds of *A Booke of Ayres* and its successors, his variety of pentameter shapes, and his structuring of a strophe by massed sounds. Many of his finest songs have these experiments behind them, as "Constant to none" lies behind "Follow your Saint." The chief emphasis in his investigations of sound here was to shape verse that would imitate its subject, as his English march imitates drum-beats, his elegiacs the slight rise and extended fall of hope, or in "Rose-cheekt *Lawra"* the "gently expanding and contracting accentual rhythm that makes this poem flow in a way so perfectly expressive of its subject matter."[32]

In 1601 and 1602 we find Campion breaking open the mystery of sound and analyzing it (not only in the *Observations* but in his English songs and Latin poems too). He was to spend the next dozen years drawing meaning after meaning out of sound, in the significances explored in the songbooks and the symbolism of the masques. Then, toward the end of his career, he was to point new directions for the history of sound to move in.

The Latin Poems

In this chapter we have been investigating things Campion thought about but did not really do, directions he pointed out and seemed to believe in, but did not himself take. By knowing what he did not do, we may gain a perspective on what he did do. For example, in veering away from his own technical experiments with prosody and his speculations about how four-part harmony might be written, he intensified his interest in cross-disciplinary matters, in the *combination* of words and music rather than their individual problems. His work on counterpoint came late in his career; probably there was no time left to develop its implications and move toward becoming a baroque composer, or one of the really important names in English music like Byrd, Dowland, or Purcell. On the other hand, the *Observations* is an early work, and there must have been a great store of common sense in him that prevented him from wasting his career trying to write English poetry as if it were Latin, as Richard Stanyhurst and Abraham Fraunce did, and ending up the sort of man Ben Jonson could dismiss as "a Foole." Instead of doing these things, he became the finest of our song-writers. But for a little while he was what we would regard today as a foreign poet. And we may fitly conclude this chapter on what he did not do with a short consideration of what he did for a little while—that is, write Latin poetry. He entered and then soon left a career as a Latin poet.

It was a common enough thing for writers of his time to do. Bacon usually published his treatises in Latin. The Latin poems of Crashaw, Cowley, Milton, and others were as well known as their English poems. The Latin epigrams of John Owen went through innumerable editions in England and on the Continent, while John

Barclay's long Latin prose romance *Argenis* rivaled Sidney's *Arcadia* in popularity. Alexander Pope even at his late date had his *Essay on Man* translated into Latin for a European audience. Latin was not so dead a language then as it is today, of course. Spoken church-Latin survived the reforms of 1558. It was the language of the universities, and it was European. If you wanted people outside the little island to read you, you wrote in Latin. If you wanted your work to survive the vagaries of linguistic change, you wrote in Latin. You knew your audience, men educated in the universities like you, maybe even your former classmates at Oxford or Cambridge. And, to put it bluntly, it was an easy literary market, like that for romance today: if you sounded a little like Ovid or Martial or Vergil your readers loved it, because they were often seeking confirmation of conventional expectations.

It may come as a surprise that Campion's Latin poetry comprises about one third of his total output. It is almost all early work done before 1595 when he was twenty-eight, while he was probably still working entirely as a poet, before combining that vocation with musical and medical careers. It appears in his first publication, *Thomae Campiani Poemata* (1595): a minor epic fragment *Ad Thamesin; Fragmentum Umbrae,* the first half of a long erotic poem after the manner of Ovid; sixteen elegies, and 129 epigrams. Late in life he revised this juvenalia as *Tho. Campiani Epigrammatum Libri II,* etc. (1619), wisely omitting *Ad Thamesin,* completing *Umbra,* revising eleven of the original elegies and adding two new ones, and swelling the number of occasional epigrams he had composed over the years to a grand total of 453.[33]

The early work reveals some of the things a young poet's work often does today—a combination of ambition and conventionality. To say of a poet working in Latin that "he has not yet found his own voice" is a solecism. He started to write in the epic voice and failed miserably. He tried to write a long erotic poem—a sort of Latin version of what Marlowe was doing in *Hero and Leander* or Shakespeare in *Venus and Adonis* or Drayton in *Endimion and Phoebe*—and succeeded. There are some surprises here: he could write like Spenser in Latin, he could imitate Ovid with remarkable fidelity. He was facile. He had no sense of structure, and was constantly yielding to the temptation of digression. He had a strong sense of myth and its potential meanings, and he loved symmetry.

The main if not the only distinction of *Ad Thamesin* ("To the

Thames") is that it is the first Latin poem devoted to the defeat of the Armada. The prose argument he prefaced to it reads, "The poem congratulates the Thames for the rout of the Spaniards. In it are outlined the reasons for which the Spaniards were led to make an expedition against England. These are greed, cruelty, pride, and envy. Then an apostrophe to the Queen ends the work like a pastoral" (*D*, 363). His concern is with moral absolutes, vice and evil. Most of the action occurs in a dark and dismal place sacred to Dis or Satan (it is identified in a marginal gloss as a poetic description of America, which Spain holds in its power). Thus the Spanish desire to conquer England in order to master the seas and the new world, as well as pure Mediterreanean viciousness, becomes the motive for invasion. Dis tries both to help the Spaniards and to whip up their courage, and he does so by a parade of vices beginning with gold and Greed, next Slaughter and Pride, then the Fountain of Envy wherein the Spanish view England with its white cliffs, serene fields, and prosperous cities. They are consumed with envy, and after a brief entertainment rush off to launch the invasion. But the river Thames disturbs the waters of the sea and brings them to shipwreck. Most of the poem is taken up with descriptive work, especially in those static absolutes defining vice rather than advancing action, those allegorical houses so frequent in Spenser—the House of Dis, the House of Avarice, the Fountain of Envy. So intent was Campion on these descriptive pieces that he left a scant eighteen lines for the defeat itself, and then broke that off for an apostrophe to Elizabeth! It begins *in medias res* and sets out an opposition of places and tries for a Vergilian style (but achieves only something like Ovid). Its presiding genius is Edmund Spenser, and behind him the Italian epic poet Troquato Tasso, whose infernal council in book 4 of *Gerusalemme Liberata* Campion is imitating (it was subsequently to influence Milton). Readers are lucky that Campion did not decide to pursue further his ambition of becoming an epic poet.

Umbra or "Shadow" is a much better poem. It has a clear symmetrical structure of two parts, one female and one male, with cross relations. The first half recounts Apollo's rape of the nymph Iole, drugged by him into a deep sleep, and the painful birth of their son Melampus, who is a sort of black Cupid (save for the image of his father the sun on his chest). The second half tells how Morpheus, the god of sleep, falls in love with Melampus and visits him, in sleep, in the form of a composite ideal of female beauty; Melampus awakens filled with desire, can find his beloved nowhere, and wastes away to become the first shadow, fleeing throughout all time, forever exiled from light. It is about sexual desire—in the female unconscious and violent possession, in the male the vain pursuit of an ideal or dream—desire imaged as dream or finally as shadow which depends on its "object" for substance, as in "Followe thy faire sunne, unhappy shaddowe." Stylistically it is like a page out of the *Metamorphoses,* full of turns on words and other types of poetic wit like Ovid's. One of the most interesting things about this poem is the archetypal quality of its myth. It bears some resemblance to Spenser's tale of Amoret and Belphoebe in book 3 of *The Faerie Queene:* Iole's conception in sleep resembles Chrysogone's, the resulting children are in each case figures of Amor, and the setting, the valley where Cybele gives the flowers their forms, is redolent of the Garden of Adonis. Campion used his characteristic light and dark imagery to infuse this myth with suggestions of cosmic archetypes, of the paradoxical relations between the cold, dark, wet female center of earth with its unawakened potentiality, and the hot, light, dry male inseminating principle in the skies, of their reluctance or eagerness to join and the fecundity or barrenness that may result. By means of such imagery and symbolism, Campion makes his own Ovidian tale and then traces in it this timeless process of great creating nature.

In the first elegy of his 1595 set Campion announces himself as the first English elegist, relates his work to a long British erotic tradition stemming from Chaucer, and links Ovidian grace to the peace of Elizabeth. Some of the thirteen poems in Campion's collection mock love and other lovers, some are frankly erotic, but most of those addressed to the wanton Mellea and the cold Caspia achieve the Ovidian tone of passion mingled with ironic self-observation that poets like Marlowe, Donne, Jonson, and later Carew tried to capture in English.[34]

The epigrams exhibit a side of Campion familiar to us in the *Observations* and the epigrammatic ayres. In fact, they lie behind them, and often announce themes that the English songs will develop. Some of them are darkly erotic, some are elegiac, many are addressed to great and obscure friends and acquaintances, among them Spenser, Bacon, Nashe, and Chapman. Their keynote is variety of subject matter: tobacco, drinking gold, London citizens, the tarantella, wrath, honor, the death of a dog, physicians, poetasters, pocket watches, cuckolds, bald men, wearing too many clothes in the summer, lawyers, bad singers, and false prophets.

The elegies sound like Ovid, the epigrams like Martial. It was hard to write poetry in a purely literary language without falling into conventions of phrasing and even feeling: we can see that if we compare Andrew Marvell's *"Hortus,"* the Latin version of "The Garden," with his English one. But taken together the elegies develop the subject matter that will eventuate in the English ayres while the epigrams develop their formal qualities: as always in Campion, it is the combination that counts. Of course, in order to find his own voice he had to turn to his native tongue, and he did that both in the English poems he was writing now and then in the 1590s and in the full phonetic and partially linguistic analysis he performed from the perspective of the Latin in *Observations.* More than that: he had to develop that voice by opening his throat in song, as it were. Then, in the court masques, he moved further through music beyond mere words into dance, light, spectacle, and movement. The progress from the written—almost inscribed—word in a monumental language to living action as mode of imitation was to become complete. And he was to emerge from the sort of cocoon of a coterie poet completely: to a song-writer whose sheet music—"after the fascion of the time"— hung in the stalls of Paul's churchyard to be handled by any hoarse rogue who thought he had a voice, then to a composer for the court stage, the center of political life in the kingdom.

Chapter Six
Masques

Campion put all his knowledge and skill—in poetry, in music, in dance—into the masque form, and either brought to light or acquired new skills in such matters as stagecraft, allegory, drama, and iconography to combine with what he already knew, when in his fortieth year he became a composer of entertainments. For the man whose interests had been in the combining of arts as much as the individual arts themselves, the masque was the perfect form.

What Is a Masque?

We must not be deceived by the printed format of a court masque in early or modern editions. It looks like a script with elaborate stage directions, rather like the printed editions of George Bernard Shaw's plays. But it in fact resembles a souvenir program rather than a script, as often narrative as dramatic in mode. It has less relation to drama than to dance, as a matter of fact, and its composers were as often poets and musicians like Campion, Daniel, and William Browne as they were playwrights like Jonson and Chapman. Moreover, it is a violently compressed form. As Stephen Orgel writes, for the dozen pages of dialogue and verse we possess, the actual audience took part in a production of three hours consisting largely of "music, dancing, pageantry, and spectacular scenic effects."[1]

Its core was the dancing. It began as dance,[2] and dance continued to convey its central action, that being replacing discord by harmony or chaos by order or the scattered by unity. Andrew Sabol (seconded by Lowbury, Salter, and Young) reduces the form to song and dance, the text functioning mainly to indicate the elements of dance and help extend its significance by myth.[3] In the classic form established by Ben Jonson in his *Masque of Queens* in 1609, the court masque had three sections: "antimasque," "masque," and "revels." The antimasque is a grotesque prologue, or mélange of characters like gypsies, witches, or men transformed into bottles. Its dances are deliberately disorderly, strange, awkward, clumsy, even threatening. They are dispelled by the entrance of the masque proper, the costumed nobility entering with a transformation of the scene to which the antimasque has formed a foil. Their entrance dances and main dance (after a conflict has been resolved) are orderly and heavily symbolic, often figured in such a way that visual iconography is reinforced by dance iconography. Order once established within the piece, it moves out to embrace society in the revels or social dances that begin with the noble masquers choosing partners from the audience. The revels had their own form, a kind of symphonic progression (leading to later codified musical forms like the baroque suite), beginning with slow dances like bass-dance or pavane, then moving into fast dances associated with youth and vitality rather than ceremony and age, like the galliard or courante, and ending with rather violent gymnastic exercises like the volta. As they moved along, more and more people took part. The revels were halted by a final return to the ceremony of the masque, and all departed to the ensuing feast together—still another form of social solidarity.

It contained as much music as a modern musical comedy. It begins with the strange instrumental music of the antimasque, often wildly rhythmical and folklike, using loud instruments like bagpipes, flutes, and drums. The masque uses the softer and more dignified stringed instruments of the viol and lute family, and combines the human voice with those instruments in the songs interspersed among the dances. The shift in instruments is a matter of significance, wind-instruments typifying human passion, stringed instruments reason and the harmony of creation. The revels switches back to instrumental music, but now it is familiar, consisting of a suite of popular tunes of the day. Music begins in dance, parts from it in order to comment on it, and finally returns to it in inviting participation.

It hinged on spectacle. The masque dispels the antimasque by a sudden introduction of stage spectacle, which shifted the audience's attention from predominantly auditory sense-experience to the visual (reflected in the text from printed dialogue to description). Conducted indoors at night, the court masque made use of advanced scenic techniques seldom attempted in the public theater (and not so very different from modern theater): movable flats, revolving stages, pageant cars, lowered machines and trap doors, wave machines, cloud machines, wind machines. Height and depth, dark and light, shallow and deep perspectives were all possible, and desirable for their spectacular and symbolic effects. The elaborateness of such machinery is well illustrated in Jonson's account of the island representing the world in the *Masque of Beauty* (1608).[4] Not only could a piece of spectacular machinery create a sensation, it could alter reality. When Inigo Jones turned from *machina versatilis* or movable stages emphasizing motion from high to low or left to right, to *scena ductilis* or the "tractable scene" of flats set in grooves that could be drawn aside to reveal scene behind scene, he could transform the entire stage and create an illusion of worlds within worlds. That is what happened in Jonson's *Oberon* (1611) which began in a wilderness, proceeded to a palace, and ended in an interior that reflected the pilastered interior of Whitehall where its audience sat and could muse at its own image.[5] Similarly, in *Pleasure Reconciled to Virtue* (1618) the scene opens up to reveal the vertical behind the horizontal (virtue behind pleasure, as it were), making heaven and earth new possibilities.[6]

Spectacle was not only plastic, it was human. The nobles who took part in a masque were gorgeously clothed: enormous headdresses, stylized helmets and cuirasses, robes conferring dignity, rich textures and colors chosen for their reflective qualities made them seem larger than life. They entered as parts of the set, either perched on the machine or surrounding it, representing such elements as pillars or stars later to be transformed into human shape. When the main machine moved into the stage with the masquers, there was not only an impressive new mass of color, stationary and in motion, but a sudden increase in light as well. For mirrors and sequins were sewn into the costumes, magnifiers and colored lights in bottles were placed in the machines, and the rather brilliantly lit hall could seem to double the intensity of its light in a blast. Jones was later to characterize the masque as "nothing else but pictures with Light and Motion" (much to Jonson's annoyance),[7] and the movement from chaos to order was likewise one from moderate to blinding light. Here it might be useful to recall the symbolism of light for Campion as comprising intellect, consciousness, divinity, and related values. When the masquers began to move in measured fashion in the dance, light suddenly burst into motion, intellect and divinity came to life and activated the stage.

It would be a mistake to conceive of these media as "extraliterary" in effect or as providing a kind of ornament or extension of literary effects, though that is a conclusion hard to avoid when it is the literary texts—not the music, choreography, costumes, or scenic designs—that have survived.[8] Each medium tended to develop a distinct but related aspect of the governing theme, all going together like a symphony of themes: music and dance developed themes of disorder-order or separateness-harmony or mechancial-human, while spectacle developed directions of transcendence from low to high or incarnation from high to low or deepening of perspective or moving from appearance to reality. Spectacular scenic shifts arrived freighted with significance expressed by iconographic details. The same is true of dance: the figured main dance frequently suggested mystical meanings, as in Daedalus's dance signifying education in *Pleasure Reconciled to Virtue*.[9]

Dance links the masque to folk customs like the agricultural rituals of Christmas or Shrovetide and thus incorporates archetypal rituals like domesticating the strange. The masques of Elizabeth I were generally linked to seasonal celebrations like Twelfth Night or Shrovetide, while James I superimposed on them specific occasions such as weddings, returns, and investures. The occasion was specific for audience and for performer—the dancers being noble friends and relatives of those persons being celebrated—and drew them together. Occasion called up ceremony, and ceremony helped shape significance. Again it was dance that brought audience and performers together in action. In the spectacular costuming of the dancers the event celebrated was raised to the level of myth, the dancers were the subjects of some grand transformation, and when at the close of the piece they moved out into the audience, they transformed, in Orgel's words, "the courtly audience into the idealized world of the poet's vision."[10]

Thus, Orgel points out, not only its ingredients but its mode made it quite different from drama: it is not entertainment like drama involving its audience vicariously, but is "a form of play" that includes its audience directly, ending as it does by "merging spectator with masquer."[11] The overarching significance of a masque owed most to the powerful (but often lost) effect of personation that made every masque move on at least two levels of significance (as did the allegorical tradition so important to the masque texts), so that in a wedding masque the noble couple see themselves personated on the stage as figures of land and sea or heaven and earth or sun and moon. In the familiar example of Milton's *Comus* the earl of Bridgewater and his wife saw their three children, personated as different versions of themselves, tracing a multiple action about Wales, about trial, about maturity, about the nature of life—all on the evening of 29 September 1634.

Guided by a sense of what their texts leave out, we now turn to Campion's three great masques themselves.

The Lord Hay's Masque

James I and his Revels Office took an old form that had existed in England for at least a century and made it serve a new and intense political purpose, that of solidifying James's kingdom, which, by the Act of Union, was to combine England, Scotland, and Wales into Great Britain. Campion was chosen to compose the masque celebrating the first of the major political weddings James was to sponsor between Scots lords and English ladies; it took place 6 January 1607, it being Twelfth night, and it was between his favorite, James Hay, first earl of Carlisle and Baron Hay, and Honora Denny, daughter of the high sheriff of Hertfordshire who had welcomed James to England back in 1603. There seems to have been some difficulty in arranging the match, for James had to create Denny a baron and grant his daughter Strixton Manor in order to gain his consent. But it must have seemed worth the trouble, for James's full intention—as it was lauded both by Campion and by Robert Wilkinson in the wedding sermon—was to strengthen the ties between his two kingdoms (see *D,* 204).

The published souvenir program moves from the visual to the auditory: it contains an engraving of one of the knights masquers as a frontispiece and five pieces of music—two songs and three dances (to which Campion wrote new words for singing)—at the back. The art of writing out an account of a masque for publication was something quite new: Daniel in *The Vision of the Twelve Goddesses* (1604) did it in two parts, a description with explanations and comments, then the script with the speeches; Jonson tended to start with his idea, then the "body" as he called it, a physical description, then the "soul" or the words. Campion sees the piece as narrative and takes his model from military history, first describing the place and then the action:

As in battailes, so in all other actions that are to bee reported, the first, and most necessary part is the discription of the place, with his opportunities, and properties, whether they be naturall or artificiall. The greate hall (wherein the Maske was presented) received this division and order: The upper part, where the cloth and chaire of State were plac't, had scaffoldes and seates on eyther side continued to the skreene; right before it was made a partition for the dauncing place . . . eighteen foote from the skreene, an other Stage was raised higher by a yearde then that which was prepared for dancing. This higher Stage was all enclosed with a double vale, so artificially painted, that it seemed as if darke cloudes had hung before it: within that shrowde was concealed a greene valley, with greene trees round about it, and in the midst of them nine golden trees of fifteene foote high, with armes and braunches very glorious to behold. From the which grove toward the State was made a broade descent to the dauncing place, just in the midst of it; on either hand were two ascents, like the sides of two hilles, drest with shrubbes and trees; that on the right hand leading to the bowre of *Flora,* the other to the house of *Night;* which bowre and house were plac't opposite at either end of the skreene, and betweene them both was raised a hill, hanging like a cliffe over the grove belowe, and on the top of it a goodly large tree was set, supposed to be the tree of *Diana;* behind the which toward the window was a small descent, with an other spreading hill that climed up to the toppe of the window, with many trees on the height of it, whereby those that played on the Hoboyes at the Kings entrance into the hall were shadowed. The bowre of *Flora* was very spacious, garnisht with all kind of flowers, and flowrie branches with lights in them; the house of *Night* ample, and stately, with blacke pillors, whereon many starres of gold were fixt: within it, when it was emptie, appeared nothing but cloudes and starres, and on the top of it stood three Turrets underpropt with small blacke starred pillers, the middlemost being highest and greatest, the other two of equall proportion: about it were plac't on wyer artificial Battes and Owles, continually moving: with many other inventions, the which for brevitie sake I passe by with silence. (*D,* 211–12)

It was the great hall at Whitehall Palace (the usual Banqueting House was being reconstructed). At one end was James's throne providing the point of view from which it will all be seen in perspective, before it the dancing area that filled the bulk of the hall; at the other end a curtain or "skreene" painted as dark clouds. The stage behind the curtain had two levels: on the lower, a yard above the dancing area, the main stage of a green valley; then above that (connected by ramps) three small stages, the bower of Flora on the right, the house of Night on the left, and between them the hill of Diana with her sacred tree.[12] From the place Campion proceeds to the persons: four speaking parts and nine dancers, including the powerful Howards: Theophilus Howard, Lord Walden; Sir Thomas Howard; and others of the king's officers:[13] "Their number Nine, the best and amplest of numbers, for as in Musicke seven notes containe all varietie, the eight being in nature the same with the first, so in numbring after the ninth we begin again, the tenth beeing as it were the Diappason in Arithmetick. The number of 9 is famed by the Muses and Worthies, and it is of all the most apt for chaunge and diversitie of proportion. The chiefe habit which the Maskers did use is set forth to your view in the first leafe: they presented in their fayned persons the Knights of Apollo, who is the father of heat and youth, and consequently of amorous affections" (*D*, 213). Now for the action. It begins with music and song: Flora and Zephirus the West Wind (a pair immortalized in Botticelli's "Primavera") are plucking and strewing flowers all over the stage while a tenor and a soprano clothed as "Silvans" or fauns and Zephirus sing a three-part song accompanied by three lutes and a bandora. It is a lovely song, in dance form of AABAAB though they are not dancing.[14] It directs the action, its refrain being the command to "strowe aboute" (*D*, 215); and it links spreading flowers to singing, as if the two can blend: "Strowe aboute, strowe aboute, / And mixe them with fit melodie." The song is about the marriage this action prepares for, and marriage is related to the political mingling of the "princely" white and red roses—the flowers of York and Lancaster that Henry VIII and then Elizabeth brought together, and that James, in seeking to unite England and Scotland, continues together.[15] The song being ended, Flora speaks of the sacred occasion of marriage marked by flowers "figuring" beauty and youth, and explains that these flowers are not subject "To winters wrath and cold mortalitie" (*D*, 216). Zephirus echoes her in the male mode, relating marriage to the time when Venus brings "Into the naked world the greene-leav'd spring" and promising fertility. Then the Silvans sing a three-part dialogue-song on maidenhood versus marriage, ending on a classical wedding chorus, "Sing Io, Hymen: Io, Io, Hymen" (*D*, 217).

The masque begins with a mythological version, by female and male deities of nature, of a wedding preparation. But it is rudely interrupted by a sudden spectacular revelation: "This song being ended the whole vale is sodainly drawne, the grove and trees of gold, and the hill with *Dianas* tree, are at once discovered. *Night* appears in her house with her 9 houres" (D, 217). Night threatens to take over the plot and thwart the marriage: she represents Diana "The Moone and Queen of Virginitie," who forbids that one of her chaste nymphs be pressed into marriage and further magnifies the depredation by pointing to the nine golden trees that are Apollo's knights transformed because they tried to seduce Diana's nymphs:

> Here they are fixt, and never may remove
> But by *Dianaes* power that stucke them here.
> *Apollos* love to them doth yet appeare,
> In that his beames hath guilt them as they grow,
> To make their miserie yeeld the greater show.
> But they shall tremble when sad *Night* doth speake,
> And at her stormy words their boughes shall breake.
>
> (D, 218)

Speech and stasis, things as they are resisting change, threaten to take over from lively song and fertile movement in this debate. The strife is soon resolved, however, by a god from the machine, Hesperus, "The Evening starre foreshews that the wisht marriage night is at hand." He explains to Night that Apollo has pacified Diana who is now

> well content her Nymph is made a Bride,
> Since the faire match was by that *Phoebus* grac't
> Which in this happie Westerne Ile is plac't
> As he in heaven, one lampe enlightning all
> That under his benigne aspect doth fall
>
> (D, 219)

—that is, King James has sponsored the marriage. He further commands that the nine knights be released from their spell.

Night will obey, and rather suddenly changes her tune:

> If all seeme glad, why should we onely lowre?
> Since t'expresse gladnes we have now most power.
> Frolike, grac't Captives, we present you here
> This glasse, wherein your liberties appeare:
> *Cynthia* is pacified, and now blithe *Night*
> Begins to shake off melancholy quite.
>
> (D, 219)

The interruption has been conceived as a clash in tone or feeling, Night at first complaining that the tragic loss of a virgin has become "sport" for Flora, Zephirus responding by words that seem to her "wanton." Now with this change of heart (like Kafka's leopards in the temple) Night becomes (naturally) the friend to lovers and will direct the remaining action of the masque, as if she were its dancing-master.[16] She asserts a wonder: the trees will dance, for "joy moun-taines moves," and it is joy that will cause dancing, while "Dancing and musicke must prepare the way" for their retransformation into living, sentient beings:

> Move now with measured sound,
>   You charmed grove of gould,
> Trace forth the sacred ground
>   That shall your formes unfold.
>   (D, 221)

The song accompanies the dance in question—probably the "mea-sures" or a slow pavane—and directs its movement, impelling the nine golden trees toward King James and the couple:

> Yet neerer *Phoebus* throne
>   Mete on your winding waies,
> Your Brydall mirth make knowne
>   In your high-graced *Hayes*.

The song is set to the same music as "The peacefull westerne winde" (*Second Booke*, 12), and beneath both one hears the traditional "Wes-tron wynde" melody that alludes to Zephirus and his power to revive natural heat.[17] The dancing long wished-for is beginning: first dance of trees setting life in motion, then transformation:

Presently the *Silvans* with their foure instruments and five voices began to play and sing together the song following, at the beginning whereof that part of the stage whereon the first trees stoode began to yeeld, and the three formost trees gently to sincke, and this was effected by an Ingin plac't under the stage. When the trees had sunke a yarde they cleft in three parts, and the Maskers appeared out of the tops of them; the trees were sodainly con-vayed away, and the first three Maskers were raysed againe by the Ingin. They appeared then in a false habit, yet very faire, and in forme not much unlike their principall, and true robe. It was made of greene taffatie cut into leaves, and laid upon cloth of silver, and their hats were sutable to the same. (D, 221–22)

Campion's marginal note indicates that they had some difficulty re-moving the trees: apparently a stage hand had forgotten to reattach the trees to an engine after displaying them to the nobility the day before (see *D,* 222, n. 44). At any rate, the transformation proceeds by stages. First Night's feelings and the nature of her involvement were changed, then the trees by her natural magic become more human, in the intermediate appearance of leafy men. The second stage is accomplished by a "Song of transformation":

> *Night* and *Diana* charge,
> And th'Earth obayes,
> Opening large
> Her secret waies,
> While *Apollos* charmed men
> Their formes receive againe.
> Give gratious *Phoebus* honour then,
> And so fall downe, and rest behinde the traine.
>
> (*D,* 222)

This song is repeated three times, as Night transforms trees into leafy men three by three (in doing so breaking down the mystic 9 into the "best of numbers . . . contained in three"), ending in a great chorus to James: "Againe this song revive and sound it hie: / Long live *Apollo,* Brittaines glorious eye" (*D,* 223). To song succeeds dancing: "as soone as the *Chorus* ended, the violins, or consorte of twelve, began to play the second new daunce, which was taken in form of an Eccho by the cornetts, and then catch't in like manner by the consort of ten; sometime they mingled two musickes together, sometime plaid all at once; which kind of ecchoing musicke rarely became their *Silvan* attire, and was so truely mixed together, that no daunce could ever bee better grac't then that, as (in such distraction of musicke) it was performed by the maskers" (*D,* 223–24). The dance is a slow measure, probably the same sort of dance as "Move now with measured sound" was.[18]

The third stage of transformation must be achieved by human action of the nine men themselves, who must make obeisance to Diana's tree and make an offering of their leaves to her. This religious procession is accompanied by "a sollemne motet" in six parts sung by six "Chappell voices" with six cornets. It is a new kind of music in the masque, sacred polyphonic music, the text celebrating chastity and temperance, its movement appropriately upward:

> With spotles mindes now mount we to the tree
> Of single chastitie.

> The roote is temperance grounded deepe,
> Which the coldjewc't earth doth steepe:
>> Water it desires alone,
>> Other drinke it thirsts for none:
> Therewith the sober branches it doth feede,
>> Which though they fruitlesse be,
> Yet comely leaves they breede,
>> To beautifie the tree.
> *Cynthia* protectresse is, and for her sake
> We this grave procession make.
> Chast eies and eares, pure heartes and voices
> Are graces wherein *Phoebe* most rejoyces.
>> (*D*, 225)

This interprets allegorically as it expresses purposeful human action. In its religious moment it fully reestablishes the wedding context, as something both in nature (as it was before the interruption) and now, also, above it in transcendence. The men can now appear in their proper ceremonial attire as Knights of Apollo in crimson satin doublets and robes "layd thicke with broad silver lace" (*D*, 224), inserted spangles reflecting the light, which was centered in the sparkling jewel of their elaborate helmets with turrets and plumes, all light and feathers swaying.[19] After a third "lively" dance, with the strong trochaic beat characteristic of a galliard,[20] they move out to blend audience and pageant: "they tooke forth the Ladies, and danc't the measures with them" (the measures being a slow and stately dance, probably a pavane: see *D*, 225, n. 55).

The piece ends with Hesperus defining "this golden dreame which I report" (*D*, 210) as a moment of "new birth," after which an elaborate farewell is given to Hesperus, the evening vanishing while full night takes over with her revels, "That th'ecclipst revels maie shine forth againe" (*D*, 226). The social occasion takes over with common dancing of pavanes, galliards, courantes, allemandes, la voltas, etc., after which Night announces an end, the chorus closes with music meant to recall the song of transformation, and all go off: "This *Chorus* was performed with severall Ecchoes of musicke and voices, in manner as the great *Chorus* before. At the end whereof the Maskers, putting off their visards and helmets, made a low honour to the King, and attended his Majestie to the banquetting place" (*D*, 227).

There survive three masques that preceeded Campion's in the new reign, one per year, it seems, each Twelfth Night. Samuel Daniel's *Vision of the Twelve Goddesses* (1604), a tentative effort in the masque form, is little more than a pageant like those performed before Elizabeth I in the 1570s: he first sets a frame for his vision by having Night rouse Somnus to create a dream, then presents the dream, Sybilla first seeing the twelve goddesses with their gifts far off and then having them appear and dance while presenting their gifts to her and the kingdom, as at Christmas. There is no conflict, and very little music or dance. Daniel in his description is concerned that his speeches be printed because attention to the spectacle might have distracted the viewers, and he is concerned to establish only one extended sense for each goddess, as Thetis is meant to symbolize only power by sea.[21]

Jonson's *Masque of Blackness* (Twelfth Night, 1605) is much more theatrical, and in it Jonson shows that he had incorporated the model of Davison and Campion's *Masque of Proteus and the Adamantine Rock* at Gray's Inn back in 1594. That masque, we may remember,[22] helped set the form exploited in King James's reign: an introductory song and dialogue that lays out the myth or "device," the entry of the masquers amid spectacle, a debate ending in a song to the monarch. *Blackness* is built on this frame: the appearance of twelve Ethiopian nymphs in their seashell, the song, Niger's explanation to Oceanus that they are seeking a land that will turn them white, their landing and presenting of gifts, and their dance and the revels. There is no transformation, for *Blackness* was to be completed by *Beauty* two years later (Jonson was already thinking in terms of antimasque and masque). Speeches take up the bulk of the text, while song and dance are not integrated into the action.

Hymenaei derives its great unity from its occasion, that being the wedding of the earl of Essex and Frances Howard (the same woman whose scandalous second marriage Campion was to celebrate in 1613) on Twelfth Night, 5 January 1606. It begins as a Roman wedding ritual, with personated bride and groom, that is broken by the eruption of eight men "out of a microcosm, or globe, figuring man,"[23] representing the four humors and four affections. Reason quells the disturbance and explicates the wedding ceremony (with an extensive disquisition on the number 5 as the union of odd and even), at which point the great world dominated by Juno or order appears, the eight men join in dance with eight women representing marital virtues, and the ceremony resumes and proceeds to its end (which blends with the participants in the wedding going to bed). Here ceremony derived from the occasion creates a total form for the action.

Campion derived many elements of his first masque from these previous productions. We can trace a direct line from Daniel's procession of twelve goddesses with their gifts to Jonson's twelve Ethiopian nymphs to Campion's nine male masquers making offering to Diana. Jonson's *Hymenaei* influenced Campion especially, with its device of the interrupted ritual and its reestablishment as beginning and end, its matching of knights and ladies, even its number symbolism—Campion's disquisition on 9 almost seems a self-conscious answer to Jonson's on 5. But when compared with Campion's predecessors, three elements of difference stand out: the great increase of ritual interest, the predominant use of music and with it dance, and the considerable extension of significance into allegorical senses.

The Lord Hay's Masque develops from *Hymenaei* the device of a wedding preparation first interrupted and finally reestablished, and here and there we can even hear an echo.[24] The descent of Hesperus performs the same function of harmonizing as Reason's descent in Jonson. But in Campion's masque the forces are those of nature—flowers, night, the evening star—and so the action becomes expressive of natural change; when Hesperus descends we see at one time a message from the god and the simple coming of evening. On this natural change is founded ritual, and Campion's masque develops a full sense of ritual as the human reproduction of natural forces; it becomes, in fact, one large ritual. The progress from interruption to reestablishment is accomplished by ritual: the song of transformation that brings green men out of the shell of golden trees, and then the ceremony of dedication to Diana that brings them further into full human shape. The device is permeated by transformation, and that transformation becomes the central action of the whole masque, which finally demonstrates how we achieve our proper humanity and harmonize our universe by means of religious dedication.

It is music and dance, rather than speech, that belong to ritual, and that in fact bring about transformation. The action Night sets out starts with joy producing the external movement of dance (by analogy and by cause from the internal increased flow of blood in joy), dance leading to song of transformation, the accomplishment of which is marked by a new dance. It is not so much that music and dance are integrated into the device, as that they carry it through,

they are the main vehicles. The *Lord Hay's* is a musician's masque.˙
When we quoted Campion's opening description earlier, we left out
a portion. Here it is restored:

> The upper part, where the cloth and chaire of State were plac't, had scaf-
> foldes and seates on eyther side continued to the skreene; right before it was
> made a partition for the dauncing place; on the right hand whereof were con-
> sorted ten Musitions, with Basse and Meane lutes, a Bandora, double Sack-
> bott, and an Harpsicord, with two treble Violins; on the other side
> somewhat neerer the skreene were plac't 9 Violins and three Lutes; and to
> answer both the Consorts (as it were in a triangle) sixe Cornets, and sixe
> Chappell voyces, were seated almost right against them, in a place raised
> higher in respect of the pearcing sound of those Instruments; eighteene foote
> from the skreene, an other Stage was raised higher by a yearde then that
> which was prepared for dancing. (*D*, 211)

Eleven violins, six cornets, at least five lutes strung low and high, a
pandora (a flat-backed instrument like a guitar), a double sackbut or
bass trombone, a harpsichord: this is a large orchestra; later we hear
of oboes (or "hoboys"), and Campion tells us that he employed a total
of forty-two voices and instruments (*D*, 223). We do not know
whether or not it was typical because no other masque composer mentions it. The musicians are made an integral part of the set: they are
placed directly on stage to the left, right, and front of the dancing
area, and they carry through the numerological design of the piece by
being set in three.

Moreover, the music carries through the theme of the masque.
Andrew Sabol points out that "the most effective musical devices he
describes in *Lord Hay's Masque* are those used to gain contrast."[25] One
form contrast takes is the three dialogue songs where two, three, or
four voices come together. Another is antiphonal music, when choirs
of voices and instruments in different parts of the hall echo each
other. This is suggested by the account of the chorus at the end of
the song of transformation:

> This *Chorus* was in manner of an Eccho seconded by the Cornets, then by the
> consort of ten, then by the consort of twelve, and by a double *Chorus* of
> voices standing on either side, the one against the other, bearing five voices
> a peece, and sometime every *Chorus* was heard severally, sometime mixt, but
> in the end altogether; which kinde of harmony so distinguisht by the place,
> and by the severall nature of instruments, and changeable conveyance of the
> song, and performed by so many excellent masters as were actors in that

musicke (their number in all amounting to fortie two voyces and instruments) could not but yeeld great satisfaction to the hearers. (*D, 223*)

It is not difficult to see how these antiphonal pieces (that accompanying the dance following this song being another example: *D,* 223–24) and dialogues mime out the theme of the diverse coming together in the masque. Moreover, it is echo that takes a part in binding the whole together, the final chorus after the revels being in itself an echo of the echoing music of transformation (*D,* 227, 223).

An unusual feature is to mark the final stage action—before it moves off stage into the audience in the common measures—by the solemn six-part motet sung by the chapel choir that was normally heard in church services (*D,* 225). The text is allegorical, it interprets the religious goal while it directs the dancers to it. The music is religious, that is, church music; we may recall that Campion thought of the motet as the musical equivalent of the epic poem, for "in Musicke we yeeld the chiefe place to the grave and well invented Motet" (*D,* 15–16). The action of the masque moves to the religious level as the masquers make offering to Diana, and it is the motet that takes them there. Here toward the end we see religious ritual as the base of dramatic ritual, expressed in the music.

Finally, Campion is unusual and influential as well in making the symbolic media that comprise a masque—traditional iconography, number symbolism, the use of music to transform emotion, and dance as an emblem of order—come together to produce a variety of significances. Daniel had been quite insistent on establishing one meaning only in 1604: "And though these images have oftentimes diverse significations, . . . we took them only to serve as heiroglyphics for our present intention, according to some one property that befitted our occasion, without observing other their mystical interpretations." Pallas was for him "armed policy" and nothing else, and he bound in his single interpretations by his verse descriptions.[26] Similarly Jonson in *Blackness* chose to label his twelve nymphs pair-by-pair by means of having each pair carry "a mute hieroglyhic" or a single symbol, such as the golden tree carried by Euphoris and Aglaia signifying fertility.[27] Though Jonson moved toward the polyseimous in *Hymenaei,*[28] it was Campion who first brought it out fully.

We know of his early admiration of *The Faerie Queene* with its multiple allegorical extensions of significance, and his use of Spenser in the allegorical houses of his early Latin poem *Ad Thamesin*. In his more mature Latin poem *Umbra* he imitated the Garden of Adonis in book 3, canto 6, of *The Faerie Queene* where form and substance, male and female, the changing and the permanent come together in the various senses of exposition. And perhaps from that Spenserian moment he derived his own myth in that poem of the paradoxical union of the cold, dark, wet female center of earth and the hot, dry, male inseminating principle in the sky.[29] Later, too, in 1609 he was to express admiration for Francis Bacon's similar exfoliation of natural myth in moral and cosmological interpretations in *The Wisdom of the Ancients* (D, 418–19). That is the background to his creation of a myth for the Lord Hay and his wife with its many extensions of significance. On stage we have the action of Flora and Night; but Flora is the agent of Apollo, Night of Diana, and such agency immediately suggests extended meanings, each visible deity being an agent of an invisible deity that is both natural and transcendent.

Most immediately, we understand this action as a psychological figure that exploits the minds of the bride and groom, who see in the masque a heightened image of their moment in time: the wedding day itself, betokening joy and fruitfulness with its scattered flowers; the coming of cool, chaste Night, which seems to destroy the aura of goodness around the wedding (perhaps because the virgin bride is fearful); and, finally, the transformation of night by the light of the occasion into a time of joy and fruitfulness. When Hesperus departs, the golden moment of the masque will dissolve and the bride and groom will depart from the hall to begin that night that will be unlike any other. To this sense belong the transformations—the change of Night herself, the reduction of discord to concord by harmonious music, and the gradual change of the masquers from golden trees to green leafy men to Knights of Apollo resplendent in crimson.

In the most general sense, Campion asks his audience to enter a "golden dreame" in which marriage is seen as the human analogue of cosmic creation, for his myth, like his *Umbra*, deals with the original opposition of principles in nature, female potential (the earth, dark, cold and wet, governed by Diana the moon, tending to stasis) and male passion (the heavens, light, hot and dry, governed by Apollo the sun, eager to move), the act of mutual love and grace by which they are reconciled, and the cosmic growth that results. Over this union rules the divine triad and its self-multiple nine, the first union of the female-even and the male-odd.

The uppermost sense of the masque in the minds of the general audience (if not the bride and groom) was the Anglo-Scottish Union James was arguing in Parliament that very year. The fact that James, the "Phoebus" of this Western Isle, has sponsored this wedding is enough to pacify Diana and Night; the fact that his nine knights have to embrace the values of chastity and temperance indicates something like advice to the Scots of his entourage. He has united chastity and love by the ceremony of marriage. He has reconciled two kingdoms—that of the hot male daylight and that of the cool female darkness that is reluctant to enter the ceremony but eventually does. If Night and night represent England in one sense, Flora and daylight Scotland, then, too, historical continuity is suggested. David Lindley reminds us that Elizabeth I throughout her career was associated with Diana goddess of chastity, and if in this masque Diana and Apollo reach concord, so too their kingdoms form a continuity that helps solidify in the minds of the audience this new reign, with all its problems and desires.[30]

The Lords' Masque

When, in The Lords' Masque of 1613, Entheus is released from the crowd of madmen, there is a strong suggestion that the palates of the masque audience have been cloyed with vanity for a while and that Entheus the poet, having regained his "libertie and fiery scope againe," will create "Inventions rare" to repair the lack. This smacks of a composer's advertisement, a heralding of Thomas Campion's return to the stage after six years' absence, with the fiery scope of his genius intact (there may even be a suggestion that his immersion in the practice of medicine was like being tossed to and fro by madmen). We know nothing of the reasons why he stayed away from the court stage for so long. His self-advertisement may have irritated Ben Jonson, who from 1607 to 1613 had dominated the masquing scene with his Beauty (1608), Queens (1609), Oberon (1611), Love Freed from Ignorance and Folly (1611), and Love Restored (1612). We do not know the circumstances, nor the nature and degree of rivalry, that might have been involved, but we do know that Jonson made fun of Campion's next masque with his Irish Masque.[31]

The suggestion surrounding Entheus seems a little uncharitable of Campion, for when he returned to the court stage after his six years of absence, the form had advanced tremendously, and he took full advantage of it. Under the hands of Jonson and Jones, it had acquired the structure of antimasque (which both contrasted and gave a foundation to the masque), masque, and revels; and it had accumulated a vast amount of theatrical technique in the forms of stage sets, machines, lighting effects, and such. Into *The Lords' Masque* Campion incorporated these elements. If in his first masque he had been a musician facing the masque, here he appears as a masque composer, in full control of the idiom that was emerging in this new genre itself.

If you were a typical Englishman, the performance on St. Valentine's Day 1613 for the wedding of the Princess Elizabeth and the Elector Palatine would have given you occasion for rejoicing. It was true that the groom was ruler of a tiny kingdom within Germany, and it might have been difficult for you to locate on a map the place along the Rhine where the borders of the Palatinate began, or its center in Heidelberg. But the Elector Palatine or the Palgrave (the name derives from *palatium,* and is related to "paladin" or palace guard) had a power that far exceeded his physical realm, having traditionally supervised the election of the Holy Roman Emperor who governed Germany and much of central Europe, and having recently become a leader of continental Protestantism. That was important. Ever since the 1580s advisors had been trying to persuade first Elizabeth and then James to make common cause with their co-religionists across the channel, joining them militarily to create something of a Protestant league against Spain and her allies. Sidney got in trouble trying to dissuade Elizabeth from marrying a French Roman Catholic, and he had died defending the Dutch against Spain. Now, after more than thirty years' delay, James was seen by many as making that much-desired move. From the eleventh century the Palgrave had been the Holy Roman Emperor's closest aide; but the role was no longer proper for Protestants, and the groom's father, Frederick IV, who ruled from 1583 to 1610 (his early death hastened by that common disease of royalty, acute alcoholism), had cast himself in the role of leader of the Protestants, establishing the Evangelical Union to combat the aggressive tendencies of Catholics within the Empire. The young Frederick V, whose uncle was the powerful Dutch Protestant leader Maurice of Nassau, continued his father's work.[32]

The masque celebrating the marriage begins as a double consort strikes up a lively tune and the curtain is raised to reveal the lower half of a perspective setting. It is a forest in deep perspective, the sides slanting inward painted with trees, the trees at the back in relief or whole round. On the left is the entrance to a cave, on the right an artificial thicket. Suddenly there emerges from the thicket the figure of Orpheus followed by tame animals. He is dressed in an antique cuirass with bases, with a robe over his shoulder, his hair long and curled with a laurel wreath on his head and a small silver bird in his hand (see *D*, 249). The consort ceases and he speaks, calling "Mania" from her dark and earthy den. The consort sounds again, and she appears out of the cave, a wild and mad old crone dressed in black, a long robe with double sleeves and a petticoat, gesturing wildly in antic fashion.[33]

He tells her that Jove (read "James," the Jove mentioned throughout as ordering the action these people accomplish for him on stage) has ordered that she set free one "Entheus" or "Poetic Fury" from the crowd of the insane she has in her charge, and that he will control the babble with the music he commands: "Let Musicke put on *Protean* changes now; / Wilde beasts it once tam'd, now let Franticks bow" (*D*, 250). And suddenly, to the tune of strange music on high wind instruments, twelve lunatics tumble out of the cave: "there was the Lover, the Selfe-lover, the melancholicke-man full of feare, the Schoole-man over-come with phantasie, the over-watched Usurer, with others that made an absolute medley of madnesse" (*D*, 250). With a change in the music, the madmen fall into a frenzied dance that exhausts them, but after a while Orpheus raises his hand and the music changes again into a soft and solemn air which quiets them. Orpheus is raising and quelling madness in them by music, and it ends when they meekly trail off the stage, back to the cave. While they were whirling about they were jostling a thirteenth figure, "*Entheus* (or Poeticke furie)," one classically dressed and very bewildered, as if he were not one of them. As they leave, he is left on stage with Orpheus. His costume shows the relation he bears to the great singer of civilization: he wears a close cuirass of the antique fashion like Orpheus's, the skin-tight sculpted cuirass that reveals the musculature of chest and shoulders like a Greco-Roman bust; he has a robe fastened to his shoulders and hanging down behind. Like Orpheus his head is encircled with laurel, but out of that wreath grows a pair of wings, and at its front it has a clasp in the shape of a star. His left arm encircles a large book, a bound folio, while he raises his right hand with a quill pen in it.[34]

These two figures face each other like person and mirror across the stage. There is a feeling of great dignity in their speeches as Orpheus explains that he has called Entheus forth at Jove's (James's) request to compose an invention to celebrate this night. Entheus replies,

> *Orpheus,* I feele the fires
> Are reddy in my braine, which *Jove* enspires.
> Loe, through that vaile, I see *Prometheus* stand
> Before those glorious lights, which his false hand
> Stole out of heav'n, the dull earth to enflame
> With the affects of Love, and honor'd Fame.
>
> (D, 251–52)

The singers burst into a song, "Come away," and after the first strophe the upper part of the curtain falls away suddenly to reveal the heavens—eight huge stars fiery on top and silver in the middle burning in the midst of varicolored clouds, in front of the scene Prometheus standing attired in cuirass, greaves, and plumed helmet like an antique hero.

Orpheus and Entheus have provided a frame. What the audience is witnessing is the process of inventing a wedding masque: what is happening on the upper stage is what those on the lower stage are imagining. The masque proper, presided over by these three great classical figures that image eternity, now begins. Prometheus has actually ordered the stars to dance. As a song urging the "musick-loving lights" to dance in honor of the confluence of the Rhine and the Thames and then to descend to human shape is sung, apparently the stars do dance: "According to the humour of this Song, the Starres mooved in an exceeding strange and delightful maner; and I suppose fewe have ever seene more neate artifice then Master *Innigoe Jones* shewed in contriving their Motion, who in all the rest of the workmanship which belong'd to the whole invention shewed extraordinary industrie and skill; which if it be not as lively exprest in writing as it appeared in view, robbe not him of his due, but lay the blame on my want of right apprehending his instructions for the adoring of his Arte" (D, 254).

The stars then vanish, as if drowned among the colored clouds, and eight masquers appear from the wings of the upper stage, while a curtain behind them resembling clouds is drawn up to reveal circles of light in motion further off in the heavens. The masquers are the transformed stars. They are dressed in cloth of silver, combining the classical cuirasses of the three presiding heroes with the more modest contemporary round breeches with bases. Around their waists are flame-shaped green leaves. What seem flames sprout from the wrists and shoulders and around their small ruffs. But their heads seem on fire, for they wear crowns of gold plate and orange enameling that seem to blend in with their hair, and a silken feather that looks like smoke emerges at the top.[35]

These are the lords who will give this entertainment its name: Lord James Hay, the king's former favorite; Philip Herbert, Sidney's nephew, now earl of Montgomery (and to be honored with his brother William as patron of Shakespeare's First Folio); and William Cecil, earl of Salisbury, son of Elizabeth's and James's secretary of state and married to one of the powerful Howard women.

Prometheus speaks again of sparks from the earth to attend the lords, and suddenly sixteen pages dart out on the lower stage. They seem half naked and all aflame, being clothed only in skin-tight cuirasses with skirts colored orange tawney like flames, wings of flame, a circlet with flames about their heads.[36] They carry large wax torches which they swing about rather dangerously, as they break into a wild and vigorous dance. Light and fire fill the room and smoke rises to the rafters.

Now a new wonder: a cloud that covers the whole stage, top to bottom, appears, and Prometheus leads the masquers down on stairs concealed within it, at the end of which procession the cloud splits in two. The lower scene has suddenly been changed, and instead of the woods there is now a two-dimensional architectural flat. It is a gorgeous facade, all gold set with rubies, sapphires, emeralds, and opals. It is Greco-Roman architecture, as if a space Orpheus and the other two have finally evoked for their exclusive use (and it may also form a compliment to the Holy Roman Empire of which Frederick is a part). There are four niches separated by gold pilasters, their capitals of the Roman composite order. Over them runs a mixed order featuring reverse scrollwork, and at the top a cornice arched slightly and touching every pilaster. In the niches stand four female statues of silver, and above each is a bas-relief in gold that seems to present part of the history of Prometheus. The statues are transformed ladies who must be awakened to love and life by the men.

The action is once more directed to the throne, where the earthly Jove sits and nods approval. Prometheus, Entheus, and Orpheus invoke Jove to release the ladies, in a brief hymn; the statues move slightly, and the men pantomime courtship of them in a galliard. It is danced to a courtly syncopated song, a rather popular contemporary cavalier piece that gives a nice sophistication to the usually less open matters of female coyness and male aggression:

> Wooe her, and win her, he that can:
>> Each woman hath two lovers,
> So shee must take and leave a man,
>> Till time more grace discovers;
> This doth *Jove* to shew that want
>> Makes beautie most respected;
> If faire women were more skant,
>> They would be more affected.
>
> Courtship and Musicke suite with love,
>> They both are workes of passion;
> Happie is he whose words can move,
>> Yet sweete notes helpe perswasion.
> Mixe your words with Musicke then,
>> That they the more may enter;
> Bold assaults are fit for men,
>> That on strange beauties venture.
>>> (*D*, 257)

The four women are transformed, and four more statues appear in their places; another invocation and courting, and all is complete. It is like rhyme. The eight ladies transformed from statues wear beautiful loose, silver dresses, with flowing gossamer veils, large fluffy ruffs, and mantles looped up on one side at the shoulder.[37]

The entertainment is moving out of the land of classical myth into the audience's world: the song is a contemporary courtly song in the meter of a galliard, and the masquers wear costumes like the clothes the fashionable audience is wearing. It becomes directed at the wedding party at this stage, for while the lords and ladies rest between dances a dialogue song with chorus wishes good luck to the bride and groom (*D*, 258–59). Also, the dancing has moved down the ramp into the dancing area of the banqueting room. The staged entertainment starts to blend with its viewers. The eight lords and eight ladies take partners from the audience, and the revels begin.

An hour passes in this social dancing. Then a brief song calls a halt, and the curtains that had been closed during the dancing rise to reveal a whole new scene—a long Greco-Roman perspective with porticos receding into the distance, in its center a large silver obelisk whose top is lost in clouds with its lights, on either side statues of the bride and groom, now mirrored in gold (*D*, 259). Now that love has been celebrated, it is time for fame. A sage old woman, the Roman Sybil, in a golden robe, and veiled, pulls the obelisk forward on the stage with a single thread of gold. She chants in a high voice after the fashion of the time a long poem in Latin about joining Great Britain and Germany in unity (*D*, 260). Then a dance, and she prophesies again, in Latin; this time Orpheus and Prometheus paraphrase her blessing of bride and groom with a large progeny. There is a song (reminiscent of one of the corontos in the revels) and a final new dance as all sixteen masquers go out (*D*, 262).

James went to great expense for his daughter's wedding. The cloth for wedding and masque was extensive, over 700 yards of satin, over 230 pounds of lace, 204 yards of copper stuffs, 318 yards of tinsel, etc. It is known that Campion was paid slightly over sixty-six pounds for his libretto, Jones fifty pounds for his designs, thirty or forty pounds each to the dancing masters Jerome Herne, Thomas Giles, one Buchan, and one Confess, ten or twenty pounds apiece to the composers Giovanni Coperario, Robert Johnson, and Thomas Giles for music, a pound apiece to the ten members of the king's violins, a pound apiece to the twelve "Madfolkes" and the five speakers of parts.

Sir John Finett, master of the ceremonies, thought that the masque "was performed with exceeding charge and commendable discharge, . . . the devyse was ingeniously cast, the dances well figured." But John Chamberlain was impatient: "That night was the Lords maske whereof I heare no great commendation, save only for riches, theyre devises beeing long and tedious, and more like a play than a maske"—he liked dancing more than dialogue. But the Venetian ambassador Antonio Foscarini focussed on the sets; for him the masque "was very beautiful, with three changes of scene. . . . certain stars danced in the heavens by a most ingenious device."[38]

It is Stephen Orgel's opinion that "the effects that Jones created for this production comprise almost an anthology of scenic machinery of that time,"[39] and we have heard how much the Venetian ambassador, who must have witnessed much sophisticated staging in his native Italy, admired its changes of setting and the "most ingenious device" by which stars were made to dance in the heavens. The first setting is divided in half horizontally, and the antimasque takes place against the lower half alone, that being a setting in depth, "a wood in pro-spective, the innermost part being of releave or whole round, the rest painted" (*D*, 249). It is all horizontal. When Entheus is freed from the limited perspective of madness and imagines for his poem the pre-siding figure of Prometheus, his vision is both literally and metaphor-ically true. The veil of imagination is the curtain of the stage, because after the first strophe of the song of invocation, "In the end of the first part of this Song, the upper part of the Scene was discovered by the sodaine fall of a curtaine; then in clowdes of severall colours (the upper part of them being fierie, and the middle heightned with sil-ver) appeared eight Starres of extraordinarie bignesse, which so were placed as that they seemed to be fixed betweene the Firmament and the Earth; in the front of the Scene stood *Prometheus*, attyred as one of the ancient Heroes" (*D*, 252). Prometheus is the surrogate figure of the poet within his fiction, the stars a reification of his fiery brain. It is a mirror and a complement. The release of imagination with its light and fire completes the lower world of earth by evoking the up-per world of the heavens in imagination and then producing it.

The world is now whole. The triad of power and poetry sets out the ceremony whose essence is bringing the stellar into human life. The Orphic song first makes the "musick-loving lights" of eight stars dance in the heavens "in an exceeding strange and delightful maner" that so impressed the Venetian ambassador. Then—probably on flats—the scene of clouds was drawn aside to reveal "an Element of artificiall fires, with severall circles of lights, in continuous motion, representing the house of *Prometheus*" (254); this scenic change accom-panies the transformation of the stars into eight masquers in costume that recall their wedding apparel.

Action now turns vertical. Prometheus from above invokes fiery spirits that "Breake forth the earth like sparks" from below (*D*, 255), and the fires of heaven and earth now combine as the fiery masquers descend to join with the fires of earth on a huge transparent cloud that fills the stage from top to bottom. The cloud—probably com-posed of a flat surrounded by smoke from a cloud machine—breaks in two and reveals the second setting. In place of the woods in the lower half of the set we now have classical architecture with four fe-male statues in niches. The set is glittering and two-dimensional. The geography is deliberately ambiguous, for this should be the House of Prometheus in the heavens but it seems to have been trans-ferred to earth, in order to be palpable. This is the scene of corresponding transformation, when eight female statues and eight male stars become human and dance together.

The varied and ingenious scenes have taken us from wild nature to civilization with its complex and harmonious architecture; it is here that the revels of the court take place. When the revels are ended we have our third setting. Gone are the divisions between upper and lower, for now the scene is one from floor to ceiling. It is a perspective scene signifying unity, "a prospective with Porticoes on each side, which seemed to go in a great way" as had the woods before (D, 259). It is about depth, reaching into the past—a Palladian perspective on a Roman piazza with the obelisk of Egypt and Rome at its center. It is here that Sybilla prophesies in Latin, evoking fame, continuity, and the permanent values.

The structure of the masque, formed on the Jonsonian model, likewise stresses evolution. It begins with Mania, a nightmare vision of mankind dominated by a chaos of passions and delusions. This antimasque is the basis of the rest, so it is not so much dispersed as purified. For Entheus or "poetic fury" or "the imagination" is filtered out of the crowd. Orpheus the primordial poet and orderer of nature purges from the primordial flux of emotions the most valuable passion placed in mankind. "Poetic Fury" creates a fiction that comes to life (as the fire in his brain leads to stars and lights): Prometheus the man of fire and power is the reification of his words, it is he who is imagined to unite heaven and earth, to bring down ethereal virtuous man from heaven and unite him with the earthly art of the beautiful female element. Gone is the original opposition of Mania-earth-low-dark and Orpheus-heaven-high-light, for they are now united in a fertility imaged as constructing a world. The poet having had a vision of reasonable, virtuous, and loving mankind and then created it as real, his work is over; it is taken up and given permanence by a female, the prophetess Sybilla, under whose aegis the masque moves from its social revels to its transcendent conclusion out of time.

What is this about? It is about language; it is about poetry; it is about civilization. It builds on the ancient myth of Orpheus to show the magical language of the poet divinely inspired bringing about a progressively more continuous and permanent civilization. It moves from the dim past to a classical present, out to a deep-resounding future. It is an ever-fuller evocation of completeness: "The number's now complete," cries Entheus (D, 258). A. Leigh DeNeef presents this masque as "a formal celebration of the nature and function of poetry."[40] For him, the four central characters represent an analysis, as in a spectrum, of four elements of poetry. Orpheus, mover of trees and tamer of beasts, represents the form-giving or shaping power of poetry, the way it makes the chaos of life's experiences yield a vision of order. Entheus, who has been released from flux by this shaping activity, is poetic inspiration, the divine spark from above that gives life to shape. His creature Prometheus represents ornament, by which DeNeef means not only the attractive surface but the principles of symmetry, completeness, and measure that control the actual poem with its encapsuled vision.[41] Finally, Sybilla represents the prophetic function of poetry when all three previous elements are in place, the power of poetry not only to embody but to extend life. From form to inspiration to a formed whole that has prophecy as its most ambitious function: this is what Elizabeth Sewell in *The Orphic Voice* calls "poetry thinking about itself,"[42] and in tracing such thought it is also tracing the progress of the civilization it sponsors. The element of ritual is strong though less overt than it was in the Lord Hay piece, but now it is shown to have power. Ritual speech creates things.

The Caversham Entertainment

When he came to publish his description of *The Lords' Masque* later in the spring, Campion included with it an account of the outdoor entertainment given to Queen Anne by Lord Knollys at Caversham near Reading on 27 and 28 April. It forms a fitting conclusion to the festivities of the wedding, for it marks the royal lady's return to private life. Two months after the marriage, Anne and James bade farewell to Elizabeth and Frederick at Gravesend; and ten days later, on 24 April, Queen Anne began her progress toward Bath, which she repeatedly visited for the gout. Of this progress, John Chamberlain wrote, "The King brought her on her way to Hampton Court; her next move was to Windsor, then to Causham, a house of the Lord Knolles not far from Reading, where she was entertained with Revells, and a gallant mask performed by the Lord Chamberlain's four sons, the Earl of Dorset, the Lord North, Sir Henry Rich, and Sir Henry Carie, and at her parting presented with a dainty coverlet or quilt, a rich carrquenet, and a curious cabinet, to the value in all of 1500 l" (*D*, 234).[43]

It is a much simpler piece than the masque, naturally employing no theatrical effects, having no governing device but only a continued cast of characters. Instead of an opening description of the scene, there is a brief description of the estate, and the bulk of the text is taken up with the speeches that were presented. Campion's goal seems to have been to surround the two-day visit with a light fiction. It falls into three parts: an outdoor piece performing a ceremony of welcome on Tuesday, an indoor piece celebrating the queen's transforming presence in a revels after supper, and a farewell ceremony with gifts on Wednesday morning.

The first piece takes Queen Anne through three stages, with pauses at the approach, at the park gate, and at the gardens before the house. For the first: "it shall be convenient, in this generall publication, a little to touch at the description and situation of *Cawsome* seate. The house is fairely built of bricke, mounted on the hill-side of a Parke within view of *Redding,* they being severed about the space of two miles. Before the Parke-gate, directly opposite to the House, a new passage was forced through earable-land, that was lately paled in, it being from the Parke about two flight-shots in length, at the further end whereof, upon the Queenes approach, a *Cynick* appeared out of a Bower" (*D, 235*). The Cynic presents a speech in favor of solitude, which is countered by "a fantastick Traveller" who has been secretly inserted into the queen's party on horseback. After the Traveller has converted the Cynic to the values of society, they go on together with the party to the park gate, where two Keepers and two "Robin-Hood-men in sutes of greene" (*D, 237*) meet the queen and offer her formal greeting, with a five-part song and a "Silvan-dance of six persons." Song and dance have succeeded to dialogue and involve the queen, and when she and her party are met in the lower garden by the Gardener and his boy language flourishes. There has been a progression in language: the Cynic had been plain and boorish—"Naked I am, and so is truth; plaine, and so is honestie" (*D, 236*)—the Traveller fantastic in his mock-logic. The Keeper and Robin-Hood-men had been plain but well intentioned—"accept such rude intertainment as a rough Wood-man can yeeld" (*D, 238*). The Gardener speaks in a homespun country version of the Euphuism that had been popular back in the 1580s: "Most magnificient and peerelesse Diety, loe, I the surveyer of Lady *Floras* workes, welcome your grace with fragrant phrases into her Bowers, beseeching your greatnesse to beare with the late woodden entertainment of the Wood-men; for Woods are more full of weeds then wits, but gardens are weeded, and Gardeners witty, as may appeare by me" (*D, 240*).

As language becomes more "flowery," it traces a rustic vision of the progress of civilization, from wilderness to forest to garden, whence Anne is guided to the door of the house. The second part of the entertainment takes place in the hall of the estate, the seat of its full civilization, and it is a miniature masque. The antimasque collects the characters of the welcoming ceremony: Traveller, Gardener, and Cynic appear, all appropriately drunk, and utter ridiculous speeches. The Traveller's mock-logic turns in on himself—"if we presse past good manners, laugh at our follies, for you cannot shew us more favour, then to laugh at us" (*D*, 243)—the Gardener becomes fulsomely self-satisfied, the Cynic rubbing his eyes in wonder at the combined effects of wine and the royal personage (*D*, 243–44). The three harmonize in a song betokening fellowship and the union of the different, and then they disperse—"Let us give place, for this place is fitter for Dieties then us" (*D*, 245). The indoor scene dominated by the presence of the queen resets rustic harmony as ridiculous.

What caused them to disperse was the appearance of a deity, the god "*Silvanus*, shapt after the description of the ancient Writers. His lower parts like a Goate, and his upper parts in an anticke habit of rich Taffetie, cut into Leaves" (*D*, 244–45). He represents myth, perhaps the myth of the world like Bacon's Pan, the lower parts linking him to earth while the upper parts reach to the sky.[44] It is his duty to present transcendence, and in his speech we observe for the first time a change from prose to verse. He praises the power of Queen Anne that transcends his, and then presents the masquers. They enter to "a great noise of drums and phifes" (*D*, 245), dance their entry, and then proceed to the little masque's third part, the revels that consume the rest of the night, the gouty queen deigning "graciously to adorne the place with her personall dancing" (*D*, 246).

The third part of the entertainment consists of a brief farewell speech by the Gardener, now speaking dignified verse about his "flowrie incantation" (*D*, 247), and the presentation of gifts, while a final three-part song is performed by three handsome country maidens. The action of transcendence that took place within the house the evening before leaves everything simple, dignified, and generous at its threshold.

The two pieces of this publication came out together printed in reverse chronological order, first the Caversham entertainment of April, then *The Lords' Masque* of the preceding February. That arrangement

seems designed to highlight a progression in tone from clowning in
the country to stately action at court. These two tones (each of which
rises, within its limitations, by deliberate modulations of style, one
from rustic pretentiousness to the high style in verse, the other from
mad babble to Latin verse) correspond to their respective occasions.
The entertainment is designed to raise the spirits of a queen who has
just lost her daughter to a husband, while the masque celebrates great
affairs of state. What the two have in common is the theme of language and its power to trace and influence the evolution of civilization. The way they go together redoubles that evolution.

The Squires' Masque

In the court masque, that form that pulled together the skills he
was master of, Campion was exploring questions of meaning or significance: his technique settled, he could plumb the problems of what
it all meant. In his first masque he was an interpreter of nature: by
evoking the allegorical senses he unfolded for his audience the nature
of nature as conjunctions of opposites in the cosmic, human, and political realms. In *The Lords' Masque* he used the nature of poetic creation as its own scaffolding, the foundation of a suggestive device
about the power of poetic language to create and make stable. His
progress is analogous to what Michel Foucault finds as a great turn
from sixteenth-century interpretation of a divinely ordered world by
finding analogies, to the seventeenth-century representation of a
world in which differences and distinctions play a major part.[45] And
in his final masque he assays a direct representation of this-our-world
as it exists, first in appearance and then in reality. This was a bold
stroke: masques never before had been dedicated to mimesis.

Campion begins his description of *The Squires' Masque* with a theoretical statement:

In ancient times, when any man sought to shadowe or heighten his Invention, he had store of feyned persons readie for his purpose, as *Satyres,
Nymphes,* and their like: such were then in request and beliefe among the
vulgar. But in our dayes, although they have not utterly lost their use, yet
finde they so litle credit, that our moderne writers have rather transfered
their fictions to the persons of Enchaunters and Commaunders of Spirits, as
that excellent Poet *Torquato Tasso* hath done, and many others.

In imitation of them (having a presentation in hand for Persons of high State) I grounded my whole Invention upon Inchauntments and several transformations. (*D*, 268)

For him, the age of myth and fiction was over—as it was for Donne, who, Carew asserted, had banished the Ovidian trains of gods and goddesses from verse.[46] He is making a statement about Jacobean society: it is much more likely to be confused by rumor and false appearance than it is to be raised to a level of vision by myth as in Elizabeth's day. Enchantment and illusion are false myths; they distort rather than ennoble life. What is needed is an accurate rendering of the life we experience—as well as the necessary appreciation of such a rendering. The change involves a stress on the psychological perception of reality rather than interpreting reality in absolute metaphysical terms.

The realism of this masque consists in its depiction of myth as falsehood and in its coasting so near the actual occasion it celebrates: for the device of the twelve Knights enchanted by the evil illusions of Rumor and freed by the sufferance of Queen Anne seems deliberately designed as a tactful attempt to lift opprobrium from the countess of Essex's remarriage. We have recounted the sordid background to the occasion before, in the murder of Sir Thomas Overbury.[47] Rumors about the actual murder did not surface until the following spring and summer, but as of 26 December 1613 there was suspicion enough. People knew that the wedding was a culmination of the attempt of the Howard family to gain influence over Robert Car, earl of Somerset, the successor to James Hay as King James's favorite. To that end they encouraged Car's passion for Frances Howard and finally even managed to have her marriage to Essex annulled in order to pave the way for Car. The annulment proceedings, which concluded on 25 September, were a messy business: it had to be proved that Essex was impotent. Furthermore, court gossips knew that the two had been sleeping together since the previous spring: no matter of cool chaste Diana opposing Flora, this. The Yuletide wedding was an unabashed and even shameless Howard triumph: four of the dancers were Howards, and four others may have been pressed into duty in order to guarantee legitimacy, since they had danced in Jonson's *Hymenaei* celebrating the countess's first marriage, that had just been so scandalously dissolved, back in 1606 (see *D*, 264, 284).

For a masque, the setting is doggedly mundane. Instead of bowers of goddesses or the heavens with moving stars which become the House of Prometheus, we have a triumphal arch as proscenium with a familiar landscape or seascape within it:

The place wherein the Maske was presented, being the Banquetting house at White Hall, the upper part, where the State is placed, was Theatred with Pillars, Scaffolds, and all things answerable to the sides of the Roome. At the lower end of the Hall, before the Sceane, was made an Arch Tryumphall, passing beautifull, which enclosed the whole Workes. The Sceane it selfe (the Curtaine being drawne) was in this manner divided.

On the upper part there was formed a Skye with Clowdes very arteficially shadowed. On either side of the Sceane belowe was set a high Promontory, and on either of them stood three large pillars of golde; the one Promontory was bounded with a Rocke standing in the Sea, the other with a Wood. In the midst betwene them apeared a Sea in perspective with ships, some cunningly painted, some arteficially sayling. On the front of the Sceane, on either side, was a beautifull garden, with six seates a peece to receave the Maskers; behinde them the mayne Land, and in the middest a payre of stayres made exceeding curiously in the form of a Schalop shell. And in this manner was the eye first of all entertayned. (D, 268–69)

This is representation. It is notable that the setting is made to include the auditorium, the pillars near the chairs of state partaking of the architectural motif set by the arch, all "Theatred." That is important, for Queen Anne will take a central part in the masque, and that will signify to the onlookers that she has overcome her initial opposition to the wedding. And instead of a ceremony—or any music or dance—the piece opens with a bare narrative report. Four Squires (hence the alternative title, *The Squires' Masque,* as well as *The Somerset Masque*) who have narrowly escaped shipwreck tell how twelve Knights who had set sail to attend the wedding have been baffled by a storm at sea caused by Error, Rumor, Curiosity, and Credulity: six of the Knights vanished into the air at sea, while the other six were transformed into the pillars the audience sees on land (and sees reflected about them in the "theatred" room). The relation is dramatized: the first Squire can scarcely finish his account to King James because of exhaustion, while the fourth breaks out in fear at the arrival of Error and his train.

The antimasque is a bit unusual in that it is concluded entirely in pantomime. The four enchanters the Squires have mentioned—Error

like a serpent (from book 1 of *The Faerie Queene*), Rumor clothed in
tongues, Curiosity in eyes, and Credulity in ears—enter and whisper
a while "as if they had rejoyced at the wrongs which they had done
to the Knights" (*D*, 271) and then begin to dance. They are joined
by three quaternities: "strait forth rusht the foure Windes con-
fusedly," "After them in confusion came the foure Elements," "Then
entred the four parts of the earth in a confused measure" (*D*, 271).
The antimasque of the world in mute confusion is dispersed by the
arrival of the delegation of value: Eternity, the three Destinies carrying a golden tree, and Harmony with nine musicians. Mere bodily
action is replaced by song, song moreover that has as its goal direction of purposeful action:

CHORUS.

Vanish, vanish hence, confusion;
Dimme not *Hymens* goulden light
With false illusion.
The Fates shall doe him right,
And faire Eternitie,
Who passe through all enchantements free.

ETERNITIE SINGES ALONE.
Bring away this Sacred Tree,
The Tree of Grace and Bountie,
Set it in Bel-Annas eye,
For she, she, only she
Can all Knotted spels unty.
Pull'd from the Stocke, let her blest Hands convay
To any suppliant Hand, a bough,
And let that Hand advance it now
Against a Charme, that Charme shall fade away.

Toward the end of this Song the three destinies set the Tree of Golde before the Queene.
(*D*, 272)

Eternity's solo song is a celebrated piece: it was set by Nicholas Lanier
in the new declamatory or monodic style, thus making the music par-
take of the realism of this masque by being reduced to heightened
unmelodic speech.[48] The musical setting gives the song a feeling of
personal urgency (one that contrasts with the dance melody of the
next song when the purpose has been happily achieved), and so in

brief space we have shifted, from a choric exorcism in the ceremonial mode, to a feeling personal persuasive lyric, to the action of setting the tree before the queen.

When "the Queene puld a branch from the Tree and gave it to a Nobleman, who delivered it to one of the Squires" (*D*, 273), the enchantments dissolve to a new melodic song in dance meter, "Goe, happy man, like th'Evening Starre": six Knights appear in a cloud, the other six are suddenly transformed out of the pillars of gold. And the wedding can now be celebrated in a combination of song and dance: the masquers perform their first dance in three sections, between them appearing three strophes of a hymn "While dancing rests" (*D*, 274). That hymn, deliberately separate from the dance mode in its religious elements, expresses marriage by an echo-effect signifying meeting and bringing in other voices that modulate from nature's meetings to the religious chorus "Io, Io Hymen." The main masque is very short, little more than an interlude between the grotesque antimasque of illusion that the world has no order, and the revels with their planned combination of social order and disorder.

The revels conclude with the entrance of twelve sailors who dance a hornpipe and then convey the twelve Knights away to their waiting ships. It is notable that the revels are brought to an end by a set of characters from the lower classes who would normally be part of the antimasque, and they have come not for a ceremonial but a practical purpose, to row people back to their ships before the tide turns. Their music, like that of "Bring away this Sacred Tree," is close to sounds the audience actually heard in life: heightened speech, a sailor's dance.[49]

The Golden Bough that is the pivot of the plot does not merely dissolve enchantments; it was the traditional guide through the underworld, but as "Grace and Bountie" it also guides us through an upper world that often seems confusing. It brings the audience into the actual world they inhabit, for at the moment when the Knights appear, "on the sodaine the whole Sceane is changed: for whereas before all seemed to be done at the sea and sea coast, now the Promontories are sodainly remooved, and London with the Thames is very arteficially presented in their place" (*D*, 273). To dissolve enchantment is not only to release the Knights but also to release us, to bring us into reality and activate the wedding celebration. In place of the confusion of the elements, we now have the natural cycle of the seasons—"Sweete springs, and *Autumn's* fill'd with due increase" (*D*,

275)—that frames love's ceremony. What had been miraculous elements become mundane: in a wedding dialogue the miraculous golden tree of Destiny is caught up in an image and becomes a natural tree serving as an emblem of fertility: "Set is that Tree in ill houre / That yeilds neither fruite nor flowre" (*D*, 275). And "Eternity" becomes a matter of blessing the couple with hopes of children so as to leave "a living Joy behind" (*D*, 275). The sailors who announce the end of the revels are ordinary sailors—"Straight in the Thames appeared foure Barges with skippers in them" (*D*, 275)—and they sing a colloquial song—"Come a shore, come, merrie mates"—while dancing a hornpipe. It ends as realistic representation: the myth was the illusion.

This is the bare bones of a masque entertainment. The text we have is one of the shortest of those publications, yet we know that it began at 11:00 P.M. and ended at 2:00 A.M.[50] One reason for its slightness is that the bulk of the action is contained and carried by music and dance, which are indicated rather than narrated in full. Another is that it is compressed, because much of the action is not explained in speeches but incorporated into the song and dance. For example, we know from their song that the sailors have come to tell the Knights it is time to embark. It was so compressed as to cause misunderstanding. The agent of Savoy attended, and to him the four Squires were merely "four men dressed poorly" who spoke in a funereal accent unsuited to a wedding, the tree "signifying the olive" of peace, the confused antimasque "a masque of twelve devils."[51] It was not simply that the agent Gabaleoni's English was at fault, for he did not attend to the visual iconography of the antimasque (iconography being in fact a science that grew up in his native Italy). The antimasque is compressed, and demands interpretation. The four enchanters form a solipsistic pattern among themselves. Credulity's ears lie open to receive the messages of Rumor's tongues, Curiosity's eyes are dazzled by the serpent Error, and the four form two couples, two men and two women for completeness. The elements of the world that enter to dance to their dance, Gabaleoni's twelve devils, represent Error's distortion of reality as something confused and chaotic. Error and Rumor not only throw one off course, but make the world seem frightening and threatening. The personified values that disperse them are abstract, but they are not so much virtues of the mind as representatives of what is—Eternity or how things have always been and will be, the three Destinies or how things must be, Harmony with nine musicians the elements of nature as it really exists with the nine spheres, and so forth. Number symbolism is involved as it was in 1607; 4 as the mundane sphere superseded by the divine number 3 and its multiples, then 12 Knights the product of their multiplication, and so on. Land and sea are disjoined by Error and his troop and rejoined by Queene Anne, under whose aegis the symbolism of 3 continues into the three sections of the wedding hymn.

The masque celebrates the reality it represents on many planes. But reality, we say, is a tricky business, by definition beyond our control. One thing Campion did not count on was the incompetence of the Florentine designer Constantine de Servi: as Gabaleoni recounts it with the relish of an Italian rival state, the device for lowering the cloud with six of the Knights in it was constructed as one makes a portcullis, and when the cloud came down the audience could see the ropes and hear the pulleys groaning away as they do when you raise the mast of a ship. The Savoyard concludes, "Apart from having seen their Majesties in good order and with great majesty, and also the great number of ladies, one could see nothing that came anywhere near meriting the inconvenience of the thousands of people who waited twelve hours without dinner."[52] Then of course the whole occasion blew up next autumn, when Campion was examined and his great patron Monson imprisoned under suspicion of having taken part in the conspiracy to murder Overbury.

Campion's big year was 1613: it was the year he published three books of songs in two volumes and composed three masque entertainments. It was marked, as we have seen, by an embracement of the psychological, of perception, of the actual. In the texts of the songs of that year he developed contrast, the literal and factual, and he was developing a style that would culminate in a dry realistic tone that encouraged a vibrant complexity of attitude. In his music he was incorporating many different voices, and was moving toward heightened speech rather than suggestive dance melody as a model for what music should be. These tendencies were to flower in his last song book in 1617. In the masques he kept throughout the overall theme of chaos yielding to order, but his means became progressively more spare, from the complex allegory of *The Lord Hay's Masque* to a naked presentation of the civilizing power of language to make a masque or a world in *The Lords' Masque*. Here in *The Squires' Masque* he stripped down the form to a spare diagram consisting of little more than an antimasque in pantomime followed by a spectacular but brief transformation scene. But the transformation did not catapult him or his audience into the wonderful; rather, it landed them in the world. What they all saw at the beginning was a tumult of elements, continents, and other personifications of the world—an illusion—and what they saw at its end was a crew of sailors coming up the Thames, disembarking, dancing a hornpipe. The masque became for Campion a means of clarifying what in fact quotidian London life was, rather than an ennoblement of it. And when the year of reality, 1613, was over, he had seen enough of it. He left the stage.

Chapter Seven
Reputation

Early Notice

During his lifetime Thomas Campion was known mainly as a Latin poet. At least, that is what the written records tell us. The first mention of him in print occurs in 1593 when he was twenty-six and virtually unpublished. In his prologue to *The Honour of the Garter* George Peele invokes the best poets of his time who are, he asserts, worthy to join Sidney in the Elisian fields and enjoy their fame. His list includes "Marley, the Muses darling," Gabriel Harvey, Sir John Harington, Thomas Watson, and a group of young poets consisting of Daniel ("Rosamond's trumpeter"), Campion, and Fraunce:

> Why thither speedes not Rosamond's trumpeter,
> Sweet as the Nightingal? Why goest not thou,
> That richly cloth'st conceites with well made words,
> Campion, accompanied with our English Fraunce,
> A peerlesse sweet Translator of our time?[1]

With the publication of the Latin *Poemata* in 1595 the tributes came fast. That same year William Covell published his *Polimanteia* in which, after praising Oxford and its poets, he turned to Cambridge in this Euphuistic passage: "I know, *Cambridge,* howsoeuer now old, thou hast some young, bid them be chast, yet suffer them to be wittie; let them be soundly learned, yet suffer them to be gentlemanlike qualified," and he clarified the reference in the margin by adding "Sweet Master Campiõ."[2] The next year Sir John Davies may have been referring to him and his poem *Umbra* when he wrote, "O could I sweet Companion, sing like you, / Which of a shadow, under a shadow sing. . .," and his friend Thomas Nashe congratulated him on showing up their mutual butt of ridicule Barnabe Barnes, in these terms:

One of the best Articles against *Barnes* I have overslipt, which is that he is in Print for a Braggart in that universall applauded Latine Poeme of Master *Campions;* where in an Epigram entituled *In Barnum,* beginning thus:—

Mortales decem tela inter Gallica caesos,

he shewes how hee bragd, when he was in *France,* he slue ten men, when (fearfull cowbaby) he never heard piece shot off but hee fell flat on his face. To this effect it is, though the words somewhat varie.[3]

His friend Charles Fitzgeffrey addressed several Latin epigrams to him in his *Affaniae* (1601); in one of them he asserts that he is the second English writer of epigrams, second to St. Thomas More, in another he reinforces Campion's claim that he is the first English elegiac poet, bringing Ovid into England.[4] By 1598 his prestige was secure, and Francis Meres in that book of lists, *Palladis Tamia,* places him in the list of poets "who have obtained renown and good place among the ancient Latine poets": "These Englishmen being Latine poets, Gualter Haddon, Nicholas Car, Gabriel Harvey, Christopher Ocland, Thomas Newton with his *Leyland,* Thomas Watson, Thomas Campion, Brunswerd and Willey have attained good report and honourable advancement in the Latin empyre."[5]

By 1605, after the *Observations* and *A Booke of Ayres,* his fame is broader, and he is included in a list not of Latin poets but of English poets generally in William Camden's *Remaines:* "These may suffice for some Poeticall descriptions of our auncient Poets: if I would come to our time, what a world could I present to you out of Sir *Philipp Sidney, Ed. Spencer, Samuel Daniel, Hugh Holland, Ben. Jonson, Th. Campion, Mich. Drayton, George Chapman, Iohn Marston, William Shakespeare,* and other most pregnant witts of these our times, whom suceeding ages may iustly admire."[6] That is very good company. Even Samuel Daniel, while disputing fiercely his program of writing in classical meters, is respectful of his English output, writing that he is "a man of faire parts and good reputation," one "whose commendable rymes, albeit now himself an enemy to ryme, have given heretofore to the world the best notice of his worth."[7] Ben Jonson held himself aloof. While many circumstances threw him and Campion together—as they had Campion and Daniel—all we know is that he parodied *The Lords' Masque* in his *Irish Masque,* and that he told William Drummond that he planned to pen an answer to both Daniel and Campion.[8]

In all this contemporary mention, only two writers considered him as a song-writer rather than a poet, and they are divided evenly into praise and blame. John Davies of Hereford penned this tribute to him in an appendix to his *Scourge of Folly:*

To the most juditious and excellent Lyrick-Poet,
                     Doctor Campion.
Upon my selfe I should *just* vengeance take
Should I omitt thy mention in my *Rimes,*
Whose *Lines* and *Notes* do lullaby (awake)
In Heav'ns of pleasure, these unpleasant *Times.*
Never did *Lyricks* more then happie *straines,*
(Straind out of *Arte* by *nature;* so with ease)
So purely hitt the *moods,* and various *Vaines*
Of *musick,* and her Hearers, as do These.
So, thou canst cure the *Body,* and the *minde*
(Rare *Doctor*) with thy two-fold soundest *Arte:*
Hipocrates hath taught thee the one kinde;
Apollo and the *Muse* the other Part:
           And both so well, that thou with both dost please:
           The Minde, *with* pleasure; *and the* Corps, *with ease.*[9]

On the other hand, about the same year, 1611, we find these lines in
a manuscript commonplace book of a Cambridge student as part of a
satire *Of London Physicions:* "How now Doctor Champion, musicks and
poesies stout Champion, / Will you nere leave prating?"[10]

It is clear that his ayres were popular. His texts were attractive to
other musicians. Robert Jones reset four of his texts to his own music, Nicholas Lanier three, William Corkine, Francis Pilkington, Al-
phonso Ferrabosco, and John Dowland one apiece. There survive more
than thirty manuscript songbooks of the seventeenth century whose
owners transcribed his songs for their own personal use and delecta-
tion, most with the music, some with words only.[11] A glance through
the seventeenth-century anthologies shows that at least six of his most
popular songs continued to be reprinted through its course: "Thou art
not faire," reset by Nicholas Lanier in *Select Musicall Ayres and Dialogues* (1652), "Though your strangeness frets my hart," reset by John
Wilson in *Cheerfull Ayres or Ballads* (1660), "If Love loves truth, then
women doe not love," with a new setting both in John Playford's
Briefe Introduction to the Skill of Musick (1660) and in his *Musical Companion* (1673), "Fire, fire," reset by Lanier in Playford's second book
of *Select Ayres and Dialogues* (1669), "Young and simple though I
am," reset by Lanier in *Select Musicall Ayres and Dialogues,* and Playford's *Musical Companion,* and a parody of "Faine would I wed a faire
young man," in Thomas Davidson's *Cantus, Songs and Fancies* (1662).

Obscurity

It will be noticed that all of these reprintings utilize new settings of Campion's texts by more up-to-date composers. This fact helps explain what so puzzles scholars (like Vivian, or Lowbury, Salter, and Young): why Campion did not remain popular through the seventeenth century as Ben Jonson and other contemporaries did. The answer is that his music was outmoded, and of course his poetry had been printed as music and was thus indissolubly linked with it, for better or worse (to recall the marriage metaphor). It was the age of the new baroque composers, heirs of the monodists, Nicholas Lanier, Henry and William Lawes, then later Henry Purcell. Neither Campion nor Dowland—to say nothing of the lesser song-writers—survived this change of musical taste.

We do find an occasional echo of Campion in the later seventeenth-century poets, especially those who maintained ties with the musical tradition. For example, Thomas Stanley's "I will not trust thy tempting graces," first printed in *Select Airs and Dialogues, set by Mr. Jeremy Savill* (1659), seems to owe something to "Thou art not faire," the third and fourth lines echoing Campion's "Thy smiles and kisses I cannot endure, / Ile not be wrapt up in those armes of thine":

> I will not trust thy tempting graces
> Or thy deceitful charms;
> Nor pris'ner be to thy embraces,
> Or fetter'd in thy arms;
> No, Celia, no, not all thy art
> Can wound or captivate my heart.[12]

Likewise Owen Felltham's "Why think'st thou (fool) thy Beauties rayes," included in John Wilson's *Cheerful Ayres or Ballads,* seems to owe something of its neatness to Campion.[13] Though Robert Herrick advertised himself as a son of Ben, here and there we find an echo of a Campion epigram or song, such as "Cherrie-ripe" from "There is a Garden in her face":

> Cherrie-Ripe, Ripe, Ripe, I cry,
> Full and faire ones; come and buy:
> If so be, you ask me where

Thy do grow? I answer, There,
Where my *Julia's* lips doe smile;
There's the Land, or Cherry-Ile:
Whose Plantations fully show
All the yeere, where Cherries grow.[14]

It was music that caused Campion to flow into the lines of these poets, especially in Herrick, who nods toward Dowland in "His Lachrimae" and writes in praise of Henry Lawes, who set his texts.[15]

Of course, as we have seen, his theoretical work on contrapuntal
harmony remained to guide composers as it was incorporated into
John Playford's *Introduction to the Skill of Musick* through its many editions from 1655 to 1694. "Never weather-beaten Saile" was used as
a devotional hymn as late as 1707, and both that hymn and "Sing a
song of joy" have reentered the hymnal and are to be found today in
Songs of Praise.[16]

But by and large Campion suffered an eclipse for over two centuries
until he was rediscovered in 1886. His music fell into obscurity with
others of his time, music being so popular and therefore much more
subject to fashion than the other arts—dependent on contemporary
performance as it is—and it can scarcely be expected that he would
survive the great age of Purcell and Handel in England, or be heard
while Haydn was in London. He achieved mere mention without
comment along with Dowland in one of the two great rival histories
of 1776, Sir John Hawkins's *History of the Science and Practice of Music,*
and he was so far abandoned not even to be mentioned among the
"obscure musicians and of mean abilities," such as Dowland and
Danyel, in Charles Burney's *A General History of Music.*[17] The Romantic interest in the Elizabethan poets caused renewed interest in their
music, and in 1837 Thomas Oliphant, secretary of the Madrigal Society, issued *La Musa Madrigalesca,* including Campion's "There is a
Garden in her face" without attribution, along with several songs of
Dowland. The next year William Chappell included an anonymous
song with words by Campion (who was not even mentioned) in his
Collection of National English Airs, and he expanded it, without high-
lighting Campion, in his *Popular Music of the Olden Times* in 1859.[18]

Rediscovery

It was only when his poetry was detached from its music that Campion could be heard again. From Edward Arber's omnibus compila-

tion of lyrics from madrigals and ayres by Byrd, Yonge, Dowland, Wilbye, and others, A. H. Bullen seized upon Campion's as being of especially high quality, and gave him prominence in his anthology *Lyrics from the English Song Books* in 1886. Three years later in 1889 he issued the very first collected edition of *The Works of Doctor Thomas Campion* from the Chiswick Press, including the ayres, the masques, and *Observations* (but not the treatise on counterpoint), along with the Latin epigrams and elegies and some other English poems attributed to him. The edition was greeted with widespread enthusiasm. Swinburne wrote Bullen upon receiving his copy, "In issuing this first edition of Campion's *Works* you have added a name to the roll of English poets, and one that can never henceforward be overlooked or erased. Certainly his long neglected ghost ought now to be rejoicing in Elysium."[19] Edmund Gosse offered him these stanzas:

> Bullen, well done!
> > Where Campion lies in London-land,
> > Lulled by the thunders of the Strand,
> Screened from the sun,
>
> Surely there must
> > Now pass some pleasant gleam
> > Across his music-haunted dream,
> Whose brain and lute are dust.[20]

Campion's ghost entered literary history with George Saintsbury's *History of English Literature* (1887), five of the nine examples of verse from the songbooks being his. Ernest Rhys in 1895 called him "perhaps the one poet who comes nearest to fulfilling, in the genre and quality of his work, the lyric canon in English Poetry," and Andrew Lang in his *History of English Literature* described him as "one of the most delightful singers in the whole of English literature."[21]

Such was the state of feeling that by 1903 his original discoverer expressed fear lest he become "the object of uncritical adultion."[22] Six years later he received his first complete and full scholarly critical edition with Percival Vivian's *Campion's Works*. Finally, in 1933, he received the accolade of T. S. Eliot, who was a close student of the *Observations;* Eliot called Campion, "except for Shakespeare . . . the most accomplished master of rhymed lyric of his time." Though Eliot put Campion firmly in his place later in 1944 with "What is Minor Poetry?" he did value Campion above Herrick though below Herbert, and asserted that "within his limits there was no more accomplished craftsman in the whole of English poetry."[23] And Campion's music reached recognition from the eminent musicologist Gustave Reese, who felt that heretofore Campion's prestige in the literary field had obscured his musical excellence.[24]

And yet, from 1909 until about 1967 there was only sporadic interest in Campion—only one substantial book, by Kastendieck in 1938. Bullen's fear ironically seemed unfounded, and Campion seemed to have settled firmly into the ranks of the minor poets. These years witnessed the rise of "modernism," and with it a solidification of a canon whose roots lay in the works and interests of T. S. Eliot and others, and whose demands dominated the academic scene, scholarship, and criticism. The "New Critics" and others elevated John Donne and the "metaphysical" poets to major status as the really important poets of the English Renaissance, and metaphysical wit and the complex image as the major evidence of literary worth. Under the shadow of Donne, even Milton's reputation paled, and lesser poets like Jonson, Campion, and Herrick, who, like Milton, subordinated image to argument, found little or no room in the literary establishment (whose very existence was a prime element in modernism) at all.

Then, at the point of Campion's quatercentenary year, the tide of taste began to turn; it seems time was preparing a birthday celebration for Campion's ghost. In the years since 1967 a new critical edition and two selections appeared, two new critical studies and the first review of scholarship.[25] The poetic climate had changed. Poetry and music were approaching each other after a long separation, with the "Beat" poets giving readings to jazz backgrounds and the lyrics of popular musicians like the Beatles and Bob Dylan starting to win the respect of readers of poetry. Poetry became vocal; public readings proliferated and replaced lonely silent reading. In 1959 Robert Lowell in *Life Studies* moved from the packed imagistic poetry typical of modernism to a relaxed and plainer epistolary style, and thereby heralded "confessional poetry." Across the Atlantic poets like Donald Davie and Philip Larkin found themselves more interested in "purity of diction" and energetic syntax than in image. The academic climate changed to welcome "postmodernism" with its distrust of absolutes and its cultivation of the human voice. Frank Kermode's *Romantic Image* was the first public assertion that an image-centered poetic was not an aesthetic absolute but a product of romantic and symbolist polemics. The canon of "Imagist" poetics—and even the idea of a canon itself—began to give way. Donne's reputation declined and in his place Renaissance poets like Sidney, Spenser, and Milton began to receive attention once again, while the taut lyric definitions of Ben Jonson and the ceremonious retreats of Robert Herrick became interesting. A good index of this change, and of its import for Campion, is that the third edition of *The Norton Anthology of English Literature* (1974) anthologized nine of Campion's lyrics, giving him a separate heading rather than lumping him together with the "minor poets," while *The Norton Anthology of Poetry* included sixteen of his songs.

Campion and Modern Poetry

Campion's ghost lay waiting in the Strand for three hundred years to become an important influence on his fellow poets, for it is only in the twentieth century that poets have found themselves attracted to Campion. Three especially have written in praise of him and have incorporated some of his techniques into their own work. They form three generations.

Ezra Pound was formulating his poetic at the moment when great enthusiasm for Campion was seizing Bullen and others. From the first, he had been convinced of the necessary connection between poetry and music; in his essay "Vers Libre and Arnold Dolmetsch," for instance, he wrote with typical dogmatism, "Poetry is a composition of words set to music. . . . Poets who are not interested in music are, or become, bad poets. . . . Poets who will not study music are defective."[26] His primary center of interest in this regard was the practice of the Provençal troubadours whom he studied assiduously from 1906 on, whom he was to translate and celebrate throughout his career; but that became coupled with an interest in Elizabethan song quite early—perhaps, as John Espey suggests, because both strains appeared together in the programmatic annual anthologies of Thomas Bird Mosher called *The Bibelot* that Pound read from 1895 to 1915.[27] Campion came to represent an ideal for him, as appears clearly in his dedication of the translation of Guido Cavalcanti's great philosophical lyric "Donna mi priegha" "To Thomas Campion his ghost, and to the ghost of Henry Lawes, as prayer for the revival of music."[28]

We do not hear Campion as clearly as we do the troubadours in the verse of *Personae,* and the one poem that seems most direct, "Apparuit" in quantitative Sapphics, owes more to Robert Bridges and what indirect influence Campion exerted through him than to Campion himself.[29] Though we may think we hear a faint echo here and there, in the translations from Propertius, it is usually only a common source, for Propertius was a favorite of Campion, too. Campion was more of an exemplar to him than the working model he was for other poets; and while Pound's own verse in *The Cantos* moved further from song and the musical toward a visual idiom, he held to the *concept* of a union of poetry and music all the more tenaciously. By 1934, in the *ABC of Reading,* Pound had constructed his own history of poetry along the lines of the marriage and divorce of words and music: "The great lyric age lasted while Campion made his own music, while Lawes set Waller's verses. . . . Music rots when it gets *too far* from the dance. Poetry atrophies when it gets too far from music."[30] On a time-line Pound established to trace the metamorphosis of English verse from Chaucer through Whitman, Campion appears after Marlowe, Shakespeare, Boyd, and Donne, just before Herrick and Waller.[31]

If Pound was the theorist of song, W. H. Auden was the practitioner. Monroe K. Spears says of him, "Auden is supreme among modern poets as a writer of songs. His songs are his most distinctive accomplishment and his most popular; in them he achieves . . . the quality of lightness that he strives for with varying success in his other works."[32] We can hear the imprint of the master of earlier song very soon in his career, as early as 1931 when we come upon this hilarious set of Sapphics modeled on Campion's second kind of Sapphic "Rose-cheekt *Lawra*":

UNCLE HENRY

When the Flyin' Scot
fills for shootin', I go southward,
wisin' after coffee, leavin'
Lady Starkie.

Weady for some fun,
visit yearly Wome, Damascus,
in Mowocco look for fwesh
a-musin' places.

Where I'll find a fwend,
don't you know, a charmin' cweature,

> like a Gweek God and devoted:
> how delicious!

> All they have they bwing,
> Abdul, Nino, Manfwed, Kosta:
> here's to women for they bear such
> lovely kiddies![33]

At some points in his career he grouped his songs together as a definite genre within his ouevre, as in the "Songs and Other Musical Pieces" of the 1945 *Collected Poetry*. They are usually allusive to music, whether to blues songs like "St. James Infirmary" or to the English song tradition; of the latter, George T. Wright says, "these songs achieve a simple and clean clarity of form and feeling, the quiet elegance common to the melodious tradition of Campion, Shakespeare, Jonson, Dryden, Tennyson, and Housman, all of whom Auden sometimes echoes."[34] In some of them he exhibited the sort of ironic lyric grace we found in Campion's late books, aphoristic, terse, free of illusion:

> Let a florid music praise,
>   The flute and the trumpet,
> Beauty's conquest of your face:
> In that land of flesh and bone,
> Where from citadels on high
> Her imperial standards fly,
>   Let the hot sun
>   Shine on, shine on.

> Underneath the abject willow,
>   Lover, sulk no more:
> Act from thought should quickly follow.
>   What is thinking for?[35]

After the 1930s his musical interests moved into opera librettos rather than songs, but he was to return to write about song—if not to write more songs—again and again, each time with a fresh and rather scholarly interest in Elizabethan music and its verse per se. In 1955 he joined Noah Greenberg in issuing *An Elizabethan Song Book,* to which he contributed an introduction, and in tandem with that volume (which included twenty-two songs of Campion with their

music, more than Dowland or any other composer) made the recording *An Evening of Elizabethan Verse and Its Music.*[36] Finally, Auden returned to the specific issue of Campion the year of his own death with
Selected Songs of Thomas Campion. Like Pound, he saw Campion as
achieving something like a limit in musical verse: he found him a
little unreal in being so musical, and concluded of him that he is "the
greatest master in English poetry of what the French symbolists called
la poésie pure." So near the end of his own life, he saw poetry reaching
toward the state of music as a set of "verbal paradises."[37]

When you first read Robert Creeley's volume *For Love* you are in
for a surprise on page 69. After amusing and trenchant enactments of
conversation like "I Know a Man" or "Wait for Me," or the oddly
apocalyptic "Oh No" or the mock-cynical "The Immoral Proposi-
tion," you come upon still another voice—and a very old one—joining his:

Air: CAT BIRD SINGING

Cat bird singing
makes music like sounds coming

at night. The trees, goddamn them,
are huge eyes. They

watch, certainly, what
else should they do? My love

is a person of rare refinement,
and when she speaks,

there is another air,
melody—what Campion spoke of

with his
follow thy fair sunne unhappie shadow . . .

Catbird, catbird.
O lady hear me. I have no

other
voice left.[38]

Actually, Campion had long been one of Creeley's favorite poets. He first encountered him through Pound, whose *ABC* was practically a bible to him.[39] In 1954 Creeley had heard similarities between Campion's "measures" and William Carlos Williams's, and juxtaposed "Kinde are her answeres" to Williams's "The World Narrowed to a Point," asserting the feel of meter without strict scansion in both; this led to an extended correspondence between Creeley and Williams in which the latter denied any connection to the Elizabethan experiments with the lyric while Creeley kept insisting.[40] In an interview with Cynthia Edelberg, Creeley expanded on his admiration for Campion, citing his diction and syntax, his following a plain style, his development of the auditory imagination, and his concept of the lyric as epigram.[41] We can hear Campion in a poem like "Air: 'The Love of a Woman' " with its light rhymes of "her," "hair," and "air," or "he" and "the," or repeated "made":

> The love of a woman
> is the possibility which
> surrounds her as hair
> her head, as the love of her
>
> follows and describes
> her. But what if
> they die, then there is
> still the aura
>
> left, left sadly, but
> hovers in the air, surely,
> where this had taken place?
> Then sing of her, of whom
>
> it will be said, he
> sang of her, it was the
> song he made which made her
> happy, so she lived.[42]

This poem shows how fully Creeley has learned to combine the lyric sound-effects of song with the colloquial (in "possibility," or "had taken place"), to learn from Campion and his own ear too, and even echo at the end sonnet 46 from Daniel's *Delia*. As for the lyric as epigram, it seems to be a constant, and a poem like "A Token" shows that it is a concept that applies as well to Creeley in his own native way as it did to Campion:

> My lady
> fair with
> soft
> arms, what
>
> can I say to
> you—words, words
> as if all
> worlds were there.[43]

Why Is He Important?

When a poet is also a musician, that fact adds a new dimension to his public fortunes. That is the element of performance that keeps his sounds echoing through our ears. Campion's songs appear now and then in recitals, both by early music groups like the New York Pro Musica or the Boston Camerata and in standard vocal programs. Entire pieces receive performance, like the New York Renaissance Band's recent performance of *The Lords' Masque,* or the Providence Early Music Consort's performance of *The Squires' Masque* on 18 March 1981. Some of his sacred songs are sung in churches by congregations to this day, and those of us who attend church may find ourselves singing a hymn by him one Sunday. "Never weather-beaten Saile" and "Sing a song of joy" are included in *Songs of Praise;* an arrangement in four parts of two of his psalm settings—"Out of my soules depth" from Psalm 130 and "As by the streames of *Babilon*" from Psalm 137—by G. W. Williams and David Pizzaro was recently published for church use.[44] The composer Paul Lansky recently reset one of the songs in "Six Fantasies on a Poem by Thomas Campion."[45]

Campion's words and tunes circulate in our air. There are recordings: the Camerata of London directed by Glenda Simpson and Barry Mason issued a recording devoted to Campion in 1979, and on 29 July 1981 the Consort of Musicke directed by Anthony Rooley recorded music from both *The Lord Hay's Masque* and *The Squires' Masque* under the title *Madrigals and Wedding Songs for Diana* as a wedding present for Lady Diana Spencer and the Prince of Wales.[46]

We have seen the fluctuations of his reputation. What is his enduring importance? It is this: he is a cynosure of sorts, or, to change the
metaphor, a term or guardian figure. The image of Thomas Campion
stands at a boundary or limit for the point at which poetry and music
meet. He is the one poet in English whose poetry is also music, not
in metaphor—as when T. S. Eliot writes of "The Music of Poetry"—
but in fact. The relation of poem and tune vary so much, and the
degree of necessity or dependence changes so much, that we have used
the rather vague metaphor of "rhyme" to indicate the relation. Sometimes we encounter a perfectly beautiful poem like "My sweetest Lesbia" or "Follow thy faire sunne" where the music heightens elements
in the verse but does not "improve" the poem in any powerful way.
At other times, we find poems like "Faine would I wed" or "So sweet
is thy discourse" that seem unremarkable on the page, but when we
sing them or hear them sung, they spring to life.

There is more to it. There are people who have never heard a Campion poem sung who yet thrill with excitement at the very idea that
the words they are reading on a page are really a song, something
with melody, something that a human voice did or will or may give
life to. Perhaps they imagine the tune while they read; perhaps they
read the poem aloud instead of silently, as they do other types of poetry. Stephen Ratcliffe somewhat wryly calls this phenomenon the
"aesthetics of ruins." He invokes fragments, the Venus de Milo, and
Keats's lines "Heard melodies are sweet, but those / Unheard are
sweeter," and he concludes: "There are some things so good that we
are willing to adore fractions of them. Indeed, by their very incompleteness they are enhanced. Since we are forced to imagine the whole
from its part—forced to become artists as audience—and since ruins
and fragments include the ideal as nothing else can, whatever is
wrong must be the remains of a former right, whatever missing perfect beyond imagining. The Parthenon can never have been as beautiful as it must have been when it was new."[47] We can give a more
positive turn to this position. After all, the two arts Campion sought
to unite are noted for their suggestiveness rather than any form of the
explicit.

Let us give one last reading to "What Epigrams are in Poetrie, the
same are Ayres in musicke." Of all the fine arts, music alone is non-
representative; while poetry and the other verbal arts imitate
thoughts, character, places, and actions, and while painting and the
plastic arts represent landscapes, people, still life—even in "abstract"

art where they are shadowy—music is not mimetic, it represents nothing. Instead, it seems to allude or evoke something like motion or muscular movement. Pound says that what stands—or moves—behind music is dance, as music stands behind poetry, and that neither must move too far beyond their source. For Campion the vector is not dance-music-poetry, but the base is the "Simmetry and proportion" of the created universe, "the motions of the Spheares" that Apollo sang, and the unfolding is world-music-poetry. Also, it lies in the art of epigram as Campion saw it to leave space for the reader to pursue suggestions, for in its very brevity there is a kind of incompleteness. That is the difference between his epigrammatic mode and Ben Jonson's. Jonson's poems are devoted to "lyric definition," they assert inclusiveness, the definite, light: "Would'st thou heare, what man can say / In a little?" Campion's are inconclusive, indefinite, suggestive, they end in open metaphors: "the strings doe breake." Perhaps in moving from the clarity of light as image of order to sound as the indicator of order not seen, he realized that. Certainly the classic epigram was suggestive, but when Campion made it incorporate lyric feeling it became doubly so: it suggested deep emotion as well as unfinished thought. What Auden says of him and what Creeley imitates in him is the suggestive. If Campion's art calls up an "aesthetics of ruins" it was partly his conscious craft that made it so: we become active in imagining the music that is not there, or imagining what is behind the music that is.

What is the importance of that? Poetry is a raid on the inarticulate, a poet said. Music is an onslaught on the inarticulate, though its spoils are less tangible than poetry's. Where poetry and music meet they establish a new boundary of human expression, where verbal articulation and the ineluctable realm of feeling join. Together they extend our sense of what can be expressed.

Notes and References

Chapter One

1. See below, chapter 7.
2. See the Latin epigram "Ad Lucium," no. 23 in *Epigrammatum Liber Secundus,* in *Campion's Works,* ed. Percival Vivian (Oxford: Clarendon Press, 1909), 275; hereafter cited in the text as *V.*
3. Peter Warlock (Philip Heseltine), *The English Ayre* (London: Oxford University Press, 1926), 98.
4. See *The Works of Thomas Campion,* ed. Walter R. Davis (Garden City, N.Y.: Doubleday, 1967), 405, 309, 64–65; hereafter cited in the text as *D.*
5. Edward Lowbury, Timothy Salter, and Alison Young, *Thomas Campion: Poet, Composer, Physician* (London: Chatto & Windus, 1970), 18.
6. It may be, however, that Percy did not attend Cambridge at all, but Oxford. The trouble is that there were so many named Percy at Cambridge.
7. See Gabriel Harvey's account of the ascendency of history over oratory in *Three Proper, and Wittie, Familiar Letters,* in *The Poetical Works of Edmund Spenser,* ed. J. C. Smith and E. De Selincourt (London: Oxford University Press, 1926), 621.
8. Thomas Nashe, *Strange Newes of the Interception of Certaine Letters* (1592), in *The Works of Thomas Nashe,* ed. R. B. McKerrow, 5 vols., 2d ed. (Oxford: Clarendon Press, 1958), 1:319.
9. Quoted by Mary Stuart, *Francis Bacon: A Biography* (New York: W. Morrow & Co., 1932), 13.
10. John Carey, *John Donne: Life, Mind, and Art* (New York: Oxford University Press, 1981), 24.
11. See Lowbury, Salter, and Young, *Thomas Campion,* 20.
12. See Enid Welsford, *The Court Masque* (Cambridge: Cambridge University Press, 1927), 163–66, and Stephen Orgel, *The Jonsonian Masque* (Cambridge, Mass.: Harvard University Press, 1965), 8–18.
13. See *Elizabethan Critical Essays,* ed. G. Gregory Smith, 2 vols. (London: Oxford University Press, 1904), 2:457.
14. Thomas Nashe, *Have with you to Saffron-Walden* (1596), in *Works,* ed. McKerrow, 3:104.
15. Nashe, *Works,* ed. McKerrow, 3:110.
16. See Ian Spink, *English Song: Dowland to Purcell* (New York: Scribner's, 1974), 15.
17. James Joyce, *Ulysses* (New York: Modern Library, 1934), 645–46.

18. See Diana Poulton, *John Dowland,* 2d ed. (Berkeley: University of California Press, 1982), 69, n.

19. Quotations from Campion's works cite page or collection of ayres and number.

20. See below, chapter 4.

21. Lowbury, Salter, and Young, *Thomas Campion,* 25.

22. On Moundeford, see William Munk, M.D., *The Roll of the Royal College of Physicians of London,* 2d ed., 5 vols. (London: the College, 1878), 1:103.

23. Frustrating and dangerous: on one occasion a nobleman practicing for Campion's *Squires' Masque* overheated himself with dancing, fell into the smallpox, and died, according to a contemporary account. See Andrew J. Sabol, *Four Hundred Songs and Dances from the Stuart Masque, With a Supplement of Sixteen Additional Pieces* (Providence: Brown University Press, 1978; reprint, Hanover and London: University Press of New England, 1982), 12.

24. See Andrew J. Sabol, *A Score for "Lovers Made Men"* (Providence: Brown University Press, 1963).

25. There are two good books on the affair: William McElwee's *The Murder of Sir Thomas Overbury* (London: Faber & Faber, 1952) and Beatrice White's *Cast of Ravens: The Strange Case of Sir Thomas Overbury* (London: John Murray, 1965).

26. Poulton, *John Dowland,* 418–19.

27. For a discussion of authorship and an interesting attempt to reconstruct the entertainment at Brougham Castle, see Ian Spink, "Campion's Entertainment at Brougham Castle, 1617," in *Music in English Renaissance Drama,* ed. John H. Long (Lexington: University of Kentucky Press, 1968), 57–74.

Chapter Two

1. Ralph W. Berringer, "Thomas Campion's Share in *A Booke of Ayres,*" *PMLA* 58 (1943):942.

2. Catherine M. Ing, *Elizabethan Lyrics: A Study in the Development of English Metres and Their Relation to Poetic Effect* (London: Chatto & Windus, 1951), 173.

3. Yvor Winters, "The 16th Century Lyric in England: A Critical and Historical Reinterpretation," *Poetry: A Magazine of Verse* 53 (1939):258–72, 320–35; 54 (1939):35–51 (see p. 37).

4. See chapter 3, below.

5. Stephen Ratcliffe, *Campion: On Song* (London: Routledge & Kegan Paul, 1981), vii–ix. For an extended thematic study of this same song, see John T. Irwin, "Thomas Campion and the Musical Emblem," *Studies in English Literature* 10 (1970):121–41.

6. Thomas Morley, *A Plaine and Easie Introduction to Practicall Musicke* (1597), ed. R. Alec Harmon (London: J. M. Dent, 1952), 291.

7. See Miles M. Kastendieck, *England's Musical Poet: Thomas Campion* (New York: Oxford University Press, 1963), 113–14, 157–58.

8. For this and other references to the music of Campion's songs, the reader should consult the editions by E. H. Fellowes listed in the selected bibliography below.

9. Lowbury, Salter, and Young, *Thomas Campion,* 61.

10. Also, the strong rhythm suggests that this is a slow dance tune like the pavan, meant to be danced by older people.

11. I am grateful to Deborah Weiner for pointing these passages out to me.

12. "Ad pulchritudinem tria requirentur integritas, consonantia, claritas" (Aquinas, *Summa Theologica,* pt. 1, question 29, article 8).

13. Abraham Cowley, "Ode: Of Wit," in *The English Writings of Abraham Cowley,* ed. A. R. Waller, 2 vols. (Cambridge: Cambridge University Press, 1905–6), 1:16–18.

14. See David A. Richardson, "The Golden Mean in Campion's Airs," *Comparative Literature* 30 (1978):108–32.

15. For example, see *Works,* ed. Davis, 15, 254, 268, 312, 323.

Chapter Three

1. *English Madrigal Verse, 1588–1632,* ed. E. H. Fellowes (Oxford: Clarendon Press, 1920), 7; see also 76, 155.

2. *Spenser's Minor Poems,* ed. Ernest De Sélincourt (Oxford: Clarendon Press, 1910), 5.

3. *The Poems of Sir Philip Sidney,* ed. William A. Ringler, Jr. (Oxford: Clarendon Press, 1962), 180.

4. Fulke Greville, *Life of Sir Philip Sidney,* ed. Nowell Smith (Oxford: Clarendon Press, 1907), 224.

5. Samuel Daniel, *Musophilus,* lines 989–1012, in *Poems and A Defence of Ryme,* ed. Arthur Colby Sprague (Chicago: University of Chicago Press, 1930), 97–98.

6. See Walter Davis, " 'Fantastickly I Sing': Drayton's *Idea* of 1619," *Studies in Philology* 66 (1969):204–16.

7. Compare Sidney, *Poems,* ed. Ringler, 30–31.

8. Sidney, *Poems,* 68–69.

9. See *Works,* ed. Davis, 9, on Latin versions of these epigrams.

10. See ibid., 10, for examples.

11. See ibid., 3–4.

12. *Syr P.S. His Astrophel and Stella* (London: Thomas Newman, 1591), sig A3.

13. David Greer, "Campion the Musician," *Lute Society Journal* 9 (1967):14.

14. *Lyrics from English Airs, 1596–1622,* ed. Edward Doughtie (Cambridge, Mass.: Harvard University Press, 1970), 110.

15. Thomas Nashe, preface to Greene's *Menaphon* (1589), in *Works,* ed. McKerrow, 3:318. For Andrewes, see George Williamson, *The Senecan Amble: A Study in Prose Form from Bacon to Collier* (Chicago: University of Chicago Press, 1951), 104, n. 3.

16. Sir Thomas Overbury, "What a Character is," in *The Overburian Characters,* ed. W. J. Paylor (Oxford: Blackwell, 1936), 92.

17. See Gwendolen Murphy, *A Bibliography of Character-Books, 1608–1700* (Oxford: Oxford University Press, 1925), and C. M. Greenough, *A Bibliography of the Theophrastan Character in English* (Cambridge, Mass.: Harvard University Press, 1947).

18. *Epigrammes,* no. 124, in *Poems of Ben Jonson,* ed. George Burke Johnston (Cambridge, Mass.: Harvard University Press, 1955), 64.

19. Overbury, *The Overburian Characters,* 92.

20. H. V. S. Ogden, "The Principles of Variety and Contrast in Seventeenth Century Aesthetics, and Milton's Poetry," *Journal of the History of Ideas* 10 (1949):159–82. See also T. E. Hulme, "Romantic and Classic," in *Speculations: Essays on Humanism and the Philosophy of Art,* ed. Herbert Read (London: K. Paul, Trench, Trubner, & Co., 1924).

21. Sir Philip Sidney *The Countess of Pembroke's Arcadia (The Old Arcadia),* ed. Jean Robertson (Oxford: Clarendon Press, 1973), 15.

22. *The Poetical Works of Sir John Denham,* ed. Theodore Howard Banks, Jr. (New Haven: Yale University Press, 1928), 77.

23. See Martial, *Epigrams,* 4.49, 10.4, and 2, prefatory letter.

24. See Ruth Wallerstein, "The Laureate Hearse: The Funeral Elegy and Seventeenth-Century Aesthetic," in *Studies in Seventeenth-Century Poetic* (Madison: University of Wisconsin Press, 1950), 59–95.

25. *Ayres and Observations: Selected Poems of Thomas Campion,* ed. Joan Hart (Cheadle: Carcanet Press, 1976), 23.

26. Ibid.

27. Ibid.

28. See Kastendieck, *England's Musical Poet,* 114–15.

29. See the comments on Sir John Davies's progress, above.

30. Thus Ezra Pound dedicated his translation of Cavalcanti's great ode "Donna mi priegha" to Campion: see below, chapter 7.

Chapter Four

1. Quoted by Bruce Pattison, *Music and Poetry of the English Renaissance* rpr. (London: Methuen, 1970), 7.

2. Kinglsey Amis, *Lucky Jim: A Novel* (Garden City, N.Y.: Double-

day, 1954), chap. 4. Jim tried to fake the tenor part of John Bartlett's "When from my love," *A Booke of Ayres* (1606), 3, then came to grief over Thomas Morley's "Now is the month of Maying" (*First Booke of Balletts* [1595], 3).

3. Oliver Strunk, *Source Readings in Music History* (New York: Norton, 1950), 408–9.

4. Howard Mayer Brown, *Music in the Renaissance* (Englewood Cliffs, N.J.: Prentice-Hall, 1976), 220.

5. Joseph Kerman, *The Elizabethan Madrigal: A Comparative Study* (New York: American Musicological Society, 1962), 43.

6. Wilfrid Mellers, *Harmonious Meeting: A Study of the Relationship between English Music, Poetry and Theatre, c. 1600–1900* (London: Dennis Dobson, 1965), 154.

7. Pepys, *Diary* 10 March 1667; quoted by E. H. Fellowes, *The English Madrigal Composers* (Oxford: Clarendon Press, 1921), 25.

8. Doughtie, *Lyrics from English Airs*, 2–3.

9. Poulton, *John Dowland*, 216.

10. Campion did this in his *Two Bookes of Ayres:* see *Works,* ed. Davis, 53, 55. The resulting part-song, however, is less like a madrigal than a homophonic song.

11. Wilfrid Mellers, "Words and Music in Elizabethan England," in *The Age of Shakespeare,* ed. Boris Ford (Harmondsworth: Pelican, 1955), 400–401.

12. Doughtie, *Lyrics from English Airs*, 101.

13. Ibid., 37.

14. W. H. Auden, Chester Kallman, and Noah Greenberg, eds., *An Elizabethan Song Book* (Garden City, N.Y.: Doubleday, 1955), xvi–xvii.

15. Pattison, *Music and Poetry of the English Renaissance,* 136.

16. David Greer, "The Lute Songs of Thomas Morley," *Lute Society Journal* 8 (1966):31.

17. Pattison, *Music and Poetry of the English Renaissance,* 136–37.

18. Doughtie, *Lyrics from English Airs*, 114.

19. Ibid., 115.

20. Edward Doughtie, "Sibling Rivalry: Music vs. Poetry in Campion and Others," *Criticism* 20 (1978):9.

21. Ibid., 11.

22. Doughtie, *Lyrics from English Airs*, 266.

23. See Poulton, *John Dowland,* 212.

24. Ibid., 135–37.

25. Ibid., 211.

26. Ibid., 233.

27. The text is quoted in chapter 3, above. See Walter Davis, "Melodic and Poetic Structure: The Examples of Campion and Dowland," *Criti-*

cism 4 (1962):89–107. Other examples are "Come away, sweet love" (*First Booke,* 11), "Come ye heavy states of night" (*Second,* 14), "Time stands still" (*Third,* 2), and "Disdain me still" (*A Pilgrims Solace,* 1).

28. See Poulton, *John Dowland,* plate 6 b, and p. 345.

29. See Mellers, *Harmonious Meeting,* 80, 82, for some other general contrasts between Campion and Dowland.

30. See chapter 2, above.

31. See chapter 2, above.

32. See Doughtie, "Sibling Rivalry," 13–14, comparing Campion's and Dowland's settings of "I must complain."

33. Ibid., 11.

34. Greer, "Campion the Musician," 7.

35. Ibid., 8.

36. Gustave Reese, *Music in the Renaissance,* rev. ed. (New York: Norton, 1959), 837.

37. Paula Johnson, *Form and Transformation in Music and Poetry of the English Renaissance* (New Haven: Yale University Press, 1972), 111.

38. Greer, "Campion the Musician," 10.

39. See chapter 2, above.

40. Mellers, "Words and Music," 407.

41. Ibid., 408.

42. Mellers, *Harmonious Meeting,* 78.

43. See Lowbury, Salter, and Young, *Thomas Campion,* 156.

44. So carefully as to criticize some of its music in his treatise on counterpoint: see *Works,* ed. Davis, 346. On Campion's music and the psalm-tunes, see Greer, "Campion the Musician," 12.

45. Hart, ed., *Ayres and Observations,* 10.

46. I am indebted to Deborah Weiner for this observation.

47. Hart, ed., *Ayres and Observations,* 10.

48. Ogden, "Variety and Contrast," 170–73.

49. Morley, *A Plaine and Easie Introduction to Practicall Musicke,* 282.

50. Lowbury, Salter, and Young, *Thomas Campion,* 150.

51. Elise Bickford Jorgens, *The Well-Tun'd Word: Musical Interpretations of English Poetry, 1597–1651* (Minneapolis: University of Minnesota Press, 1982), 177.

52. Ibid., 183.

53. See McD. Emslie, "Nicholas Lanier's Innovations in English Song," *Music and Letters* 41 (1960):21–22, and Jorgens, *The Well-Tun'd Word,* 190–201.

54. See Jorgens, *The Well-Tun'd Word,* 201.

55. Manfred F. Bukofzer, *Music in the Baroque Era from Monteverdi to Bach* (New York: Norton, 1947), 11.

56. See Spink, *English Song: Dowland to Purcell,* 100–103; the songs are "Thou art not faire," "Fire, fire," and "Young and simple though I am."

57. Greer, "Campion the Musician," 14.

58. See Stanley Boorman, "Notari, Porter, and the Lute," *Lute Society Journal* 13 (1971):28–29.

59. See Pattison, *Music and Poetry of the English Renaissance,* 139.

60. Greer, "Campion the Musician," 14.

61. Lowbury, Salter, and Young, *Thomas Campion,* 163–64.

62. Spink advances the theory that monody in England develops out of the masques and plays (*English Song,* 45–49).

63. See Jorgens, *The Well-Tun'd Word,* 145–46.

64. See Lowbury, Salter, and Young, *Thomas Campion,* 156, and Greer, "Campion the Musician," 8, also Sabol, *Four Hundred Songs and Dances,* 680.

65. Glenda Simpson and the Camerata of London, *Thomas Campion: Songs, Consort Pieces, and Masque Music,* Musical Heritage Society recording, MHS 7146 K, 1979. This recording contains generous selections from all five books of ayres. See also Ian Partridge (tenor) and Jakob Lindberg (lute), *It Fell on a Summer's Day: Songs by Dowland and Campion,* Musical Heritage Society, MHS 7201 Z, 1985, and Rene Soames (tenor) Walter Gerwig (lute) and Johannes Koch (viola da gamba), *Nine Songs from Rosseter's "Book of Ayres,"* Archive, ARC 3004, 1955.

Chapter Five

1. See Jorgens, *The Well-Tun'd Word,* 84–90.

2. Ibid., 176.

3. Pattison, *Music and Poetry of the English Renaissance,* 128.

4. Strunk, *Source Readings in Music History,* 317.

5. Ibid., 319.

6. Matthew Arnold, sonnet "To a Friend."

7. See W. H. Auden and John Hollander, eds., *Selected Songs of Thomas Campion* (Boston: David R. Godine, 1973), 11.

8. For the specifics, see *Works,* ed. Davis, 320–22, 341, 349.

9. Morrison Comegys Boyd, *Elizabethan Music and Musical Criticism* (Philadelphia: University of Pennsylvania Press, 1940), 255–58; Lowbury, Salter, and Young, *Thomas Campion,* 171–78.

10. Lowbury, Salter, and Young, *Thomas Campion,* 173.

11. *A Plaine and Easie Introduction,* ed. Harmon, 226; this is indebted to Zarlino, as Harmon notes.

12. Kastendieck, *England's Musical Poet,* 178.

13. Jorgens, *The Well-Tun'd Word,* 81.

14. See Bukofzer, *Music in the Baroque Era,* 12.

15. Giovanni Coperario, *Rules How to Compose,* ed. Manfred Bukofzer (Los Angeles: E. E. Gottlieb, 1952), 19; Reese, *Music in the Renaissance,* 838.

16. See *Works,* ed. Davis, 53, and plate 2.

17. Ezra Pound, canto 81 from *The Pisan Cantos,* 96: in *The Cantos of*

Ezra Pound (New York: New Directions, 1948). See William McNaughton, "Ezra Pound's Meters and Rhythms," *PMLA* 78 (1963):136–46.

18. Paul Fussell, *Poetic Meter and Poetic Form* (New York: Random House, 1965); J. V. Cunningham, "How Shall the Poem Be Written?" *Denver Quarterly* 2 (1967):45–62.

19. George Gascoigne, *Certaine Notes of Instruction,* in *Elizabethan Critical Essays,* ed. Smith, 1:49–51; Puttenham, *The Art of English Poetry,* in ibid., 2:129–31.

20. Jonson, *The Under-wood,* 29, in *Poems,* ed. Johnston, 157.

21. See Thomas O. Sloan, "The Crossing of Rhetoric and Poetry in the English Renaissance," in *The Rhetoric of Renaissance Poetry,* ed. Thomas O. Sloan and Raymond B. Waddington (Berkeley: University of California Press, 1974), 212–42. On the grammatical rather than rhetorical form of the *Observations,* see Jane K. Fenyo, "Grammar and Music in Thomas Campion's *Observations in the Art of English Poesie,*" *Studies in the Renaissance* 17 (1970):46–72.

22. Sidney, *Poems,* ed. Ringler, 68.

23. The scansion is by Derek Attridge, *Well-weighed Syllables: Elizabethan Verse in Classical Metres* (Cambridge: Cambridge University Press, 1974), 226.

24. The scansion is by Attridge (ibid., 227).

25. *The Prose Works of Sir Philip Sidney,* ed. Albert Feullerat, 2d ed., 4 vols. (Cambridge: Cambridge University Press, 1963), 3:11.

26. *Arcadia,* ed. Robertson, 89.

27. Attridge, *Well-weighed Syllables,* 170.

28. Samuel Daniel, *A Defence of Ryme,* in *Elizabethan Critical Essays,* ed. Smith, 2:376–77.

29. Ibid., 377.

30. Attridge, *Well-weighed Syllables,* 228.

31. See *Works,* ed. Davis, 288. T. S. Eliot used the conflict between Campion and Daniel to begin the second lecture of *The Use of Poetry and the Use of Criticism* (London: Faber & Faber, 1933), 37–40.

32. Attridge, *Well-weighed Syllables,* 226.

33. For details, see *Works,* ed. Davis, 359. *Works,* pp. 362–443, contains *Ad Thamesin, Umbra,* and selections from the elegies and epigrams, with facing-page translations.

34. J. W. Binns has an interesting discussion of the elegies in his essay on Campion in *The Latin Poetry of English Poets* (London: Routledge & Kegan Paul, 1974), 3–12.

Chapter Six

1. Ben Jonson, *The Complete Masques,* ed. Stephen Orgel (New Haven: Yale University Press, 1969), 1.

2. See the record of the interruption of a dance in progress by disguised or "masked" strangers who then join the dance, in Henry VIII's time, circa 1512: *Hall's Chronicle,* ed. Henry Ellis (London, 1809), 526.

3. Sabol, *Four Hundred Songs,* 7, and Lowbury, Salter, and Young, *Thomas Campion,* 93.

4. Jonson, *Complete Masques,* ed. Orgel, 69–70.

5. See ibid., 18–20.

6. See ibid., 36.

7. Ibid., 15. On light, see John C. Maegher, *Method and Meaning in Jonson's Masques* (Notre Dame: University of Notre Dame Press, 1966), 107–24.

8. Though we have, thanks to Sabol, a record and archive of *Four Hundred Songs and Dances from the Stuart Masque,* we do not have enough from any single masque to form a complete sense of its music. The case is similar with respect to Inigo Jones's sets and costumes, all the surviving examples of which are contained in Stephen Orgel and Roy Strong's *Inigo Jones: The Theatre of the Stuart Court,* 2 vols. (London: Sotheby Park Bernet Publications, Ltd., 1973).

9. Jonson, *Complete Masques,* ed. Orgel, 272–76.

10. Ibid., 2.

11. Ibid., 1–2.

12. See the conjectural diagram in Orgel and Strong, *Inigo Jones,* 1:120.

13. For details, see *Works,* ed. Davis, 212–13.

14. For the music, see Sabol, *Four Hundred Songs,* no. 2.

15. See *Works,* ed. Davis, 207, for the epigram to James prefixed to the masque, in which he is compared to King Arthur, as Henry VIII was.

16. See Franz Kafka, *Parables and Paradoxes* (New York: Schocken Books, 1947), 92–93.

17. See Sabol, *Four Hundred Songs,* no. 3.

18. I assume that this is the third piece of music printed with the masque, the first being a song, the second the first new dance with its lyrics, the third, fourth, and fifth being the second, third, and fourth new dances; for the music, see ibid., no. 4.

19. See the illustration in Orgel and Strong, *Inigo Jones,* 1:121.

20. See Sabol, *Four Hundred Songs,* no. 5.

21. See Joan Rees, ed., "Samuel Daniel, *The Vision of the Twelve Goddesses,*" in *A Book of Masques in Honour of Allardyce Nicoll* (Cambridge: Cambridge University Press, 1967), 26, 33–35.

22. See chapter 1, above.

23. Jonson, *Complete Masques,* ed. Orgel, 79.

24. "This sacred place, let none profane" (*Works,* ed. Davis, 216) and "Bid all profane away" (Jonson, *Complete Masques,* 77), for example.

25. Sabol, *Four Hundred Songs,* 25.

26. See Rees in *A Booke of Masques,* 26, 36.

27. Jonson, *Complete Masques,* ed. Orgel, 56–57.

28. See D. J. Gordon, *"Hymenei:* Ben Jonson's Masque of Union," *Journal of the Warburg and Courtauld Institutes* 8 (1945):107–45.

29. See chapter 5, above.

30. See David Lindley, "Campion's *Lord Hay's Masque* and Anglo-Scottish Union," *Huntington Library Quarterly* 43 (1979):1–11.

31. See *Works,* ed. Davis, 264, 267, n., 269, n., 270, n.

32. On Elizabeth and Frederick, see Josephine Ross, *The Winter Queen: The Story of Elizabeth Stuart* (New York: St. Martin's Press, 1979).

33. See Orgel and Strong, *Inigo Jones;* 1:242.

34. See the illustration in ibid., 1:248.

35. See the illustrations in ibid., 1:249, and color plate of no. 80.

36. See the illustrations in ibid., 1:250, and color plate of no. 81, reproduced as the frontispiece to the present text.

37. See ibid., 1:44, and illustrations on 1:247, 251.

38. These accounts of expenses and opinions appear in ibid., 1:241–42.

39. Jonson, *Complete Masques,* ed. Orgel, 22.

40. A. Leigh DeNeef, "Structure and Theme in Campion's *Lords Maske,"* *Studies in English Literature* 17 (1977):95.

41. Ibid., 101.

42. Elizabeth Sewell, *The Orphic Voice* (New Haven: Yale University Press, 1960), 60.

43. On the entertainment as a genre, see Mary Ann McGuire, "Milton's *Arcades* and the Entertainment Tradition," *Studies in Philology* 75 (1978):451–71.

44. Francis Bacon, *De Sapientia Veterum,* chap. 6, "Pan sive Natura," in *The Works of Francis Bacon,* ed. James Spedding, R. L. Ellis, and D. D. Heath, 15 vols. (Cambridge: Riverside Press, 1863), 13:92–101.

45. Michel Foucault, *The Order of Things: An Archaeology of the Human Sciences* (New York: Random House, 1970), 17–76.

46. Thomas Carew, "An Elegie on the death of the Deane of Pauls, Dr. Iohn Donne," in *The Poems of Thomas Carew,* ed. Rhodes Dunlap (Oxford: Clarendon Press, 1949), 71–74.

47. See chapter 1, above.

48. For the music, see Sabol, *Four Hundred Songs,* no. 20; on the song, see *Works,* ed. Davis, 266.

49. See ibid., no. 23.

50. John Orrell, "The Agent of Savoy at *The Somerset Masque,"* *Review of English Studies,* n.s. 28 (1977):304.

51. Ibid.

52. Ibid., 304–5.

Chapter 7

1. *The Life and Minor Works of George Peele,* ed. David H. Horne (New Haven: Yale University Press, 1952), 246.

2. Quoted by Vivian, in *Works,* xxxvi.

3. Davies, *Orchestra* (1596), in *The Poems of Sir John Davies,* ed. Robert Krueger (Oxford: Clarendon Press, 1975), 124, 376, n. Nashe, *Have with you to Saffron-Walden* (1596) in his *Works,* ed. McKerrow, 3:110.

4. Quoted by Vivian, in *Works,* xxxvii.

5. Francis Meres, *Palladis Tamia, Wits Treasury* (1598), in *Elizabethan Critical Essays,* ed. Smith, 2:315.

6. Quoted by Vivian, in *Works,* xxxviii.

7. Daniel, *A Defence of Ryme,* in *Elizabethan Critical Essays,* ed. Smith, 2:358.

8. Ben Jonson, *Conversations with Drummond of Hawthornden,* in *Ben Jonson,* ed. C. H. Hereford and Percy Simpson, 11 vols. (Oxford: Clarendon Press, 1925–52), 1:132.

9. John Davies of Hereford, *The Scourge of Folly* (London, 1611), 204.

10. Quoted by Vivian, in *Works,* xl.

11. See *Works,* ed. Davis, 485–87, for details.

12. *The Caroline Poets,* ed. George Saintsbury, 3 vols. (Oxford: Clarendon Press, 1921), 3:142.

13. *The Poems of Owen Felltham,* ed. Ted-Larry Pebworth and Claude J. Summers (University Park: Pennsylvania State University Press, 1973), 5.

14. *The Complete Poetry of Robert Herrick,* ed. J. Max Patrick (Garden City, N.Y.: Doubleday, 1963), H–53.

15. See ibid., H–371, H–851. With the former, compare Edward Lord Herbert's "Tears, flow no more," in *Minor Poets of the Seventeenth Century,* ed. R. G. Howarth (London: J. M. Dent, 1931), 19.

16. See *Works,* ed. Vivian, 363; Lowbury, Salter, and Young, *Thomas Campion,* 157. See also Muriel T. Eldridge, *Thomas Campion, His Poetry and Music (1567–1620)* (New York: Vantage Press, 1971), 123, 129, on reprintings in hymnals.

17. See Lowbury, Salter, and Young, *Thomas Campion,* 6–7.

18. Ibid., 10–11.

19. *The Swinburne Letters,* ed. Cecil Y. Lang, 6 vols. (New Haven: Yale University Press, 1959–62), 5:257.

20. Quoted by Ratcliffe, *Campion,* 180.

21. *The Lyric Poems of Thomas Campion,* ed. Ernest Rhys (1895); Andrew Lang, *History of English Literature* (1912); cited by Lowbury, Salter, and Young, *Thomas Campion,* 12.

22. Thomas Campion, *Songs and Masques, with Observations in the Art of English Poesy,* ed. A. H. Bullen (London: A. H. Bullen, 1903), viii.

23. T. S. Eliot, *The Use of Poetry and the Use of Criticism* (London: Faber & Faber, 1933), 37; *On Poets and Poetry* (New York: Farrar, Strauss, 1957), 46.

24. Reese, *Music in the Renaissance, 839.*

25. *The Works of Thomas Campion,* ed. Davis (1967); *Ayres and Observations: Selected Poems of Thomas Campion,* ed. Hart (1976); *Selected Songs of Thomas Campion,* ed. Auden and Hollander (1973); Lowbury, Salter, and Young, *Thomas Campion* (1970); Ratcliffe, *Campion* (1981); and Margaret B. Bryan, "Recent Studies in Campion," *English Literary Renaissance* 4 (1974):404–11.

26. Ezra Pound, reprinted from *The Egotist* of 1917 in *Pavanes and Divisions* (New York: Alfred A. Knopf, 1918), 151.

27. See John Espey, "The Inheritance of Tò Kalón," in *New Approach to Ezra Pound: A Co-ordinated Investigation of Pound's Poetry and Ideas,* ed. Eva Hesse (Berkeley: University of California Press, 1969), 323–24.

28. The poem is printed in *Make it New: Essays of Ezra Pound* (London: Faber & Faber, 1934), 353 ff., in an essay, "Cavalcanti," dated "1910/1931."

29. See *Poetical Works of Robert Bridges,* 2d ed. (London: Oxford University Press, 1953), 437–38. On Bridges and Campion, see Edward Thompson, *Robert Bridges* (London: Oxford University Press, 1944), 12, and Albert Guérard, Jr., *Robert Bridges: A Study of Traditionalism in Poetry* (New York: Russell & Russell, 1965), 287. Harvey Gross compares Pound's and Swinburne's Bridges-inspired Sapphics in *Sound and Form in Modern Poetry* (Ann Arbor: University of Michigan Press, 1964), 141–42.

30. Ezra Pound, *ABC of Reading* (New York: New Directions, n.d.), 60–61; see also 156. See also *Literary Essays of Ezra Pound,* ed. T. S. Eliot (New York: New Directions, 1968), 113.

31. Pound, *ABC of Reading,* 173.

32. Monroe K. Spears, *The Poetry of W. H. Auden: The Disenchanted Island* (New York: Oxford University Press, 1963), 105.

33. W. H. Auden, *Collected Poems,* ed. Edward Mendelson (London: Faber & Faber, 1976), 60–61.

34. George T. Wright, *W. H. Auden,* rev. ed. (Boston: Twayne, 1981), 88.

35. Auden, *Collected Poems,* ed. Mendelson, 117, 119.

36. *An Elizabethan Song Book,* music edited by Noah Greenberg, text edited by W. H. Auden and Chester Kallman (Garden City, N.Y.: Doubleday, 1955); *An Evening of Elizabethan Verse and Its Music,* Columbia, ML 5051, 1955.

37. *Selected Songs of Thomas Campion,* ed. Auden and Hollander, 11.

38. Robert Creeley, *For Love: Poems 1950–1960* (New York: Scribner's, 1962), 69.

39. Robert Creeley, *Contexts for Poetry: Interviews 1961–1971,* ed. Donald Allen (Bolinas, Calif.: Four Seasons Foundation, 1973), 212.

40. "William Carlos Williams: *Selected Essays,*" in *A Quick Graph: Collected Notes and Essays,* ed. Donald Allen (San Francisco: Four Seasons Foundation, 1970), 107–9; Paul Mariani, " 'Fire of a Very Real Order': Creeley and Williams," in *Robert Creeley: A Gathering,* ed. William V. Spanos, *boundary 2* 6, no. 3–7, no. 1 (double issue, spring–fall 1978):184–87.

41. Cynthia Dubin Edelberg, *Robert Creeley's Poetry: A Critical Introduction* (Albuquerque: University of New Mexico Press, 1978), 167–68.

42. Creeley, *For Love,* 142. See Hugh Kenner's review of *Collected Poems, 1945–75,* in *New York Times Book Review,* 7 August 1983, 13.

43. Creeley, "A Token," in *For Love,* 123.

44. G. W. Williams and David Pizzaro, *Choral Settings of Psalms* (Minneapolis: Augsburg Publishing House, 1982).

45. See *New York Times,* Sunday, 5 June 1983, H25.

46. Consort of Musicke, *Madrigals and Wedding Songs for Diana,* Hyperion, A 66019, 1981; see also Concentus Musicus of Denmark, *Masque Music,* Nonesuch, H 71153, 1967.

47. Ratcliffe, *Campion,* 14.

Selected Bibliography

PRIMARY SOURCES

Campion's Works. Edited by Percival Vivian. Oxford: Clarendon Press, 1909. Reprint. 1966. Complete, including all the English and Latin texts, but without music.

The Works of Thomas Campion. Edited by Walter R. Davis. Garden City, N.Y.: Doubleday, 1967. Complete English works with some music for the songs, selected Latin poems with translations by Phyllis S. Smith.

Songs from Rosseter's Book of Airs. Edited by Edmund Horace Fellowes. 2 pts. English School of Lutenist Song Writers, 1st ser., nos. 4, 13. London: Stainer & Bell, 1922.

First Book of Airs. Edited by E. H. Fellowes. English School of Lutenist Song Writers, 2d ser., no. 1. London: Stainer & Bell, 1925.

Second Book of Airs. Edited by E. H. Fellowes. English School of Lutenist Song Writers, 2d ser., no. 2. London: Stainer & Bell, 1925.

Third Book of Ayres. Edited by E. H. Fellowes. English School of Lutenist Song Writers, 2d ser., no. 10. London: Stainer & Bell, 1926.

Fourth Booke of Ayres. Edited by E. H. Fellowes. English School of Lutenist Song Writers, 2d ser., no. 11. London: Stainer & Bell, 1926. Fellowes's editions contain the complete songs with their music in modern transcription.

Four Hundred Songs and Dances from the Stuart Masque: With a Supplement of Sixteen Additional Pieces. Edited by Andrew J. Sabol. Providence: Brown University Press, 1978. Reprint. Hanover and London: University Press of New England, 1982. All the surviving music to Campion's court masques.

Selected Songs of Thomas Campion. Edited by W. H. Auden and John Hollander. Boston: David Godine, 1973. A tasteful selection, with music to twenty of the songs.

Ayres and Observations: Selected Poems of Thomas Campion. Edited by Joan Hart. Cheadle: Carcanet Press, 1976. A good selection with a fine introduction.

SECONDARY SOURCES

Attridge, Derek, *Well-weighed Syllables: Elizabethan Verse in Classical Metres.* Cambridge: Cambridge University Press, 1974. Comprehensive study of quantitative experimentation, discussing Campion's *Observations* and its context.

Berringer, Ralph W. "Thomas Campion's Share in *A Booke of Ayres*." *PMLA* 58 (1943):938–48. On the basis of exhaustive stylistic analysis, assigns part 2 of *A Booke of Ayres* to Philip Rosseter rather than Campion.

Binns, J. W. "The Latin Poetry of Thomas Campion." In *The Latin Poetry of English Poets*. London: Routledge & Kegan Paul, 1974, 1–25. A good general discussion, focusing on the elegies.

Bradner, Leicester. *Musae Anglicanae: A History of Anglo-Latin Poetry, 1500–1925*. New York: Modern Language Association of America, 1940. Provides a good context for Campion's Latin poetry and a general discussion of it.

Bryan, Margaret B. "Recent Studies in Campion." *English Literary Renaissance* 4 (1974):404–11. Useful bibliography and discussion of canon.

Coperario, Giovanni. *Rules How to Compose*. Edited by Manfred F. Bukofzer. Los Angeles: E. E. Gottlieb, 1952. Shows an interesting relation with Campion's treatise on counterpoint.

Davis, Walter R. "Melodic and Poetic Structure: The Examples of Campion and Dowland." *Criticism* 4 (1962):89–107. Compares and contrasts the ways in which music highlights poetic structure in these two composers.

DeNeef, A. Leigh. "Structure and Theme in Campion's *Lords Maske*." *Studies in English Literature* 17 (1977):95–103. Full critical discussion of this masque, centering on the theme of language and poetry.

Doughtie, Edward. "Sibling Rivalry: Music vs. Poetry in Campion and Others." *Criticism* 20 (1978):1–16. Illuminating comparisons of Campion's settings of his own verse with settings by other composers.

Eldridge, Muriel T. *Thomas Campion, His Poetry and Music (1567–1620)*. New York: Vantage Press, 1971. Amateur appreciation, containing some interesting remarks on the music of twelve songs (89–135).

Fenyo, Jane K. "Grammar and Music in Thomas Campion's *Observations in the Art of English Poesie*." *Studies in the Renaissance* 17 (1970):46–72. Detailed comparison of the *Observations* to William Lily's Latin grammar in content and stucture.

Greer, David. "Campion the Musician." *Lute Society Journal* 9 (1967):7–16. Excellent introduction to the music.

Hollander, John. *Vision and Resonance: Two Senses of Poetic Form*. New York: Oxford University Press, 1975. On the auditory element in Campion's song-texts, and on the theory of *Observations* (71–90), in a book on the poem, the ear, and the eye.

Ing, Catherine M. *Elizabethan Lyrics: A Study in the Development of English Metres and Their Relation to Poetic Effect*. London: Chatto & Windus,

1951. Contains an intersting chapter on Campion's metrics and sound effects (151–77).

Irwin, John T. " Thomas Campion and the Musical Emblem." *Studies in English Literature* 10 (1970):121–41. An exhaustive analysis of the sound effects of "Now winter nights" (*Third Booke of Ayres*, 12).

Jorgens, Elise Bickford. *The Well-Tun'd Word: Musical Interpretations of English Poetry, 1597–1651.* Minneapolis: University of Minnesota Press, 1982. Contains perceptive comments on Campion's musical settings of his verse, as well as an excellent general treatment of the whole problem of words and music.

Kastendieck, Miles M. *England's Musical Poet, Thomas Campion.* 1938. Reprint. New York: Oxford University Press, 1963. A good survey emphasizing the combination of poetry and music.

Lindley, David. "Campion's *Lord Hay's Masque* and Anglo-Scottish Union." *Huntington Library Quarterly* 43 (1979):1–11. Illuminating discussion of the politics in this masque.

Lowbury, Edward, Salter, Timothy, and Young, Alison. *Thomas Campion: Poet, Composer, Physician.* London: Chatto & Windus, 1970. A survey emphasizing the music.

MacDonagh, Thomas. *Thomas Campion and the Art of English Poetry.* Dublin: Hodges, Figgis, & Co. 1912. An early appreciation.

Mellers, Wilfrid. *Harmonious Meeting: A Study of the Relationship between English Music, Poetry, and Theatre, c. 1600–1900.* London: Dennis Dobson, 1965. Contains brilliant analyses of words and music in four Campion songs (70–80).

Nicoll, Allardyce. *Stuart Masques and the Renaissance Stage.* New York: Harcourt, Brace, 1938. Excellent survey of the masque as a stage phenomenon, with suggestions about the staging of Campion's masques.

Orgel, Stephen, and Strong, Roy. *Inigo Jones: The Theatre of the Stuart Court.* 2 vols. London: Sotheby Park Bernet Publications, Ltd., 1973. Collects all of Jones's designs and other documents for *The Lord Hay's Masque* and *The Lords' Masque.*

Pattison, Bruce. *Music and Poetry of the English Renaissance.* 1948. Reprint. London: Methuen, 1970. A pioneering study with many perceptive comments on Campion and other composers.

Peltz, Catherine W. "Thomas Campion, An Elizabethan Neo-Classicist." *Modern Language Quarterly* 11 (1950):3–6. Examines Campion's models in Catullus, Propertius, and others, and argues that he recaptures their tone brilliantly.

Ratcliffe, Stephen. *Campion: On Song.* Boston: Routledge & Kegan Paul, 1981. An analysis, even more exhaustive than Irwin's, of a single song, "Now winter nights" (*Third Booke of Ayres*, 12).

Richardson, David A. "The Golden Mean in Campion's Airs." *Comparative Literature* 30 (1978):108–32. On the complementarity of words and music, centering on the ways music reflects text in a general but telling manner.

Short, R. W. "The Metrical Theory and Practice of Thomas Campion." *PMLA* 59 (1944):1003–18. How Campion's quantitative experiments produced metrical freedom in his accentual poetry.

Smith, Hallett D. *Elizabethan Poetry: A Study in Conventions, Meaning, and Expression.* Cambridge, Mass.: Harvard University Press, 1952. Contains an excellent chapter on words and music, with comments on Campion (257–89).

Spink, Ian. "Campion's Entertainment at Brougham Castle, 1617." In *Music in English Renaissance Drama,* edited by John M. Long, 57–74. Lexington: University of Kentucky Press, 1968. Argues Campion's authorship of an entertainment at Brougham Castle, and attempts an interesting reconstruction of it.

Winters, Yvor. "The 16th Century Lyric in England: A Critical and Historical Reinterpretation." *Poetry: A Magazine of Verse* 53 (1939):258–72, 320–35; 54 (1939):35–51. A pioneering study of the plain style in Renaissance poetry, placing Campion in that movement.

Index